LARRY A. RAGELS

THERE ARE MANY ROADS TO RECOVERY

THE STORY OF OVER 100 ADDICTION RECOVERY PROGRAMS THAT WORK — AND A FEW THAT DIDN'T

There Are Many Roads to Recovery
The Story of Over 100 Addiction Recovery Programs That Work --- and a Few That Didn't
All Rights Reserved.
Copyright © 2019 Larry A. Ragels
V3.0

The opinions expressed in this manuscript are solely the opinions of the author and do not represent the opinions or thoughts of the publisher. The author has represented and warranted full ownership and/or legal right to publish all the materials in this book.

This book may not be reproduced, transmitted, or stored in whole or in part by any means, including graphic, electronic, or mechanical without the express written consent of the publisher except in the case of brief quotations embodied in critical articles and reviews.

Milky Way Books

ISBN: 978-0-578-22231-8

Cover Photo © 2019 www.gettyimages.com. All rights reserved - used with permission.

PRINTED IN THE UNITED STATES OF AMERICA

Dedication

To the 515 AA group – thank you for being there.

To William L. White – for his pioneering work.

To Amazon and Google – for making so much research possible.

To my proofreaders, Deborah and Joyce – many thanks.

To my family, nuclear and extended – whose love and support are unbelievable.

Table of Contents

Introduction i

Preface ix

CHAPTER 1:
Native North Americans: First Nations – First Recoveries 1

    The Code of Handsome Lake: The Longhouse Religion 4

    John Slocum and the Indian Shaker Church 7

    Native American Church: The Peyote Road 9

    Indianized AA 12

    The Good Red Road 19

    The Recovery Medicine Wheel 25

    Wellbriety! 28

    Taking These Roads 33

    Chapter Endnotes 38

CHAPTER II:
Alcoholics Anonymous and Other Twelve Step Programs: The Great Granddaddy 45

    AA and The Oxford Group 47

    How it Works: Twelve Steps – Two Interpretations 52

    AA's Culture and Traditions 62

    Programs Patterned after AA 65

    Taking These Roads 76

    Chapter Endnotes 78

CHAPTER III:
The McGoldrick Method and Bridge House:
A Forgotten Treasure 83

    Edward J. McGoldrick, Jr. – The Man Behind the Method 84

    Bridge House: A Treatment Center Before Its Time........................85

    Managing the Mind: The Program Theory..87

    McGoldrick's Diagram of the Mind..88

    The Conscious Mind and the Subconscious Mind 90

    The Laws of Learning 92

    William James' Rules for Breaking Old Habits 93

    The Mental Diet: Capsules of Thought 94

    Absorbing the Mental Diet: From Theory to Practice....................105

    Taking This Road 109

    Chapter Endnotes..111

CHAPTER IV:
Synanon: The Rise, The Fall and The Legacy........................115

    The TLC Club and Synanon I: How it Started 117

    Three Synanons 120

    The Synanon Game 121

    The Fall of Synanon 123

    Taking These Roads 124

    Chapter Endnotes..126

CHAPTER V:
Women's Recovery Programs: *By* Women, Primarily *for* Women –
and Men Use Them Too..128

    Women in AA: Long Road to Success..129

    Women For Sobriety: The First Alternative....................................133

Men For Sobriety: Men Suffer Too 140

Twelve Steps for Women Alcoholics: AA's Steps Blended with Kirkpatrick's Statements 141

Sixteen Steps for Discovery and Empowerment: Saying No to Patriarchy 143

My Way Out: A Four Step Program 147

Taking These Roads 149

Chapter Endnotes 153

CHAPTER VI:
Secular and Rational Programs: Believe It or Not 157

SOS: Making Sobriety Your Priority 159

Rational Recovery: Defeat the Beast 162

SMART Recovery: REBT for Everyone 165

LifeRing Secular Recovery: Sobriety, Secularity and Self-Help .. 167

IACT: The International Association for Clear Thinking, Inc. 168

YES Recovery and the YES Recovery Document 169

Pathways to Sobriety: A Workbook for Change 171

Recovery International: A Mental Health Program for Recovery .. 174

Secular Psychologists: Self Help Guidance From the Pros 176

Taking These Roads 179

Chapter Endnotes 184

CHAPTER VII:
Moderation and Controlled Drinking: An Enduring Quest 188

Charles Clapp's Square Pegs: A "Screwy Theory" 190

The Society of Seven Sinners: Arthur Cain's "Tragic Fiasco" 192

Alcoholic Games: TA Challenges AA 195

Drinkwatchers and Similar Programs: Moderation Unlimited 199

Moderation Management: The Promise and the Peril 203

HAMS: Reducing the Harm 209

Taking These Roads 214

Chapter Endnotes... 216

CHAPTER VIII:
FAITH-BASED RECOVERY:
"BE NOT AMONG WINEBIBBERS"[1] 221

Jerry McAuley and Gospel Rescue Missions:
But for the Grace of God… 223

The Salvation Army: "Go See Sally" 226

America's Keswick Colony of Mercy 228

A First Century Christian Fellowship, The Oxford Group,
Moral ReArmament and Initiatives of Change:
One Program with Many Names 229

The Venerable Matt Talbot: Patron of Alcoholics and Addicts 234

The Calix Society: "Replacing the Cup that Stupefies
with the Cup that Sanctifies" 238

Alcoholics Victorious: We Are Free in Christ 239

Alcoholics for Christ 242

"Overcomers" Recovery Groups 243

Celebrate Recovery® 247

LDS Recovery: The Mormon Way 250

Millati Islami 251

Bahá'í Faith.. 253

Taking These Roads 254

Chapter Endnotes... 260

CHAPTER IX:
Afrocentric Recovery: From Frederick Douglass to Malcolm X and Beyond 267

Malcolm X and the Nation of Islam:
"Recovery by Any Means Necessary" 273

Glide Memorial Church: "Telling the Truth and
Living in the Spirit" 277

Free N One: Free from Drugs and Alcohol, and One in Christ 281

One Church - One Addict 283

African American Survivors Organization 284

Taking These Roads 284

Chapter Endnotes 288

CHAPTER X:
New Age Recovery: Ancient Wisdom for Modern Times 295

Abraham-Hicks and Their New Twelve Steps 297

Addiction Alchemy:™ The True Gold of Recovery 300

TM:® Transcendental Meditation 303

Deepak Chopra: Quantum Recovery? 305

The Sedona Method:® The Art of Letting Go 315

Emotional Freedom Technique: The Tapping Solution 318

Drum Therapy: "Drumming Out Drugs" 322

Pagan Recovery: "Here There Be Pagans," *Sober* Pagans 325

Buddhist Recovery: Noble Paths to Overcome Suffering 331

Taking These Roads 336

Chapter Endnotes 339

Introduction

"This one's going into DTs," the doctor said.

He was talking about me, predicting that I'd have *delirium tremens*, the most feared and serious form of alcohol withdrawal. Six years earlier I had been through a typical Twelve Step treatment program. I'd joined AA and stayed sober for about five years, of which only the first year or so was very agreeable. Although I enjoyed the company of others who stayed sober like me, I grew increasingly dissatisfied with the Twelve Step program. It just didn't seem to be designed for an ambitious young man looking for a toe-hold on life, like I was at the time.

I had been through treatment, and it worked, more-or-less, as it was supposed to. But the treatment providers only seemed to know one way to manage recovery: go to AA. That's all anybody seemed to know. I searched and asked. What else is there? But the quest just seemed to go in circles. Everything led back to another Twelve Step program. Have you tried Narcotics Anonymous? How about Al-Anon?

Finally, my search for an alternative brought me to experiment with controlled drinking, which was getting big publicity at the time. And guess what? For me, it worked! – uh, for a while. I believe it's a common enough outcome: a few months of moderate drinking, then drinking a little bit more, a little bit more, a little bit more, and a little bit more. Then the next thing I knew, I'm hooked too bad to sober up without medical assistance.

My M.D. wasn't such a good doctor and I didn't actually have the DTs as predicted, but I was sick enough to spend some time in the hospital's intensive care unit. It wasn't fun. When I regained sobriety, I started looking in earnest for different alternatives and I have been looking ever since. I started reading. I filled up the house with books. The result, after nearly three decades of sober research, is this book: *The Roads to Recovery Are Many: The Story of Over 100 Addiction Recovery Programs That Work, and a Few That Didn't.*

The phrase "roads to recovery are many" did not originate with me. To the best of my knowledge it was first use by William Griffith Wilson, alias Bill W, cofounder of Alcoholics Anonymous. Wilson used it in a 1944 *AA Grapevine* article. In the September issue of that year, the magazine included a piece by Philip Wylie, a well-known writer. Wylie wrote about his own solo recovery from alcoholism, which did not include reliance on AA or the Twelve Steps. Then, according to historians Bill White and Earnest Kurtz: "Anticipating some potential resistance among AA readers, the *Grapevine* editor asked Bill Wilson to offer comment on Wylie's story."[i] Bill took the opportunity to declare that *all* recoveries are a cause for celebration, not just those achieved through AA. "No AA should be disturbed if he cannot fully agree with Mr. Wylie's truly stimulating discourse," Wilson counseled. "Rather shall we reflect that the roads to recovery are many."[ii]

On numerous other occasions Bill reiterated his belief that the roads to recovery are not in any way limited to Twelve Step programs. In the same article, Wilson declared that: "AA has no monopoly on reviving alcoholics."[iii] Furthermore, in a piece written in 1963 he declared that: "it would be a product of false pride to believe that Alcoholics Anonymous is a cure-all, even for alcoholism."[iv] And a couple of years later he declared: "In no circumstance should members feel that Alcoholics Anonymous is the know-all and do-all of alcoholism."[v]

Do these statements by AA's co-founder guarantee that AA groups and other Twelve Step institutions are never subject to excess hubris — what some modern scholars have termed "recoveryism"?[vi] Unfortunately, no. And Bill himself saw how easily this could happen: "Simply because we have convictions that work well for us," he wrote, "it becomes very easy to assume that we have all the truth."[vii]

Unfortunately, this still aptly describes the mind set of some Twelve Step members, groups and institutions.

But the Twelve Steppers are not alone. Those who crow that everyone can recover through the pathway of moderation, for example, are practicing recoveryism. So are those who mock and deride spiritual or religions recovery roads. There are also those who proclaim that prescribed medications are the only way out, and so forth. Alas, recoveryism, like its sister ailments of racism and sexism, is hard to eradicate.

Many of these well-intentioned folks are forgetting that *all* pathways to recovery that work for some people are worth applauding. Bill White, an eminent historian of all things recovery, put it this way: *"Recovery by any means necessary under any circumstances. All pathways and styles of recovery are cause for celebration."*[viii]

This book describes over 100 recovery programs and ideas, the vast majority of which really work and are available for use today. There are so many that there almost has to be something for everybody: something that's totally different or maybe something that's just tweaked a little.

If you are committed to the Twelve Step philosophy, you will find ways here to enrich your program. If you are struggling with the Twelve Steps, but wanting to stay with that popular program, you may find things that will help to clarify your chosen path. And if you are one of those who object to the ubiquitous Twelve Step method, you will be pleased to know that there are many, many alternatives to it — a great many more than are usually reported, even in books and articles that claim to be complete guides to alternative recovery. The roads to recovery truly are many. There are choices.

Right now, few of the alternative programs are as readily available as your local Twelve Step group, but different programs do exist, they do work, and you can use whichever of them you find appealing, with or without group support. The more aspiring among you may even find yourselves starting a group based on your favorite recovery program or idea. But recovery groups are not for everyone and they may not be for you. This book contains the information individual seekers need to follow up on the recovery ideas that are of interest to them. Each chapter ends with writer-to-reader comments and, where available, relevant websites that can be visited.

As the book's subtitle suggests, included are some programs that didn't work. These stories are told for the lessons they teach, and perhaps to slow the re-invention of square wheels, which the addictions field may be inclined to do from time to time.

For some time it's been suggested that there is a need to broaden the base for substance abuse treatment. Reading this book is a long step in that direction. If you are a professional therapist or counselor, this book will help you to better hone your practice. It will help you to help your clients, who need to know as much as possible about what's available. The same is true if you are a family member or a loved one of a person who needs help. Helping them find the program that is right for them is much better than trying to force them into something they just don't like.

The Roads to Recovery Are Many may be read in two different ways. In one sense it is a report on most of the known addiction recovery ideas that have been used in America and elsewhere. It may be read as such and if you choose to do so, you will gain a better-than-average understanding of what's been tried, what's failed, and what remains as viable pathways for those seeking recovery programs that suit their individual needs.

But for those who want immediate help with finding a way for themselves or a loved one, any chapter can be read alone, by itself. You can read about what interests you. If you are uninterested in religion, there is no need to visit the chapter on religious programs. If you think the New Age is looney, there is no need to go there. If you are a woman or a feminist, you may — or may not — want to concentrate your attention on that chapter.

But a note of caution concerning the chapter titles is needed. Not all of the programs are limited to just one category. For instance the My Way Out (MWO) program is included in the chapter on women's programs. I decided to put it there because the founder is a woman and the vast majority of its members are female. However, a substantial minority of those following the program are men; and since the program has no theism, it could be included in the secular chapter. MWO also allows for moderate drinking for those who choose it, so it could be of interest to those seeking moderation pathways. It may be worthwhile to at least skim the chapters to make sure that you don't miss out on a program that is right for you. Another helpful comment: there is nothing the footnotes that is of interest to the average reader. They are citations and that is all. Feel free to ignore them.

Preface

Larry Ragels' family is pleased to see the book to which he devoted several years of research, study and writing published. It is with regret and great sadness that it did not occur before his passing in March of 2017. He was in the process of finding a publisher when he became too ill. This is his work entirely, from the title through chapter ten. We make no assurances that the websites and phone numbers referred to are still accurate. However, we encourage further exploration of any topic that may be of interest to you.

The introduction to this book gives the reader suggestions about how best to use or read the book. The following is taken from a brief autobiographical account so that the reader may get to know Larry's background. He became the person he was through these struggles and experiences. "Author" is the title he prized, just after the titles of husband, father, and grandfather.

Best regards, Tetiana V. Ragels, Gina Ragels Penisten, Joyce Ragels Darling

Larry A. Ragels knows what it's like to live with an alcoholic. He knows what it's like to desperately wish the loved ones would get sober. He knows what it's like to have that wish fulfilled. He knows what it's like when they relapse. He knows what it's like to experience the early years of heavy drinking leading to alcoholism. He knows the pride of being able to handle his liquor. He knows what it's like to have that control slip away. He will tell you that he never drank more than he wanted, but that he often wanted more than he should. He knows what it's like to have others complain about his drinking. He knows what it's like to misuse other drugs. He knows what it's like to go through twenty-eight days of Twelve Step rehab. He knows what it's like to join AA, finding a fellowship he enjoyed, but not the personal growth he wanted and needed. He knows what it's like to be branded alcoholic for life. He knows what it's like to choose controlled drinking as an alternative. He knows what it's like for the experiment to succeed initially, then fail spectacularly. He knows what it's like to need medical detox in an intensive care unit.

Ragels has been collecting and studying alternative recovery programs since attaining full and permanent sobriety in the early 1980's. He collected well over fifty. In these times when experts need to know more and more about less and less, no one can be an expert in all these programs. But Ragels is the one person who surely knows more about this broad subject than anyone else.

Ragels was born and grew up in South Dakota. He's a graduate of Northern State University in Aberdeen, South Dakota. His B.S. degree in secondary education was never used. Instead he embarked on a public service career. Starting at one of the lowest rungs on the ladder, he climbed to the highest general schedule grade attainable. His governmental career was the equivalent of a soldier starting as a private and earning promotions to the rank of colonel.

In the 1990's Ragels contributed numerous articles and book reviews to *The Journal of Rational Recovery, The Bottom Line on Alcohol in Society, and S.M.A.R.T. Recovery News & Views*. In 2008 he retired from public service to pursue a full-time writing career. His self-imposed research and preparation for this includes taking the classes that are required of Certified Addiction Counselors.

Today Ragels' recovery lifestyle is best described as near-abstinent. He doesn't drink alcohol as a beverage, but he will sometimes participate in legitimate ceremonies and toasts. At times in the past he's attended Alcoholics Anonymous, Al-Anon, Secular Organizations for Sobriety, and SMART Recovery meetings. He's not now a member of any particular recovery organization or fellowship.

Larry A. Ragels (April 29, 1947-March 11, 2017)

CHAPTER 1:
Native North Americans:
First Nations – First Recoveries

In 1798 a child was born to Candace Apes of Colrain, Massachusetts – a baby boy. He was named William after his father and later in life he would change the spelling of his last name from Apes to Apess: William Apess. The boy's father was half Pequot Indian, half Anglo. His mother was of mixed heritage but according to William, in her veins flowed, "not a single drop of white man's blood."[1]

Life was hard for many at the turn of the Nineteenth Century, but even by the standards of his time, William Apess had a difficult life. He was not more than four years old when his parents separated, sending their children to live with grandparents. Unfortunately, those relatives were as poor as they were addicted to alcohol. They were barely able to meet the children's basic needs, while abusing them terribly. One day William's grandmother came home drunk and beat poor William nearly to death. Although his grandmother's beating almost cost Apess his life, he did not blame her. He blamed the alcohol that she drank and the European culture that supplied it.

In 1829 Apess published *A Son of the Forest*, the first autobiography to be written in English by a Native American. In it, he described his views on the beatings he received at the hands of his grandparents:

> [T]his cruel and unnatural conduct was the effect of some cause. I attribute it in great measure to the whites, inasmuch as they introduced among my countrymen that bane of comfort and happiness, ardent spirits – seduced them into a love of it and, when under its unhappy influence, wronged them out of their lawful possessions... Now many [Natives] were seen reeling

about, intoxicated with liquor, neglecting to provide for themselves and [their] families ... I do not make this statement in order to justify those who had treated me so unkindly, but simply to show that inasmuch as I was thus treated only when they were under the influence of spiritous liquor, that the whites were justly chargeable with at least some portion of my sufferings.[2]

After that terrible beating, the Apes children were taken from their grandparents. In those days the customary way of dealing with indigent children was to bond them out to other families as indentured servants. This is what was done with the Apes children, they were bonded out to various neighbors. Although William's life was a little improved by this circumstance, he was still abused sometimes by his new masters. He eventually ran away and joined the army, where he fought in the War of 1812. Though only a teenager, it was in the military that he developed his own habit of alcoholic drinking. In his autobiography, Apess wrote: "In a little time I became almost as bad as any of them [I] could drink rum, play cards, and act as wickedly as any."[3]

After he left the army Apess traveled about, somehow learned good English, and became an ordained Methodist minister and temperance reformer. His strong religious faith seems to have kept him sober. In *A Son of the Forest*, Apess wrote:

I abstained entirely and found that I could not only stand labor as well but perform more than those who drank the spirits. All the hands exclaimed against me and said that I would soon give out; but I was determined that *touch not, taste not, handle not,* should be my motto; God supported me and I can truly say that my health was better, my appetite improved and my mind was calm.[4] [emphasis in the original]

That decision must have been made when Apess was still in his twenties. Its importance is shown by his liberal use of italics. It appears that Apess kept his vow for at least a decade, but after about

1836, the record becomes unclear. Apess died in 1839 at the young age of 41. It is often speculated that his death was alcohol-related.[5] The truth may never be known. As Barry O'Connell wrote in his introduction to a modern printing of Apess' works, "all we can … know with certainty is that he no longer practiced his ministry and had no evident role in a community of native people or among reformers." But whatever else may have occurred, O'Connell said, the tale of William Apess "is a remarkable story."[6]

Indeed, whatever his failings – if any – Apess' successes are extraordinary given his disadvantaged youth and scant education. Contrary to his views regarding his grandparents' drinking, however, the history of First Nations struggle with alcohol is not one of helplessness. Indian resistance to alcohol began early and continues to this day.[7] In fact, the lives of William Apess and other Indian ministers such as George Copway and Samson Occom help to demonstrate that.[8]

Although the record is incomplete, there is evidence that First Nations people have resisted alcohol for several centuries. Years ago, Choctaw Indians in Oklahoma said that Neal Dow (a temperance reformer who was born in 1804) was no more than a boy when the first council fires against whiskey were held by them.[9] More than a century and a half before that, in 1648 according to Ernest Cherrington, an Algonquin chief exhorted his tribe to total abstinence.[10] Some years later, wrote John Allen Krout, "the Alleghenies adopted a plan for spilling all the rum that was brought amongst them."[11] And shortly after that, in 1754, a pamphlet was published in London titled "The Speech of a Creek-Indian Against the Immoderate Use of Spiritous Liquor, Delivered in a National Assembly of the *Creeks*."[12] Although it was published in England, this speech was surely delivered in the United States.

The eighteenth century also saw the emergence of Indian recovery circles led by Native prophets such as the six Delaware Prophets, the Shawnee Prophet, and the Kickapoo Prophet. According to Don Coyhis and Bill White: "These prophetic leaders used their own recoveries from alcoholism to launch abstinence-based, pan-Indian movements that called for rejection of alcohol and return to ancestral traditions."[13] As those recovery advocates put it: *"Early indigenous responses to Alcohol problems included the development of sobriety-based religious/cultural revitalization and healing movements that constitute the first [successful] recovery mutual aid societies in the world."*[14] [emphasis in original]

Other early Native leaders started anti-alcohol religious movements that remain in existence today. This chapter will discuss those movements, along with modern, Indian-led programs that are using indigenous ceremonies and traditions to overcome alcoholism and other addictions.

The Code of Handsome Lake: The Longhouse Religion

"Niio!" (so be it) Handsome Lake shouted as he stumbled from his bed to the door of the longhouse. He got far enough for his married daughter and her husband to see him. Then he collapsed. He had lain sick in bed for four years, suffering from alcoholism and a "wasting disease." Perhaps his time to die had come. His faithful daughter and her husband carried him back to bed, certain that he was dead or dying.

Handsome Lake was a chief among the Senecas. Arthur Parker, a fellow Seneca Indian and a Native America scholar, wrote about his sickness. As Parker described it, the daughter said to her husband: "Run quickly and notify his nephew … [tell him] that he who has lain so many years in bed has gone. Bid him come immediately." So the husband ran to carry the message to the nephew, Blacksnake, and also to Cornplanter, Handsome Lake's half-brother.[15]

Blacksnake came and touched Handsome Lake on every part of his body. The body was cold as death, but he found one warm spot over the heart. "Hold back your sadness, friends," Blacksnake said.[16] Cornplanter also touched the body and found a warm spot.

It was about noon when Blacksnake noticed that the warm spot was spreading. "Are you well? What think you?" he asked

Handsome Lake. "Yes I believe myself well," the man answered. Then he spoke of a vision, saying: Never have I seen such wondrous visions! Now at first I heard some one (sic) speaking. Some one spoke and said "Come out awhile" and said this three times... So I called out boldly *"Niio!"* and arose and went out[;] there I saw three men clothed in fine raiment... Never before have I seen such handsome commanding men ....[17]

The men in the vision told Handsome Lake: "He who created the world at the beginning employed us to come to earth... He commanded us saying 'Go once more down upon the earth and visit him who thinks of me. He is grateful for my creations, moreover he wishes to rise from sickness and walk upon the earth. Go you and help him recover."

"Take these berries and eat of every color," the messengers told Handsome Lake. "They will give you strength." The men also told him that they would appoint someone to make medicine and that: "Early in the morning ... you will have the medicine for your use, and before noon the unused medicine will be cast away because you will have recovered."[18] And so it was. Handsome Lake recovered to walk again upon the earth.

This was the first of Handsome Lake's three visions. In one of the visions, a fourth messenger appeared. He was like the others, but he had wounds on his hands, feet, and side. This messenger was thought to be Jesus.

The messengers gave Handsome Lake instructions on how the Iroquois were to live. Once a powerful confederacy of six tribes (including the Senecas), the Iroquois had been reduced to a handful of Natives living on scattered reservations in the United States and Canada. Their very existence was in jeopardy.

The messengers' instructions are called the Code of Handsome Lake or the Longhouse Religion (because meetings are held in the "long houses" built by the Iroquois). The message combined traditional Iroquois ceremonies with ways to adapt to the realities of life with the European settlers. It is often credited with saving the Iroquois from cultural extinction.

The main objective of the new religion was temperance. "The first word is *one'ga* [alcohol]" the messengers told Handsome Lake. "It seems that you never have known that this word stands for a great and monstrous evil and has reared a high mound of bones... You lose your minds and *one'ga* causes it all... So now all must say, 'I will use it nevermore. As long as I live, as long as the number of my days I will never use it again. I now stop.'"[19]

The messengers also gave reasons for their instructions: "Now some have said that there is no harm in partaking of fermented liquids," the messengers told Handsome Lake. "Then let this plan be followed: let men gather in two parties, one having a feast of food ... and the others have cider and whiskey... When the feast is finished you will see those who drank the fermented juices murder one of their own party but not so with those who ate food only."[20]

> After his return to life in 1799, Handsome Lake spent the rest of his years preaching the *Gaiwiio* or "good message" that he received from the four heavenly beings. According to Elias Johnson, himself a chief of one of the Iroquois tribes, by the time of Handsome Lake's death in 1815, "the whole unchristianized portion of the Six Nations [the Iroquois] had become firm believers in the new religion."[21]

The success of Handsome Lake's reformation received recognition and praise from Quaker missionaries and even from president Thomas Jefferson. In a letter to Handsome Lake, Jefferson wrote: "Persuade our red brethren then to be sober and to cultivate their lands; and their women to spin and weave for their families. You will soon see your women and children well fed and clothed, your men living happily in peace and plenty, and your numbers increasing from year to year."[22]

Elias Johnson reported that as a result of Handsome Lake's teachings: "Many abandoned their dissolute habits and became sober and moral men; discord and contentions gave place to harmony and order, and vagrancy and sloth to ambition and industry."[23]

In addition to forbidding alcohol, the "good message" outlawed witchcraft, promiscuity, gambling, quarreling and other such evils. It emphasized the importance of the nuclear family – father, mother and children – as opposed to the extended matriarchal clans that were traditional with the Iroquois. It taught that men as well as women should engage in planting and husbandry, not limiting their activities to hunting wild game and fishing. These changes helped the Iroquois adapt to life after 1800.

Today, the Longhouse Religion is still practiced by approximately 5,000 people.[24] A modern leader of the Longhouse Religion, when interviewed by Brian Maracle, reaffirmed the church's stance against alcohol: "A person must not drink at all. These are Longhouse people I am talking about. No drinking at all. Not a drop. That's our belief. It's not for us."[25]

John Slocum and the Indian Shaker Church

Although the names are similar, the Indian Shaker Church should not be confused with the Shakers of New England. And although their stories are somewhat similar, John Slocum should not be confused with Handsome Lake. John Slocum of the Northwest and Handsome Lake of the Northeast were born in different centuries and separated by more than 2,500 miles.

John Slocum, a member of the Squaxin tribe, was born in 1838 in what is now the state of Washington. He was a logger by trade and widely known as a "bad" Indian. According to a nearly contemporary report by Charles Rakestraw: "Slocum was a well-to-do Indian but also a very bad Indian. He drank whiskey, gambled, swore, raced horses, and engaged in other evil practices which make up a generally reckless life." Slocum was distinguished from the rest of his tribe, Rakestraw wrote, "by being rather worse than any of the others"[26]

In 1881 or 1882 (accounts vary) Slocum was involved in a logging accident and was thought to have died. He revived as the family was awaiting his casket and told of an out of body or near-death experience. During his trance or actual death, Slocum reported that he journeyed to heaven where he was refused entry due to his many sins. An angel, sometimes said to be Saint Peter, gave Slocum the choice of going to hell or returning to earth for the purpose of starting a church to convince his people to believe in Jesus and lead moral lives. Slocum chose to return to earth.

Slocum's church did well enough for a couple of years, but then it seems that Slocum himself began to backslide (as least as far as his gambling was concerned). He fell ill and for a second time and for a second time his family thought that he was dead. His wife Mary prayed for him and soon she began to tremble or shake in a most violent manner. This is what gave the society its name: Shakers. As she trembled or shook over the seemingly lifeless body of John Slocum, the man apparently "rose from the dead" once again. This second resurrection reenergized the church and it began spreading along the Northwest coast.

> The church Slocum founded is a mixture of Protestantism, Catholicism, and traditional Indian practices. Rakestraw compared it to Christian Science because there is a strong emphasis placed on healing the sick.[27]

The Shaker church services and healing ceremonies can be noisy affairs. Bells are rung, feet are stamped and, of course, people shake. The religion also places a very strong emphasis on moral and upright behavior. To quote again from Rakestraw:

> This very practical and effectual religion requires that its adherents shall not swear, lie, steal, nor fight; that they shall not work on Sunday, nor gamble, nor use either whiskey or tobacco; and that they shall not oppress anybody nor do anything which they know to be wrong. But especial emphasis is

placed upon abstinence from tobacco and whiskey. And to the credit of the Indians who have become converted it may truthfully be said that after their conversion they immediately and permanently eschew all of their former vices and evil practices and live exemplary lives, no matter how disreputable the individuals may have been before the conversion, or the taking of "the shake."[28]

The importance that the Indian Shakers place upon abstinence from alcohol cannot be over-emphasized. In 1922 T. T. Waterman wrote: "The one virtue of non-indulgence in alcohol has served to make the members of the Shaker church the most prosperous of the Indians."[29]

A good percentage of today's church members are said to be former drunkards or alcoholics. Logan Slagle and Joan Weibel-Orlando even compared the Indian Shaker Church to Alcoholics Anonymous and the Shaker testimonials to the stories heard in AA.[30]

A number of years ago, a disagreement arose over the use of the Bible in Shaker church services. The result was a schism, so now there are two branches of the church: the original Indian Shaker Church and the Indian Full Gospel Church.[31]

Native American Church: The Peyote Road

On May 19, 1836 a group of Comanche warriors raided Ft. Parker, Texas. Several members of the Parker family were killed that day and nine-year-old Cynthia Ann Parker was taken captive. The Comanches adopted her and renamed her Nadua (someone found). When Nadua became a young woman, she married Peta Nocona, a Comanche war chief. Sometime around 1845, or perhaps as late as 1850, she gave birth to a boy, Quanah, whose name means "fragrant."

Cynthia Ann Parker was rescued by the Texas Rangers in 1860, but after 24 years with the Comanches, she never readjusted to life with her White family.

Quanah, the only one of her three children to survive to adulthood, was one of the last Comanches to consent to life on a reservation, but when he finally accepted reservation life, he adjusted remarkably well. In addition to becoming Chief of the Comanches, he seems to have been one of the richest Indians in America; his friends included president Theodore Roosevelt, with whom he went wolf hunting, and several influential Texas ranchers.

He took his mother's maiden name, Parker, as his own, but he never gave up some of his Indian customs, such as polygamy – which was practiced by some, though not all, Native tribes – and he chose for his religion what was known at the time as the "Peyote Cult." In fact, he was one of the foremost leaders of the peyote movement that spread to many Indian reservations across North America.

Quanah Parker was not the only early leader of what was to become the Native American Church (NAC). John Rave, who quit drinking with the use of peyote, carried its use north to the Winnebagos, and John Wilson, a Caddo, introduced a new peyote ritual called the "Big Moon" (or "Cross Fire") ceremony. Previously the Caddo and other tribes had known only the "Half Moon" peyote ceremony popularized by Parker. According to Omer Stewart, an historian of the peyote religion:

> The theologies of both ceremonies were similar. Peyote is good; peyote comes from God; peyote heals. Peyote teaches one to think good thoughts; it teaches one to know good from evil. It can cure anything … Both ceremonies were strongly opposed to the use of liquor and claimed that peyote destroyed the taste for alcohol.[32]

The ceremonies are also similar, except that the "Big Moon" ceremony has a different altar and is said to be more complex, include more Christian elements and the preaching of a sermon. William Hagan, a biographer of Quanah Parker, provided a description of Parker's "Half Moon" ceremony, which is sometimes called the "Tepee Way":

The ceremony took place in a tepee. On entering, the communicant faced a raised altar that among Quanah's people took the form of a horseshoe whose open end faced the tepee entrance. Atop the altar would have been a single large peyote button, the "peyote chief," or "father peyote," and in front of it a fire. The ceremony required a minimum of a drum, a rattle, a staff, an eagle-bone whistle, a quantity of sage, and a supply of [peyote] buttons. As the participants entered, they would move to their left and proceed to their sagebrush-filled cushions behind and on the sides of the altar.[33]

Parker's ceremony was an all-night affair that concluded with a communal breakfast. The same can be said for many peyote ceremonies today, which usually commence on a Saturday evening at sunset and conclude with sunrise on Sunday morning. Peyote ceremonies are led by a "Road Chief" who is in charge of the ceremony and may make minor ceremonial changes.

Generally, peyote use is illegal, but an exception is made for legitimate use by the Native American Church. Peyote may not be the drug of choice for many people anyway. As the introduction to an on-line version of Paul Radin's 1925 book, *The Peyote Cult,* states: "Peyote has never been a drug for thrill seekers. The small, hard cactus is difficult to obtain. It tastes vile, ingestion normally leads to painful vomiting, and the effects are more subtle than other psychedelics."[34]

It is, of course, possible, to take enough of the drug so that the effects are not subtle. The only example I found of this, however, dates back to the beginning of the twentieth century. This was an account of a Tonkawa Peyote Meeting held in 1902. The witness was Samuel Kenoi, a Chiricahua Apache. He attended a peyote meeting where "the chief man of the peyote rite," a Corporal Jesse, consumed many peyote buttons. According to this first-person account given to Morris Opler, an American cultural anthropologist:

> The fourth day ... I didn't eat any [peyote]. I just watched for about three hours, and everyone was affected... Corporal Jesse ate forty peyotes that night. He was making all kinds of animal sounds. Once in a while he fell over. He was seeing visions.

Before I left he went out of his mind. He just lay there. And the rest were praying and singing.

None ate as many as he did... Jesse was the only one who made noises... They said, "he's up somewhere talking with visions."[35]

The use of Peyote in this manner definitely appears to be the exception. To quote Omer Stewart again, in both the Big Moon and Half Moon ceremonies, "peyote was eaten not for visions but to concentrate and learn from peyote. Visions and nausea were an indication that the mind was wandering from a devotion to peyote, or that the body was trying to rid itself from some bad thing."[36]

There appears to be no misuse or abuse of peyote in the modern Native American Church. Edward Anderson, who wrote a book on Peyote and attended at least one peyote ceremony, reported that the ceremony, "was *not* a dangerous or wild orgy in which there was intoxication, sexual license, and other immoral activities." According to Anderson: "Peyotism clearly demands much of its followers: physical endurance, patience, confession, and repentance."[37] Today, the NAC is one of the largest pan-Indian spiritual movements in North America.[38]

Many recovered and recovering Indian alcoholics attribute their sobriety to the Native American Church, whose congregations have been found to be "rich with recovered alcoholics."[39] Matthew Kelley, Clinical Director of the Na'nizhoozhi treatment center in Gallup, New Mexico, writes that "active participation in the Native American Church is considered to be more effective than standard 12-step treatment or medical treatment protocol."[40]

Indianized AA

Phyllis Chelsea knew that she had to quit drinking. Her seven-year-old daughter had given an ultimatum: Mommy and Daddy had to stop drinking or she would not come home.

Phyllis and her husband Andy, members of the Alkali Lake Band of Shuswap Indians, had taken the child to her grandmother's for the week-end so the two of them could party. "I don't want to come home with you," seven-year-old Ivy told her parents when they came to pick her up. "Not until you quit drinking." Phyllis quit right away, to be followed by Andy four days later.

The Alkali Lake Band in north-central British Columbia, Canada was so besotted that neighboring communities called it "Alcohol Lake." But prior to the 1940s, "Alcohol Lake" had almost no alcoholism. Then a European immigrant opened a general store and trading post. The trader gradually introduced alcohol to soften up his customers and by the 1960s, Alkali Lake had acquired a very big drinking problem.

When Phyllis and Andy sobered up in 1971, they were the only non-drinkers in the whole Band of about 400 Shuswap people. The only bright spot the first year was when Andy was elected tribal Chief. The community had long talked of doing something about its "problem," but nothing was done because no one was sober enough to do it. When Andy won an election after campaigning on a sobriety platform, it was at least some indication that the community was finally getting ready to address its problems – but it would be a full year before another Alkali Lake resident would join the sober couple.

Over the years, a few more Indians, and then a few more than that, joined with Phyllis and Andy. Professor Dennis Kelley, a Cumash Indian, provided a summary of the gradual but profound changes: "By 1973, the group had increased to 12, and by 1975, 40 percent of the reserve was sober. That number reached 98 percent by 1979[!]"[41]

Several factors contributed to the victory at Alkali Lake, including AA, economic incentives and a revitalization of the traditional life of the community. The Four Worlds International Website describes "a strong AA program (*culturally adapted and changed to fit the community's reality*)."[42] [emphasis added]

What the Alkali Lake Band did in creating a culturally-relevant version of AA is sometimes called the Indianization (Indian-i-ZAshun) of Alcoholics Anonymous. According to Coyhis and White, the first Indianized AA Group was started in Oneida, Wisconsin back in 1953.[43] The movement has been expanding ever since. But why the need for specialized Indian meetings? In a paper titled "The Healing Circle: An Alternative Path to Addiction Recovery," Ronald D. Smith, et al. described two sources of conflict:

> First, individuals who are raised in traditional ways are taught a value system in which each person has sole responsibility for living his or her life in the proper manner; the development of group dependency does not fit well with this value... Second the AA practice of identifying oneself as an **alcoholic** directly contradicts the Lakota belief in the sanctity and power of words; if a person continues to say that he or she is an **alcoholic**, then he or she will, in fact, be a drinking **alcoholic**.[44]

Furthermore, traditional people are sometimes uncomfortable with a number of other things about AA, such as the public disclosures of personal problems, the confession of powerlessness, certain Christian elements of the AA program, and its predominately White demographics.[45] Finally, Native Americans are sometimes indifferent to the principle of anonymity, which may be perceived as coldness or standoffishness on the part of White members.[46]

How then does Indian AA differ from regular AA? Coyhis and White,[47] along with Louise M. Jilek-Aall,[48] described several differences:

- Regular AA meetings usually start and end at a specific time. Indian meetings often start late, after everyone has arrived, and end later than scheduled.
- At regular AA meetings coffee breaks, if any, are usually short and self-served. Indian AA meetings provide long breaks for socializing. Women serve the others.

- Regular "closed" AA meetings are attended by AA members only. Indian meetings may include family members, friends, teenagers and children.
- Regular "speaker" meetings usually adhere to a specific predetermined schedule. Indian meetings usually have no set schedule for speakers, who may speak for as long as they want.
- As a rule, most standard AA meetings adhere rather closely to AA's ideas, principles, slogans and sayings. Indian meetings may blend AA with Indian ideas and slogans, replace references to a Christian God AS WE UNDERSTOOD HIM with references to the Creator or Great Spirit, and replace affirmations of powerlessness with an emphasis on the acquisition of personal and cultural power.

For example, Louise Jilek-Aall, in her paper on "Acculturation, Alcoholism and Indian-Style Alcoholics Anonymous," described an AA meeting of the Coast Salish Indians: [M]embers come and go as they please. The meeting is constantly interrupted by people entering and leaving, mothers bring their babies and small children, teenagers, their friends. Young people having private fun in a corner, or children crying and doors being slammed, irritate non-Indian speakers, while Indian members feel relaxed and at home.

> Coffee-breaks are drawn-out affairs and the chairman often has difficulty getting the meeting going again. There is no time limit to speechmaking and people will disband only when overcome by fatigue.[49]

Other Indian recovery groups may use a revised and acculturated version of the Twelve Steps. Here, side-by-side with the Twelve Steps of AA, is one such revision called "Sobriety Through the Sacred Pipe."

ALCOHOLICS ANONYMOUS	SOBRIETY THROUGH THE SACRED PIPE
1) We admitted we were powerless over alcohol—that our lives had become unmanageable.	1) We admit we are powerless over demon alcohol and that our Native Way of Life had become unmanageable.
2) Came to believe that a Power greater than ourselves could restore us to sanity.	2) We came to believe that the Power of the Pipe is greater than ourselves and can restore us to our Culture and Heritage.
3) Made a decision to turn our will and our lives over to the care of God AS WE UNDERSTOOD HIM.	3) We made a decision to turn our will and our lives over to the care of the Great Spirit through the Sacred Pipe.
4) Made a searching and fearless moral inventory of ourselves.	4) We make a searching and fearless moral inventory of who we are, and understand the symbolic meaning of the Four Directions.
5) Admitted to God, to ourselves, and to another human being the exact nature of our wrongs.	5) We acknowledge to the Great Spirit, to ourselves and to the Native American Brotherhood/Sisterhood, our struggles against the tide and its manifest destiny.
6) Were entirely ready to have God remove all these defects of character.	6) Be entirely ready for the Great Spirit to remove all the defects of an alien culture.
7) Humbly asked Him to remove our shortcomings.	7) We humbly ask the Great Spirit to remove all the defects of an alien culture.
8) Made a list of all persons we had harmed, and became willing to make amends to them all.	8) Make a list of all the harm that has come to our people from demon alcohol and become willing to make amends to them all.

9) Made direct amends to such people wherever possible, except when to do so would injure them or others.	9) Make direct amends to our people that struggle against the alcohol disease, whenever possible, except when to do so would injure them or others.
10) Continued to take personal inventory and when we were wrong promptly admitted it.	10) Continue to take a personal searching and fearless inventory of who we are, and when we sell ourselves out, promptly admit it.
11) Sought through prayer and meditation to improve our conscious contact with God AS WE UNDERSTOOD HIM, praying only for knowledge of His will for us and the power to carry that out.	11) Seek through prayer and meditation to improve our conscious contact with the Equality and Brotherhood/Sisterhood of all Mother Earth's Children and the Great Balancing Harmony of the Total Universe.
12) Having had a spiritual awakening as the result of these steps, we tried to carry this message to alcoholics, and to practice these principles in all our affairs.[50]	12) Having the universal understanding and wisdom of our hearts, minds, and spirits of all the People, we carry this message to Native alcoholics and addicts, and practice these principles in all Native affairs.[51]

Another adaption of the Steps was made by Mickey M. in his *Medicine Wheel of My Recovery*, a fairly routine "how I recovered" autobiography. Except for changing "*God*" to "Father Spirit," Mickey M.'s steps remain largely unchanged, but he makes an interesting correlation of each of the Twelve Steps with a totem animal:

Step 1 – "equals the medicine of the bear... The spiritual message from the bear is, 'without truth there is no change.'"

Step 2 –   "equals the medicine of the deer… 'come to the Father Spirit weak and humble and [He will] give you strength.'"
Step 3 –   "equals the medicine of the horse… 'when you're weak, I will carry you.'"
Step 4 –   "equals the medicine of the fox… To be unseen and observant … 'see yourself in your own mind's eye.'"
Step 5 –   "equals the medicine of the buffalo. Unity and harmony…"
Step 6 –   "equals the medicine of the owl… wisdom, the death of something whether it's bad or good."
Step 7 –   "equals the medicine of the coyote, shortcoming, opening the same door and expecting something different."
Step 8 –   "equals the medicine of the wolf, a loyal friend…"
Step 9 –   "equals the medicine of the mountain lion, courage…"
Step 10 – "equals the medicine of the crow… don't be afraid of change…"
Step 11 – "equals the medicine of the eagle… let the warm breath of the Great Spirit's words under your wings keep you from falling…"
Step 12 – "equals the medicine of the hawk, the messenger…"[52]

    The opening and closing ceremonies may be another area where Indian AA meetings differ from regular AA meetings. Regular meetings are usually opened with the Serenity Prayer* and closed with the Lord's Prayer. Indians may perform these ceremonies differently or use something else altogether. If the Serenity Prayer is used, it may be called the "Sobriety Prayer" and ended with a loud AMEN! – something not often heard at regular AA meetings.

    Meetings may also be opened or closed with totally different prayers. Here's one from Robert Blackwolf Jones (Ojibway) that

---

* God grant us the serenity to accept the things we cannot change, the courage to change the things we can, and the wisdom to know the difference.

may be read at Indian AA meetings. Such prayers may be recited in English or a Native language.

> *O Great Spirit, whose voice I hear in the winds,*
> *and whose breath gives life to all the world,*
> *Hear me! I am small and weak.*
> *I need your strength and wisdom.*
> *Let me walk in beauty and make my eyes ever*
> *behold the red and purple sunset.*
> *Make my hands respect the things you have made*
> *and my ears sharp to hear your voice.*
> *Make me wise so that I may understand the*
> *things you have taught my people.*
> *Let me learn the lessons you have hidden in*
> *every leaf and rock.*
> *I seek strength*
> *Not to be greater than my brother, but to fight my*
> *greatest enemy – myself.*
> *Make me always ready to come to you with clean*
> *hands and straight eyes,*
> *so when life fades, as the fading sunset,*
> *my spirit may come to you without shame.*
> *Mitakuye-Oyasin* [53]
> (mah-tah-kee–o-ah-sin — "all are related")

The Good Red Road

The *Red Road* (the *Good Road* or the *Good Red Road*) is a way of living in accordance with tribal or pan-Indian traditions and customs. Gene Thin Elk (Lakota) pioneered the Red Road approach to addiction recovery. Thin Elk is the director of Native Student Services at the University of South Dakota. According to him:

The Red Road Approach is a holistic approach to spiritual, mental, physical and emotional wellness based upon Native

American healing concepts and traditions and uses prayer as the basis for all healing....

To ensure that healing continues after spiritual awareness, mental cognition, physical recovery, and emotional release, the Native American must have a lifestyle (culture) that is harmonious with self, community, and the cosmos. The traditions and values of the Native American People ensure balance by living these cultural traditions through the Red Road...[54]

The Red Road might be considered the treatment version of Indianized AA and it has naught to do with skin color. The Red Road concept is based on the Native tradition of correlating colors with the four directions of the Medicine Wheel (to be discussed shortly). The Red Road is said to be "good" and runs north to south. There is also a Black (or Blue) Road that is "bad" and runs east to west. Black Elk, a Lakota Holy Man of the Oglala Band, described the Red Road and the Black Road he saw in his Great Vision:

> And now the fourth Grandfather spoke .... "Behold the Earth!" So I looked down and saw it lying yonder like a hoop of peoples, and in the center bloomed the holy stick that was a tree, and where it stood there crossed two roads, a red one and a black. "From where the giant lives (the north) to where you always look (the south) the red road goes, the road of good," the Grandfather said, "and on it shall your nation walk. The black road goes from where the thunder beings live (the west) to where the sun continually shines (the east), a fearful road, a road of troubles and of war. On this also shall you walk ..."[55]

The Red Road approach includes a number of Native healing ceremonies and rituals that are useful in restoring health, including recovery from addictions. Among the things that might be used in addition to, or instead of, standard Twelve Step Facilitation programs are: sweat lodges, smudging, talking circles, sacred pipe ceremonies, pow-wows, sacred dances, and Native healers (medicine men or medicine women).

There are many different styles of *sweat lodges*, but the one most often mentioned seems to be the *Inipi* (purification) ceremony developed by the Plains Indians. These Indians construct a sweat lodge with supple willow posts, bent to create a low dome structure about four to five feet high and approximately 10 feet in diameter.

The frame was originally covered with buffalo hides or the skins of other large animals, but today heavy blankets, canvas tarps, or other such materials may be used. Inside the structure, a pit about one foot deep is dug to hold the hot rocks that are brought in after being heated red hot in an outside fire. Water is sprinkled or poured on the rocks to create steam. The sweat lodge ceremony usually includes four sessions or rounds, each lasting about 30 to 45 minutes. Almost everything about the *Inipi*, from the building of the lodge to the final round of the ceremony, has a spiritual significance.[56]

Smudging is a ceremony for cleansing people, objects or places (buildings or rooms). The cleansing is done with smoke. Traditionally, one or more of four sacred herbs are used. The herbs are: sage, cedar, sweet grass and tobacco. Some traditions omit tobacco and one Native group in Saskatchewan substitutes willow fungus. The herbs are bound together into a smudge stick or allowed to smolder in a ceramic or rock bowl. Some traditions use abalone shells, but others warn against its use because abalone is said to represent "Grandmother Ocean." They say it should be used in ceremonies involving water, not burning.

The smudge stick may be lit and allowed to smolder. Similarly, loose herbs in a bowl may be made to smolder, thus creating the most smoke with the least amount of flame. The smoke may be guided or "pushed" with your hands, a feather, or feather fan. The smoke may be pushed into the corners of a room, or used to "wash" your hands and body.[57]

Talking Circles are a way of managing meetings. Two elements are critical to having a talking circle: 1) the participants sit in a circle, if possible; and 2) the participants pass a significant object from person to person and whoever holds the object has the right to speak; the others are to listen. The significant object may be a decorated stick, a feather, a wampum belt, a sacred shell, or something else. Generally, it is passed in a clockwise direction and may go around the circle more than once. There is no time limit on speaking and *only the person holding the special object may speak.* He or she may say anything that is "in the heart or on the mind." No one has to stay on a specific topic. According to Don Coyhis (Mohican), "Indians will talk in circles more than they will talk at tables or respond to lectures."[58] Recently, the talking circle idea has gone almost mainstream, even occasionally showing up in corporate boardrooms.

Even those who know very little about Indian cultures probably think they know something about the *peace pipe*. Actually, "peace pipe" is a misnomer (incorrect name) for the *sacred pipe*. Smoking the pipe is a way of meditation or prayer. It is also used to seal agreements such as treaties, hence the name "peace pipe." The smoke is regarded as a visible prayer and also a means of carrying prayers to the Great Spirit.

Keeping in mind that the cultures of Native American tribes are incredibly diverse, a sacred pipe ceremony may go something like this: The pipe carrier or leader assembles the pipe and ritually fills the bowl a pinch at a time. The bowl may be filled with tobacco, red willow bark, or some mixture of herbs. Next, the leader beseeches the seven powers (east, south, west, north, above, below, and the Great Spirit or Creator at the center) and sends his own prayers. The pipe is then passed clockwise to all the participants who may smoke it or just hold it and pray. The shortest prayer is simply to say "all my relations," meaning that all things are related. After everyone has had a chance to meditate or pray and all the tobacco or willow bark has been smoked, the pipe is ritually disassembled and put away. A sacred pipe is never stored with the stem attached to bowl.[59]

Regarding the pipe's use in sealing promises, Indians say that it is dangerous to lie while smoking the pipe. They tell this story about General George Custer: Custer smoked a pipe with a Cheyenne holy man. While smoking the pipe, Custer vowed, "I will never harm the

Cheyennes again. I will never point my gun at a Cheyenne again." As Kenneth Cohen, a well-known health educator, dryly noted: "The Battle of Little Big Horn[*] tells the story of the price Custer paid for his deceit."[6]

Pow Wows are large gatherings of Native North Americans and people of other backgrounds. They involve dancing, drumming, singing and socializing. They may also feature giveaways, feasting and concession sales of Indian arts and crafts. Estimates are that 90 percent of all Indians attend Pow Wows but Pow Wow attendance is not limited to Indians; the general public is also invited.

The peak season for Pow Wows is Memorial Day through Labor Day, but Pow Wows may be held year round, including Thanksgiving and Christmas Holidays. All, or almost all, Pow Wows are alcohol and drug free. This provides a sober social environment for many. Some spend an entire summer traveling from one Pow Wow to another. A few dedicated Pow Wow goers say they have achieved sobriety just by following this "Pow Wow trail."[61]

While Pow Wows are meant to be social events, *sacred dances* are deeply spiritual. Non-Indians are not always invited to attend spirit dances such as the Gourd Dance, Stomp Dance, Ghost Dance or Sun Dance. The Sun Dance is perhaps the most holy of the sacred dances. It may include fasting, singing, praying and, in some cases, piercing of the skin and small flesh offerings to the Creator. Participants in the Sun Dance willingly undergo these sacrifices for the good of their families and communities.[62]

Native *medicine people* take a different view of healing than do most western doctors, claims Mohawk elder Ernie Benedict. Specifically, he said:

The difference that exists is that the white doctor's medicine tends to be very mechanical. The patient is repaired, but he is not a better person than he was before. It is possible in the Indian way to be a better person after going through a sickness followed by the proper medicine.

---

[*] Commonly known as "Custer's Last Stand." General Custer, two of his brothers, and five Seventh Cavalry companies were killed by Indian warriors on June 25 and 26, 1876.

According to Kenneth Cohen, who has trained with elder healers, "several broad categories of intervention are considered important among virtually all Native American healers, including vision-seeking, smudging, prayer, music, counseling, massage, ceremony, and herbs."[64] In *Black Elk Speaks*, Heháka Sápa (Black Elk), described one of his first cures. Although this was not a treatment of an addiction problem *per se*, it does show, in a general way, some of the methods that may be used by Indian medicine people. As Black Elk recalled the event:

> [I was out hunting for a sacred herb and] There right on the side of the bank the herb was growing, and I knew it, although I had never seen one like it before, except in my vision.... Something must have told me to find the herb just then, for the next morning I needed it and could have done nothing without it.
>
> I was eating supper when a man by the name of Cuts-to-Pieces came in, and he was saying: "Hey, hey, hey!" for he was in trouble. I asked him what was the matter, and he said: "I have a boy of mine, and he is very sick and I am afraid he will die soon."....
>
> [W]e went into [Cuts-to-Pieces'] teepee... The sick little boy was on the northeast side, and he looked as though he were only skin and bones.... I made low thunder on the drum, keeping time as I sent forth a voice. Four times I cried "Hey-a-a-hey," drumming as I cried to the Spirit of the World, and while doing this I could feel the power coming through me from my feet up, and I knew I could help the sick little boy.... Now I walked to the north and to the east and to the south, stopping there where the source of life is and where the good red road begins. Standing there I sang thus:

"In a sacred manner I have made them walk.

A sacred nation lies low.

In a sacred manner I have made them walk.

A sacred two-legged, he lies low.

In a sacred manner, he shall walk." ....

I next took [a] cup of water, drank a little of it, and went around to where the sick little boy was. Standing before him, I stamped the earth four times. Then, putting my mouth to the pit of his stomach, I drew through him the cleansing wind of the north. I next chewed some of the herb and put it in the water, afterward blowing some of it on the boy and to the four quarters. The cup with the rest of the water [was given] to the sick little boy to drink.... He got well and lived to be thirty years old.[65]

The Recovery Medicine Wheel

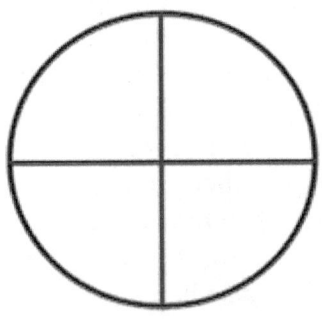

MEDICINE WHEEL

According to Mohican Elder Don Coyhis, about 80 percent of all Native tribes have Medicine Wheels and *all* tribes practice some form of circle teaching.[66] He also says that the tribes who do have Medicine Wheels often assign different interpretations to the wheel.[67] In its simplest form, the Medicine Wheel is a circle containing an equal-armed cross (see diagram on left). The circle represents the universe or the "circle of life," which the cross divides into quadrants. This very basic symbol speaks two profound truths: 1) all living phenomenons are cyclic; and 2) a good analysis of any subject can often be made by considering the subject as having four parts or stages. Thus we have the yearly cycle of nature, which can be studied and understood by dividing the year into four seasons: spring, summer, fall and winter. There are also four cardinal directions: east, south, west and north, which are correlated with the seasons and other growth cycles. For human life, infancy is in the east; childhood occupies the south; adulthood lies in the west; and north is the position of the elder. (In Anglo terms, the stages of human life are baby, child, adult and senior.) There are also four directions of human growth: emotional, mental, physical and spiritual; and four aspects of human societies: individual, family, community and nation. These too are correlated with the four directions.

Different colors are assigned to the stations of the wheel, but there are several different schemes for doing this. Coyhis gives red to the east, yellow to the south, black to the west, and white to the north. He credits this to "the Lakota Nation of the Northern Plains."[68] But another source, also crediting the Lakota Medicine Wheel, assigns yellow to the east and red to the south.[69]

The object of studying the Medicine Wheel is to bring all these different forces and stages into balance. Disharmony can lead to addiction and all sorts of other problems, but as Don Coyhis puts it: "The Medicine Wheel teachings are a way to get back to the harmony which the Great Spirit placed in life."[70]

The Medicine Wheel has been adopted by numerous New Age groups who may or may not have an adequate acquaintance with Native cultures. An explicitly First Nations approach to recovery through the Medicine Wheel was created by Kip Coggins (Ojibway and Ottawa) and set forth in his book, *Alternative Pathways to Healing: The Recovery Medicine Wheel.*

Coggins' pan-Indian approach utilizes the four quarters of the Medicine Wheel, but he gives slightly different meanings to the four directions than do some other models. He assigns four steps for each of the four directions, creating a program of sixteen steps. According to Coggins: "The individual steps are guides for those who seek spiritual, emotional, psychological and physical growth or improvement."[71] His interpretation of the four directions and his sixteen steps are:

NORTH (The Physical Realm)

1. Beginning today I will take good physical care of myself.
2. Beginning today I will regain balance in my life by developing an understanding of the important connection between the physical, psychological, spiritual, and emotional parts of my existence.
3. Beginning today I will stop inflicting pain (either physically or emotionally) on others or myself.
4. Beginning today I will come to an understanding that change is a process I can't expect miracles overnight.)

EAST (The Realm of Knowledge and Enlightenment)

1. Beginning today I will reawaken to all of creation and to all of the beauty that exists in the world around me.
2. Beginning today I will make a commitment to release myself from a narrow view of life and begin to grow, learn and gain new knowledge.
3. Beginning today I will remember that I have a sacred right to live my life as I wish and the need to bring harmony and balance to my existence by respecting the life rights of others.
4. Beginning today I will work on understanding the changes I must make in order to achieve personal harmony, balance, and freedom.

SOUTH (The Spiritual Realm)

1. Beginning today I will come to an understanding of my special relation to Mother Earth. (Release my pain to Mother Earth.)
2. Beginning today I will come to an understanding of my special relation to Father Sky.
3. Beginning today I will seek a greater understanding of my sacred connection to all of the universe.
4. Beginning today I will reconnect with and nurture my own Spirit.

WEST (The Realm of Introspective Thought)

1. Beginning today I will speak honestly with myself.
2. Beginning today I will look at my problems and my accomplishments with a willingness to commit myself to positive growth and change.
3. Beginning today I will examine the ways in which I have tried to manipulate, control or manage the lives of others and make a commitment to stop this behavior.
4. Beginning today I will acknowledge that change in my life must begin with me.[72]

Since these steps are circular and not linear, you can begin the program at any point and then proceed clockwise around the circle.

Wellbriety!

An Indian man was sober but he wasn't content in AA. When he was awarded the distinguished Purpose Prize[*] in 2008, it was said of him: He "felt emptiness in sobriety. He found himself going

---

[*] The Purpose Prize is an award for social innovators over the age of sixty.

through the motions at support group meetings, disconnected from the reasons why he shouldn't drink."[73]

He also wondered why the support group he attended wasn't full of Indians. He wondered if other Indians who wanted to quit drinking also thought that something was missing from AA. Eventually he met "Johnny," another Native American in the AA program. Johnny took him on a five-day fast – a "vision quest" – up in the mountains. It was there that he had a vision of a white bison rising from the ground. "It was like my angel," he said. To him, this vision meant that his sobriety program would not be complete without acknowledging his Indian culture.[74]

He began devoting all his spare time to working with Indian alcoholics until, eventually, the task became overwhelming. He used up all his annual vacation and still did not have enough time for his job *and* his passion. At about this time, the corporation he worked for announced layoffs. They offered him a $141,000 buyout, which he took. After that he devoted all his time to White Bison, Inc., a nonprofit corporation he founded for the purpose of helping Indians and Native communities combat the many problems stemming from addictions.[75]

The Indian man in the above story is someone we have already heard from: Don Coyhis. His other accomplishments notwithstanding, Coyhis's greatest contributions to recovery are undoubtedly White Bison, Inc. and the growing Wellbriety movement that it birthed.

As Coyhis grew his organization, he consulted with many tribes and tribal elders. Among the first teachings he received from the elders are the Four Laws of Change. Coyhis received the Four Laws of Change from an elder in New Mexico, far removed from his Mohican heritage in Wisconsin. The Four Laws of Change apply to all four aspects of human societies (individual, family, community and nation) but their most important application is to the community. The Four Laws of Change are:

1. *Change comes from within* - True change starts with a desire to change. Change begins with a change of heart.

2. *In order for development to occur it must be preceded by a vision* - The vision may be a spiritual experience, a carefully thought-out business plan, or a combination of both. Whatever the seed event, the principle is this: "we move towards and become like that which we think about."
3. *A great learning must occur* - When applied to communities, this means that all parts of the cycle of life (baby, youth, adult and elder) must participate in the learning experience.
4. *You must create a healing forest* - The "healing forest" and the "sick forest" are metaphors for healthy and sick communities. Consider a "sick" forest. The trees are sick because there is something lacking or something amiss in the environment. The soil is poor; there is too much or two little sunshine or rain, etc. If young trees are taken from this forest and put into a nursery where they get proper nutrients, water and sunshine, they get better. But when they return to the forest, they get sick again. This is a metaphor for many communities. The community is sick with alcoholism, family violence, and so forth. Some "trees" are taken out of this forest and sent to a treatment center, where they get better. But when replanted back in the sick community, they get sick again. The message is that it is insufficient to just treat individuals – healing communities ("forests") must be created.[76]

In the course of his work with White Bison and Wellbriety, Coyhis had other visions. Richard Simonelli described one:

> In 1994 [Don Coyhis] had a vision. In his visionary experience, he saw a small tree shed its leaves and form itself into a circle of about four feet in diameter. As the vision continued, he saw the feathers from both Golden and Bald eagles fly through the air and arrive at the willow hoop. One by one the feathers attached themselves to the hoop until a total of 100

feathers fastened around the circumference of the willow...

After speaking about his vision with elders in order to understand its significance, word went out on the "moccasin telegraph" that eagle feathers were needed. One by one, they began to arrive from Native peoples around North America and even from around the world. The visionary hoop became a reality.[77]

Coyhis and others took this sacred hoop on numerous "hoop journeys" across the U.S.A. and Canada. Everywhere they went, they received publicity and promotion for the Wellbriety movement.

Although Coyhis didn't feel that AA gave him totally good sobriety, he remains an admirer of the program and readily credits it with saving many Indian lives, now and prior to the growth of the Wellbriety movement. In 2002 White Bison, Inc. published *The Red Road to Wellbriety: In the Native American Way*, which is sometimes called the "Indian Big Book." This book is the first complete offering of a culture-specific approach to the Twelve Steps. It closely follows the revered "Big Book" of AA, with the addition of chapters on codependency and adult children of alcoholics. Eighteen recovery stories written by Native North Americans are included.[78]

"Wellbriety" means to be both sober and well. *The Red Road to Wellbriety* states that, according to Indian elders, the Twelve Steps of AA are not an exclusively White man's way, they are also an Indian way, with one change: the Steps should be placed in a circle. Says the anonymous author of *The Red Road to Wellbriety*, the Indian Big Book "is written for those who choose to use the 12 Steps in a circle and the teachings the Elders have given to us."[79]

The White Bison version of the Steps revises some of the wording and names a specific Principle for each Step. The Twelve Steps and Twelve Principles of Wellbriety, along with their positions on the Medicine Wheel, are:

EAST – Finding the Creator

STEP 1	Honesty	— We admitted we were powerless over alcohol – that we had lost control of our lives.
STEP 2	Hope	— We came to believe that a power greater than ourselves could help us regain control.
STEP 3	Faith	— We made a decision to ask for help from a Higher Power and others who understand.

SOUTH – Finding Ourselves

STEP 4	Courage	— We stopped and thought about our strengths and our weaknesses and thought about ourselves.
STEP 5	Integrity	— We admitted to the Great Spirit, to ourselves, and to another person the things we thought were wrong about ourselves.
STEP 6	Willingness	— We are ready, with the help of the Great Spirit, to change.

WEST – Finding our Relatives

STEP 7	Humility	— We humbly ask a Higher Power and our friends to help us to change.
STEP 8	Forgiveness	— We made a list of people who were hurt by our drinking and want to make up for these hurts.
STEP 9	Justice	— We are making up to those people whenever we can, except when to do so would hurt them more.

NORTH – Finding the Elders' Wisdom

STEP 10   Perseverance — We continue to think about our strengths and weaknesses and when we are wrong we say so.

STEP 11   Spiritual Awareness — We pray and think about ourselves, praying only for the strength to do what is right.

STEP 12   Service — We try to help other alcoholics and to practice these principles in everything we do.[80]

The Red Road to Wellbriety gives specific instructions on how to work these steps. In keeping with First Nations' circle philosophy, the instructions are designed so that the recovering person can go through the steps numerous times, gaining a deeper understanding of Wellbriety with each cycle.

Coyhis is adamant that Wellbriety is not just for Indians. The program is for all races. Coyhis says that the Great Spirit did not create different races. Regarding the Creator, he says:

"He made only one race, the human race, but he made humans to wear different earth suits."[81]

Taking These Roads

While I have attended a few pow wows, I am not a Native North American nor a First Nations scholar. What I have written in this chapter is the result of considerable study of the references cited, as well as numerous other books, articles, videos – and nothing else. I apologize for any errors.

The **Longhouse Religion** is practiced on eight reservations in New York state and the Quebec and Ontario provinces of Canada. They are:

- The Allegany Reservation near Salamanca, New York
- The Cattaraugus Reservation near Gowanda, New York

- Tonawanda near Buffalo, New York
- The Onondaga Reservation near Syracuse, New York
- Oneida on the Thames River in Ontario
- St. Regis along the St. Lawrence River, New York
- Grand River near Brantford, Ontario
- Caughnawaga near Montreal, Quebec[82]

There is also a 2004 book, *The Path of Handsome Lake: A Model of Recovery for Native People*, by Alf H. Walle. Like Handsome Lake, Walle recommends restructuring and revitalizing Native cultures. Unfortunately, his book is written in an academic style, but Walle says that his methods are intended for use by addiction counselors *and* self-help groups. He gives a six-step program that he calls "The Path of Handsome Lake." The steps are:

1. I possess a culture and a tradition. Embracing them is sacred, meaningful, and joyful.
2. All cultural traditions change and are under attack. I will strive to help my culture evolve and flourish.
3. I will break the cycle of personal and cultural decay by ceasing to abuse alcohol.
4. I recognize my past errors and I will remember them when choosing a more noble and fulfilling path.
5. Having chosen a more noble and fulfilling path, I will strive to keep my errors in the past and correct them as soon as they occur.
6. My heritage and my traditions give me a spirituality. By denying them, I deny my own self and become vulnerable to relapse. By embracing them, I can better succeed in recovery and in life.[83]

The program has another part, the six "Landmarks of the Path." These are:

1. We recognize who we are.

2. We acknowledge that our heritage, culture, and traditions are our strength.
3. We reject the vulnerability that comes from ignoring our roots.
4. We realize that our brothers and sisters may have their own traditions and we respect them.
5. We understand that strength comes not in retreating from challenges, but from embracing ourselves.
6. While Handsome Lake was an American Indian, his example may be useful to others who face cultural and personal disruptions in their lives.[84]

The ***Indian Shaker Church*** may be on the decline, but according to David Wilma, there are approximately 21 congregations and 3,000 members in Washington, Oregon, Northern California, and British Columbia."[85]

Neither the *Longhouse Religion* nor the *Indian Shaker Church* have a presence on the Internet.

The ***Native American Church*** boasts a number of websites. An important site is: http://nativeamericanchurches.org/. There is also a listing of Native American Churches:
http://web.archive.org/web/20050308162749/www.utah-nac.org/nacindex.html

Many *Native American Church* congregations do not restrict membership based on race. However, the question of the legality of peyote use remains. Peyote is governed by a complex array of state and federal laws. Peyote is classified a Schedule 1 hallucinogen by the U.S. Government. This means that it is illegal to buy, sell or possess peyote without a DEA license. However, the listing of peyote as a controlled substance does not apply to use by the Native American Church. Nevertheless, there are state and local laws that apply in various jurisdictions. Unless you are sure of your status and the status of the ceremonies you are – or will be – attending, it is suggested that you seek competent legal counseling. I am not a lawyer and nothing written in this book should be taken as legal advice. The same goes for the possession of eagle feathers and some other wild animal parts. Generally, it is illegal for non-Indians to possess eagle parts and violators may be fined up to $25,000. But don't take my word for it. Unless you are sure that what you are buying, receiving, or possessing is legal, seek competent legal advice.

Indianized AA meetings may be available on reservations or in urban communities with a high percentage of Native Americans. Indianized AA meetings may not be just for Indians. One White man who attended Indian AA meetings said this:

> I used to go to our own A.A. meetings for years. I would listen to the speeches and despise the speakers. I felt lonely even in A.A. and I could not stop drinking. When I came to your [Indian] group it was different. I feel you are true friends. Your talks really sink in. I feel that what you say is honest. Through you people I have gained sobriety. You have taught me to be honest within myself. Your friendship has kept me from killing myself. I thank every one of you Indian friends for my sobriety.[86]

When walking the **Good Red Road,** you should know that *sweat lodge* ceremonies can be hazardous if they are not supervised by a properly trained leader. Between 1996 and 2009 seven deaths are known to have occurred at improperly performed, non-traditional sweat events, including three victims who died at a sweat conducted by James Arthur Ray in Sedona, Arizona.[87] Arvol Looking Horse, the nineteenth keeper of the Sacred White Buffalo Calf Pipe Bundle,[*] and other Indians, were appalled by this and concerned that the Sedona tragedy was being confused with their traditions. Said Looking Horse:

> Our First Nations people have to earn the right to pour the mini wiconi (water of life) upon the inyan

---

[*] This refers to the legend of the White Buffalo Calf Woman, who brought the Sacred Pipe to the Lakota/Dakota/Nakota people many generations ago.

oyate [stone people] in creating Inikaga [life within] by going on a vision quest for four years and four years to a Sundance. Then you are put through a ceremony to be painted – to recognize that you have now earned the right to take care of someone's life through purification... What has happened in the news with the makeshift sauna called the "sweat lodge" is not our ceremonial way of life.[88]

Kip Coggins' ***Recovery Medicine Wheel*** program is available through his book, *Alternative Pathways to Healing: The Recovery Medicine Wheel.* It may be out of print but there are some new and used copies available. There is also a second edition: *The Recovery Medicine Wheel: An Alternative Pathway to Healing and Wellness,* which was published by Ventajas, L.L.C. in Boston, Virginia (www.SocialWorkInfo.com). New and used copies of this edition are available too. There are also a few articles posted on the Internet that discuss Kip Coggins' program.

The website for ***White Bison, Inc.*** and the ***Wellbriety*** movement is: http://www.whitebison.org. The email address is info@whitebison.org. The phone number is 719-548-1000 (toll-free: 1-877-871-1495). The street address is: 701 N. 20th Street, Colorado Springs, CO 80904.

There are quite a few *Wellbriety* group meetings. An Internet site for finding these is:

http://www.whitebison.org/firestarter-resources/wellbriety-recovery-meetings.php.

There are many exciting things happening in Indian country, both for you, my Indian brothers and sisters, and for others. If you are Native and want to be part of this, good for you! If you are not Indian, but still want to be a part of it all, be polite, be respectful, be willing to learn and, with all you heart, seek to be sober. Whatever pathways you choose, I wish you well.

Mitakuye Oyasin!

Chapter Endnotes

1. Apess, William, author, and Barry O'Connell, editor (1997) *A Son of the Forest and Other Writings,* Amherst: University of Massachusetts Press, page 4.
2. Apess and O'Connell (1997) pages 6 - 7.
3. Apess and O'Connell (1997) page 25.
4. Apess and O'Connell (1997) page 47.
5. *Wikipedia* (1Aug 2010) *"William Apess."* Retrieved 9/15/2010 from: http://en.wikipedia.org/wiki/William_Apess. And "Seneca nation" (30 Jan 2009) *New World Encyclopedia.* Retrieved 9/15/2010 from: http://www.answers.com/topic/william-apess
6. Apess and O'Connell (1997) page xxii.
7. Coyhis, Don L. and William L. White (2006A) *Alcohol Problems in Native America: The Untold Story of Resistance and Recovery–The Truth About the Lie,* Colorado Springs, CO: White Bison, Inc., page 67.
8. Coyhis, D. and W. White (2002) "Addiction Recovery in Native America: Lost History, Enduring Lessons," *Counselor,* 3(5):16-20.
9. Foreman, Grant (1934) "A century of Prohibition" *Chronicles of Oklahoma, Volume 12, No.2,*June.Retrieved6/2/2013from: http://digital.library.okstate.edu/Chronicles/v012/v012p133.html
10. Cherrington, Ernest (1920) *The Evolution of Prohibition in the United States of America,* Montclair, NJ: Patterson Smith Publishing Corporation, page 21.
11. Krout, John Allen (1925) *The Origins of Prohibition,* New York: Russell and Russell, page 47.
12. Coyhis, Don and William L. White (2006B) "Alcohol Problems in Native America: A New and Provocative History," *Counselor,* 7(4), 54-56.
13. Coyhis, Don and William L. White (2002) "Addiction and Recovery in Native America,"*Wellbriety! White Bison's*

Online Magazine, Vol. 3, No. 5, page 4. Retrieved 9/15/2010 from: http://www.whitebison.org/magazine/2002/fall/Wellbriety!vol3no5.pdf
14. Coyhis and White (2006B).
15. Parker, Arthur C. (1913) *The Code of Handsome Lake, The Seneca Prophet,* page 23. Retrieved 8/21/2010 from: http://www.aren.org/prison/documents/american-indian/31/31.pdf
16. Parker (1913) page 23
17. Parker (1913) page 24
18. Parker (1913) page 24
19. Parker (1913) page 27.
20. Parker (1913) page 45.
21. Johnson, Elias (1881) *Legends, Traditions and Laws of the Iroquois or Six Nations And History Of The Tuscarora Indians,* Lockport, NY: Union Printing and Publishing Co., page 186.
22. "Jefferson-Handsome Lake Letter," November 3, 1802, in Coyhis and White (2006A) page 329.
23. Johnson (1881) page 187.
24. *Wikipedia* (20 Oct 2010) "Longhouse Religion." Retrieved 12/21/10 from: http://en.wikipedia.org/wiki/Longhouse_Religion
25. Maracle, Brian (1993) *Crazywater: Native Voices on Addiction Recovery,* New York: Penguin Books, page 22.
26. Rakestraw, Charles D. (1900) "The Shaker Indians of Puget Sound," in *The Southern Workman and Hampton School Record,* Vol. 29, No. 1, page 702.
27. Rakestraw (1900) page 708.
28. Rakestraw (1900) page 703.
29. Waterman, T. T. (1924) "The Shake Religion of Puget Sound," from *The Smithsonian Report for 1922,* Washington, DC: Government Printing Office, pages 499-507.
30. Slagle, A. Logan and Joan Weibel-Orlando (1986) "The Indian Shaker Church and Alcoholics Anonymous:

Revitalistic Curing Cults," *Human Organization,* Vol. 45, No. 4, pages 310 - 319.
31. Jilek-Aall, Louis M. (1972) "Alcohol and the Indian-White Relationship: The Function of Alcoholics Anonymous in Coast Salish Society," Master's Thesis, The University of British Columbia, page 73.
32. Stewart, Omer C. (1987) *Peyote Religion: A History,* Norman, OK: University of Oklahoma Press, page 91.
33. Hagan, William T. (1993) *Quanah Parker, Comanche Chief,* Norman, OK: University of Oklahoma Press, page 56.
34. Radin, Paul (1925) *The Peyote Cult.* Retrieved 1/26/2011 from: http://www.sacred-texts.com/nam/pla/pey/index.htm
35. Opler. Morris E. (July-Sept 1939) "A Description of a Tonkawa Peyote Meeting Held in1902," *American Anthropologist.* Reprinted in 2010 *American Ethnography Quasiweekly.* Retrieved 3/24/2011 from: http://www.americanethnography.com/article.php?id=24.
36. Stewart (1987) page 91.
37. Anderson, Edward F. (1996) *Peyote: The Divine Cactus,* second ed., Tucson: The University of Arizona Press, page 72.
38. Ojibwa (2009) "The Native American Church." Dec 15, Retrieved 3/26/11 from: http://www.nativeamericannetroots.net/showDiary.do?diaryId=312.
39. Pascarosa, P., S. Futterman and M. Halsweig (1976) "Observations of Alcoholics in the Peyote Ritual: A Pilot Study." *Annals of the New York Academy of Sciences,* 273:518-24. Quoted in Coyhis and White (2006A) page 124.
40. Kelley, Matthew J. (1977) "Native Americans, Neurofeedback, and Substance Abuse Theory," *Journal of Neurotherapy,* Vol. 2, Iss. 3. Retrieved 7/6/2013 from: http://www.tengerresearch.com/grow/supportinginfo/Kelley-Native_Amer_NF_and_SUD.pdf
41. Kelley, Dennis F. (2008) "Alcohol Abuse Recovery and Prevention as a Spiritual Practice," in *Religion and Healing*

in *Native America: Pathways for Renewal,* Suzanne J. Crawford O'Brien, editor, Westport, CN: Praeger, page 67.

42. "The Alkali Lake Community Story" (n.d.) The Four Worlds International Web page, PartIV. Retrieved 6/23/2013 from: http://4worlds.org/4w/ssr/partiv.htm.
43. Coyhis and White (2006A) page142.
44. Vick, Ronald D., Linda M. Smith and Carol Iron Rope Herrera (1998) "The Healing Circle: An Alternative Path to Alcoholism Recovery," *Counseling and Values,* 01607960, Jan., Vol. 42, Issue 2.
45. Coyhis and White (2006A) pages 140-141.
46. Jilek-Aall, Louise (1981) "Acculturation, Alcoholism and Indian-style AlcoholicsAnonymous," *Journal of Studies on Alcohol,* Suppl. No. 9.
47. Coyhis, Don and William White (2002) "Alcohol Problems in Native America: ChangingParadigms and Clinical Practices," *Alcoholism Treatment Quarterly,* 20(3/4), 157-166.
48. Jilek-Aall (1972) page 23.
49. Jilek-Aall (1981) page 154.
50. [Wilson, Bill, et al.] (1955) *Alcoholics Anonymous,* 2nd Edition, New York: Alcoholics Anonymous World Services, Inc., pages 59-60.
51. Womack, Marie-France Lisette (1996) *The Indianization of Alcoholics Anonymous,* Native American Research and Training Center, page 48. Retrieved 6/25/2013 from: http://library.ncrtm.org/pdf/M106.0001.01.pdf.
52. M., Mickey (2012) *Medicine Wheel of My Recovery,* Bloomington, IL: Author House, pages ix - xi.
53. Jones, Robert Blackwolf and Gina Jones (1995) *Listen to the Drum: Blackwolf Shares His Medicine,* Salt Lake City: Commune-A-Key Publishing.
54. Thin Elk, Gene (n.d.) quoted in: Arbogast, Doyle (1995) *Wounded Warriors: A Time for Healing,* Omaha: Little Turtle Publications, page 318.

55. Neihardt, John G. (1972) *Black Elk Speaks: Being the Life Story of a Holy Man of the Oglala Sioux As Told through John G. Neihardt (Flaming Rainbow),* Lincoln, NB: University of Nebraska Press, pages 28-29.
56. "The Native American Sweatlodge, A Spiritual Tradition" (n.d.). Retrieved 8/7/2003 from: http://www.barefootsworld.net/sweatlodge.html
57. Native American Information (n.d.) "Smudging Ceremony." Retrieved 7/27/2013 from: http://www.snowwowl.com/nainfosmudging.htm
58. Coyhis, Don (2000) "Culturally Specific Addiction Recovery for Native Americans," in *Bridges to Recovery,"* edited by Jo-Ann Krestan, New York: The Free Press, page 110.
59. Wood, Nicholas Breeze (2000) "The Sacred Pipe," *Sacred Hoop,* Issue 31, pages 19 - 21 and "The Native American Pipe Ceremony," *Native Americans Online.* Retrieved 7/27/2013 from: http://www.native-americans-online.com/native-american-pipe-ceremony.html
60. Cohen, Kenneth "Bear Hawk" (2003) *Honoring the Medicine: The Essential Guide to Native American Healing,* New York: One World Ballantine Books, pages 264-265.
61. "Wacipi-Powwow" (1994) *TPT Documentaries,* video 56 min 11 sec. Viewed 8/16/2013 at: http://video.tpt.org/video/2256819604/. And Schultz, Becky Olvera (n.d.) "Native American Powwow History & Description," *Pow Wow Power.* Retrieved 8/14/13 from: http://www.powwow-power.com/powwowhistory.html
62. "Native American or Indian Dance" (n.d.) Retrieved 8/17/2013 from: http://www.learningace.com/doc/781104/fd31121466a0b477cecdccbe0503ec20/native-americanor-indian-dance-htm
63. Quoted in Achterberg, Jeanne (1985) *Imagery in Healing: Shamanism and Modern Medicine,* Boston: Shambhala, page 146.
64. Cohen (2003) page 145.
65. Neihardt (1972) pages 197-203.

66. Coyhis (2000) page 92
67. Coyhis (2000) page 89.
68. Coyhis (2000) page 89.
69. "Lakota (Sioux) Medicine Wheel" (n.d.) *St. Joseph's Indian School*. Retrieved 8/21/2013 from: http://www.stjo.org/site/News2?page=NewsArticle&id=6459
70. Coyhis (2000) page 93.
71. Coggins, Kip (1990) *Alternative Pathways to Healing: The Recovery Medicine Wheel,* Deerfield Beach, FL: Health Communications, Inc., Page 15.
72. Coggins (1990) pages 16-36.
73. "Founder White Bison Purpose Prize Winner 2009" (n.d.) Retrieved 8/27/2013 from :http://www.encore.org/don-coyhis-purpose-prize
74. "Founder White Bison Purpose Prize Winner 2009" (n.d.)
75. "Founder White Bison Purpose Prize Winner 2009" (n.d.)
76. Coyhis and White (2006A) pages 157-158.
77. Simonelli, Richard (2000) "Journey of the Sacred Hoop," *Canku Ota - A Newsletter Celebrating Native America,* March 11, Issue 5.
78. Coyhis and White (2006A) page 193.
79. White Bison, Inc. (2002) *The Red Road to Wellbriety: In the Native American Way,* Colorado Springs, CO: White Bison, Inc., pages 47-48.
80. White Bison, Inc. (2002) pages 50-51.
81. Coyhis, Don (1999, 2006) "The Wellbriety Journey: Nine Talks by Don Coyhis," Colorado Springs, CO: White Bison, Inc., page 20. Retrieved 8/30/2013 from: http://whitebison.org/2006pdf/WellJourney10_3_06.pdf
82. Martin, John H. (2005) "Handsome Lake: A New Religion for the Seneca," Chapter 3 in *Saints, Sinners and Reformers: The Burned-Over District Re-Visited,* Fall, page 4. Retrieved 7/10/2013from: http://www.crookedlakereview.com/books/saints_sinners/martin3.html

83. Walle, Alf H. (2004) *The Path of Handsome Lake: A Model of Recovery for Native People,* Greenwich, CT: IAP, Information Age Publishing, page 190.
84. Walle (2004) page 191.
85. Wilma, David (18 Apr 2006) "Native Americans organize the Indian Shaker Church in 1892," *HistoryLink: the Free Online Encyclopedia of Washington State History.* Retrieved 10/11/2010 from: http://www.historylink.org/index.cfm?DisplayPage=output.cfm&file_id=2640
86. Quoted in Jilek-Aall (1981).
87. *Wikipedia* (29 May 2013) "Sweat Lodge." Retrieved 7/27/2013 from: http://en.wikipedia.org/wiki/Sweat_lodge
88. Looking Horse, Arvol (16 Oct 2009; 8 Jan 2010) "Concerning the deaths in Sedona." Retrieved 8/31/2013 from: http://www.fusioncash.net/forum.php?topic=20648.0;wap2

CHAPTER II:
Alcoholics Anonymous and Other Twelve Step Programs:
The Great Granddaddy

As the youngest child and only son of billionaire John D. Rockefeller, *Sr.*, John D. Rockefeller, *Jr.* could have been or done almost anything that he wanted.

What he chose was to devote his life to polishing up and restoring his father's and his family's image. He divested himself of almost all his business interests in order to give more of his time to philanthropy and improving the Rockefeller image. Ironically, one of the few businesses he remained active in almost became his undoing.

On April 20, 1914, a firefight broke out between the Colorado militia and striking coal miners living in a tent encampment near Ludlow, Colorado. Several miners, a bystander, and one Colorado guardsman were killed that day, but the real tragedy was discovered the next morning when the bodies of two women and eleven children were found dead under the charred remains of a tent that had been set ablaze. This tragic event is known as the Ludlow Massacre, one of history's bloodiest confrontations between labor and capital.

Be it right or wrong, the tragedy was blamed on John D. Rockefeller, Jr., who sat on the board of directors and owned the largest interest in Colorado Fuel and Iron, the company the miners were striking against.

Rockefeller was shocked at the outrage expressed against him. Socialist writer Upton Sinclair "indicted" Rockefeller for the murders of the women and children.[1] Helen Keller called him a "monster of capitalism."[2] And the International Workers of the World (IWW) picketed his mansion, making Rockefeller a virtual prisoner in his own home.³ To help quell the uproar, Rockefeller hired Ivy Lee, one of the first public relations experts in the country. Guided by Lee, Rockefeller made some concessions and admitted some fault. The savvy Ivy Lee made the most of this to get Rockefeller better press and media coverage. As a result, the Rockefeller family name and the junior Rockefeller's reputation were saved and possibly enhanced by his handling of the scandal. According to William Lyon MacKenzie King, a future Prime Minister of Canada who also advised Rockefeller during the crisis, the event was a turning point in the young Rockefeller's life.⁴

Ivy Lee died in 1934, but it was to his firm that the junior Rockefeller turned when he wanted to help promote Alcoholics Anonymous. In 1940, Rockefeller gave a dinner party to introduce the fledgling and largely unknown Alcoholics Anonymous (AA) organization to New York's moneyed elite. The dinner was a success and after that AA was put in touch with the public relations firm of Ivy Lee. According to AA historian Earnest Kurtz: "Marked by the Ivy Lee touch, the ensuing publicity was widespread and generally favorable… Requests for help and orders for the Big Book [AA's newly printed basic text] 'poured in…'"⁵

AA itself lists other significant founding moments, but some scholars and old time AA members believe it was the Rockefeller dinner that really founded AA by putting it on the road to establishment recognition and success.⁶ Hence the Ludlow Massacre and the interventions of Ivy Lee are significant, if somewhat indirect, critical moments in the chain of events leading to the huge success and dominance of AA and the Twelve Steps.

This chapter will examine the Twelve Step program and some of the history and philosophy of Alcoholics Anonymous, one of the largest and longest-lived recovery programs ever. It will also introduce some of the many the other programs that are patterned after AA.

AA and The Oxford Group

"Frank [Buchman, the Oxford Group's founder,] had been drying out drunks since before Bill [Wilson, AA's co-founder,] had his first cocktail."[7] So wrote an authority on Oxford Group history, T. Willard Hunter, in a 1978 unpublished manuscript.

The Oxford Group (OG) was a nondenominational Christian fellowship founded by Frank N. D. Buchman in the early part of the Twentieth Century. It reached its peak of popularity in the 1920s and 1930s.

AA credits several sources for the spiritual and intellectual ideas embodied in its program, but none comes close to outweighing the Oxford Group. As AA writes its history, it began in Zurich, Switzerland, where a wealthy American went to be treated by the famous psychiatrist, Dr. Carl Jung. After failures at treatment, Jung informed the man, Rowland Hazard, that he was hopelessly alcoholic unless he had a religious conversion. He advised Hazard to look for a religious organization to join. Hazard joined the Oxford Group and, as part of the group's practices, he set about trying to convert others. One of his successes was Ebby Thacher, another drunk, who carried the message to Bill Wilson. Wilson remained sober but was unable to convert others until he met Dr. Bob Smith while on a business trip to Akron, Ohio. These two, Wilson, known as "Bill W.," and Smith, known as "Dr. Bob," remained dry throughout their lifetimes and became AA's official co-founders. Of the two, Wilson is considered the more important because he lived longer and wrote much more prolifically. Smith was more important to AA's early growth, but it was Wilson who most influenced AA as it is today – and it was Wilson who wrote the famous *Twelve Steps,* which are the heart of the AA program.

AA's Twelve Steps were included in the previous chapter, Chapter One on Native North American recoveries, but for those who missed it, or who want a refresher, the Twelve Steps of Alcoholics Anonymous are:

1. We admitted we were powerless over alcohol—that our lives had become unmanageable.
2. Came to believe that a Power greater than ourselves could restore us to sanity.
3. Made a decision to turn our will and our lives over to the care of God AS WE UNDERSTOOD HIM.
4. Made a searching and fearless moral inventory of ourselves.
5. Admitted to God, to ourselves, and to another human being the exact nature of our wrongs.
6. Were entirely ready to have God remove all these defects of character.
7. Humbly asked Him to remove our shortcomings.
8. Made a list of all persons we had harmed, and became willing to make amends to them all.
9. Made direct amends to such people wherever possible, except when to do so would injure them or others.
10. Continued to take personal inventory and when we were wrong promptly admitted it.
11. Sought through prayer and meditation to improve our conscious contact with God AS WE UNDERSTOOD HIM, praying only for knowledge of His will for us and the power to carry that out.
12. Having had a spiritual awakening as the result of these steps, we tried to carry this message to alcoholics, and to practice these principles in all our affairs.[8]

Wilson gave generous credits to Dr. Jung (even though Jung admitted that his methods failed) and to William James, an American psychologist and philosopher (even though of James' many books, Wilson apparently read only one, *Varieties of Religious Experiences,* which he read while sobering up). Wilson downplayed the OG's contribution,[9] but the fact remains that Wilson, Smith and the other early AAs were all members of the Oxford Group for several years.

The Oxford Group, however, was not intellectually respected and not universally popular – especially with some religious denominations such as the Catholic church, which virtually banned Catholics from attending OG meetings.

Eventually Wilson did give credit to the Oxford Group, though not to Frank Buchman. At AA's twentieth anniversary Wilson said, "the important thing is this: the early AA got its ideas of self-examination, acknowledgment of character defects, restitution for harm done, and working with others straight from the Oxford Groups and directly from Sam Shoemaker, their former leader in America, and from nowhere else."[10] Bill Wilson never did acknowledge or thank Frank Buchman, but after Buchman's death he expressed regret that he had not done so.[11] In 1960, Wilson finally got to the truth of the matter, admitting that almost all of the Twelve Steps came from the Oxford Group.[12]

This is entirely true. It can be shown by a careful reading of accounts left by Oxford Group members who overcame their drinking problems. Among the more important and enlightening of these – which were written before Bill Wilson penned the Twelve Steps – are *Life Began Yesterday* by Stephen Foot and *The Big Bender* by Charles Clapp, Jr. These volumes, along with *I was a Pagan* by V. C. Kitchen, may have been the inspiration for AA's "Big Book" or basic text, *Alcoholics Anonymous.*

Since Clapp's book seems to offer the most examples, we will first follow its outline in showing how Oxford Groupers worked the steps. Even Clapp's description of the Oxford Group gives several clear examples of working the steps:

The Group believed God has a plan, not only for the world, but for each individual; that it was not possible to obtain a clear understanding of that plan until the individual had let God completely clean up his own life [*Steps Six* and *Seven*]; that the way to clean it up was completely to share (talk out) one's life with another individual [*Step Five*]... Then the group believed that one should completely surrender (turn over) his life to God [*Step Three*], sincerely trying to find out, day by day, hour by hour, God's plan for him. The latter was done by praying and listening [*Step Eleven*]...[13]

Clapp's first contact with the Oxford Group was when a friend of his expressed amazement that a former business partner had written to apologize for a disagreement they had years ago. It seems that this fellow had joined the OG. It is unknown whether he was alcoholic or not, but in making his apology he was doing what AA would later call its *Ninth Step,* making direct amends to those he had harmed.

Clapp's next exposure was when a fellow stockbroker, Shepherd Cornell, invited Clapp to an OG meeting. Cornell was thereby working a part of AA's Twelfth Step, which says to carry the message.

Oddly, Clapp's next experience was not AA's First Step (surrender) but a portion of AA's Twelfth Step, which says that one should have a *spiritual awakening* (or spiritual *experience*). Clapp had spent part of an evening talking with Rev. Sam Shoemaker, who is described above as the leader of the Oxford Group in America. Soon after leaving Shoemaker, Clapp had this experience:

> Suddenly the street lights grew dim, the most overwhelmingly powerful feeling gripped me, something inside me said, "you must surrender your life to Me!" Gradually the lights returned to their natural brightness, the gripping feeling left, and I was sitting bolt upright, tingling all over...[14]

Clapp sought out Shepherd Cornell and Sam Shoemaker again, both of whom described the event as a spiritual experience. When he met with Shoemaker for a second time, they prayed: "At last we got down on our knees. I prayed out loud for the first time in my life, simply asking God to take my life and run it..."[15] Clapp had performed AA's *Third Step*, which is to turn one's will and one's life over to the care of God.

A little later on, Clapp expressed the conviction that: "In so far [sic] as I was concerned, there was no longer any doubt of the existence of God."[16] Here we see that Clapp had worked part of AA's *Second Step,* which has members come to believe in God or a Power greater than themselves. A little while later Clapp had some doubts about God's plan for him, and so he prayed about it. This would be AA's *Step Eleven.*

Clapp next apologizes to his family, from whom he was estranged, and to a girl he had been seeing. This is an example of Clapp working *Step Nine,* making amends.

After two or three years, Clapp still had not gotten completely sober. Then he reported that "a former drunk who had completely given up drinking after coming in touch with the group cornered me." It so happened that this former drunk was AA co-founder-to-be Bill Wilson. Only after talking with Wilson did Clapp admit that "drinking had me licked."[17] In other words, Oxford Group member Wilson worked AA's *Step Twelve,* carrying the message, and got Oxford Group member Charles Clapp to work *Step One,* admitting he was powerless. Although Clapp did not remain sober for the rest of his life, he reported that from that day in October 1935 to at least 1938 (the publication date of his book) he did not have a drink.

Clapp went on to tell about his talking over his life completely with someone (*Step Five*) and the difficulty of trying to make complete amends or restitutions (*Step Nine*). Finally, Clapp mentions his "countless chances to help others,"[18] thereby demonstrating that he too worked AA's *Step Twelve.*

Stephen Foot also practiced some – maybe all – of AA's Twelve Steps. For example he worked *Steps One* and *Two*: "One decides that one has not controlled one's life particularly well hitherto, and therefore it had better be put under new management;"[19] and *Step Three*: "God broke through [and] I surrendered my life to Him;"[20] He also worked *Step Five:* "When for the first time in my life I had been completely honest about myself, with another man, I felt like Christian [a character in John Bunyan's *Pilgrim's Progress*] when the load rolled off his back;" and *Step Eleven:* "I… ask[ed] God to show me His purpose for my life and claim[ed] from Him the power to carry that out."[21]

Another Oxford Grouper who left a record of his sobriety achieved in the OG was V. C. Kitchen. Kitchen worked *Steps One and Two:* "I then and there admitted my inability to quit [drinking alcohol] of my will and asked God to take charge of the matter;"[22] and *Step Three:* "I surrender [to] Thee my entire life, O God. I have made a mess of it, trying to run it myself. *You* take it – the whole thing – and run it for me, according to Your will and plan."[23] He also worked *Step Five:* "I found myself blurting out the whole story I was never going to tell anybody;"[24] *Step Seven:* "[God] satisfied unsound desire by *removing* the desire itself and that has given me the only genuine satisfaction I have ever found;"[25] and *Step Nine:* "[God] gave me courage to hand my partner a check for the estimated discrepancy in my expense account."[26] Finally, he worked *Step Eleven:* "I have learned the secret of two-way praying. I have learned not only to pray *to* God but to *listen* to Him."[27]

Other Oxford Groupers made written inventories of their sins (*Step Four*). Rev. Sam Shoemaker advised in his book *How to Become a Christian:* "It would be a very good thing if you took a piece of foolscap [large format] paper and wrote down the sins you are guilty of."[28] Kitchen himself left a fascinating account of what may be an early version of a written Fourth Step. He described what the OG called the game of "truth": "You write down the five things you honestly like the most in life. And you write down the five things you most hate. Then – if any change has come into your life – you write them down again to show the comparison between your old life and the new."[29] For example, in his old life Kitchen most liked himself and in his new life he most liked God. In his old life he most hated poverty (for himself) and in his new life he most hated sin.

According to prolific writer and AA member Dick B., one of Kitchen's daughters "specifically confirmed… that Kitchen 'drank too much and quit drinking 100% soon after meeting the Oxford Group and remained sober until he died.'"[30]

How it Works: Twelve Steps – Two Interpretations

There must be hundreds if not thousands of books and articles written about the famous Twelve Steps of Alcoholics Anonymous.

To summarize or analyze them all here would be impossible. This section will concentrate on two *official* interpretations of the steps, one found in *Alcoholics Anonymous,* AA's beloved "Big Book," and the other in AA's later testament, the *Twelve Steps and Twelve Traditions,* popularly known in AA as the "Twelve and Twelve." Both books were largely written by Bill Wilson, but the interpretations of some of the steps are surprisingly different.

The "Twelve and Twelve" was written thirteen years after the "Big Book." In it, Wilson briefly explained the reason for the differences. According to Wilson, the *Twelve Steps and Twelve Traditions,* "proposes to broaden and deepen the understanding of the Twelve Steps as first written in the earlier work."[31] Other than that statement, Wilson made few attempts to tie the two interpretations together. The following brief discussion will concentrate mostly on pointing out the significant differences; differences which often seem to be overlooked. It is not an instruction guide for working the steps, nor a criticism of either set of instructions.

#STEP ONE: We admitted we were powerless over alcohol – that our lives had become unmanageable.

AA's Step One is not specifically addressed in the "Big Book." Instead, the reader is referred to "our description of the alcoholic" (Chapters 2 and 3). In these chapters, Wilson was at pains to distinguish a "real alcoholic" from "a certain type of hard drinker [who] may have the habit badly enough to gradually impair him physically and mentally."[32] At the time, Wilson must have thought that one could be such a hard drinker and still not be an alcoholic. AA, Wilson maintained, is only for the *real* alcoholics.

In the "Twelve and Twelve," Wilson took a different approach. There he emphasized the "fatal progression" of alcoholism and the possibility of "raising the bottom" for alcoholics who are not the worst off. In both volumes he recommended that doubters "try some controlled drinking," thereby, he thought, either proving or disproving their alcoholism.[33]

#STEP TWO: Came to believe that a Power greater than ourselves could restore us to sanity.

AA's "Big Book" does not directly address this step either. It refers readers back to the fourth chapter, titled "We Agnostics." Chapter four is a relatively standard argument against agnostic or atheistic materialism and in favor of belief in a spiritual reality. Wilson pointed out times when material science has been wrong, such as the scientists who "proved" airplanes could not fly.[34] He reminded the reader that physical appearances can deceive: "The prosaic steel girder," he wrote, is not what it seems, but "a mass of electrons whirling around each other at incredible speed."[35]

In the "Twelve and Twelve," Wilson made the same sorts of arguments, but there he emphasized the large number of believers in AA. He pointed out that the spiritual life makes sense because it works for so many people who were former atheists or agnostics. In the "Twelve and Twelve," Wilson offered the somewhat controversial invitation that someone could, if he or she wished, make AA itself their "higher power."[36] This was generally meant to be a temporary state of affairs. Wilson believed that an AA member would eventually come to accept a more traditional concept of the deity. In fact, later on in the "Twelve and Twelve," Wilson wrote that as a result of working the steps, doubters would come to "love God and call Him by name."[37]

#STEP THREE: Made a decision to turn our will and our lives over to the care of God AS WE UNDERSTOOD HIM.

As explained above, the "Big Book" covers the first three steps quite succinctly: "Our description of the alcoholic, the chapter to the agnostic, and our personal adventures before and after, make clear three pertinent ideas: a) That we were alcoholic and could not manage our own lives. b) That probably no human power could have relieved our alcoholism. c) That God could and would if He were sought."

"Being convinced," Wilson declared, "WE WERE AT STEP THREE."[38]

After a brief argument that the drinker must "quit playing God,"[39] Wilson offered a suggested prayer to say when taking this step:

> God, I offer myself to Thee – to build with me and to do with me as Thou wilt. Relieve me of the bondage of self, that I may better do Thy will. Take away my difficulties, that victory over them may bear witness to those I would help of Thy Power, Thy Love, and Thy Way of life. May I do Thy will always![40]

The above is the "Big Book's" version of Step Three. In the "Twelve and Twelve" the third Step is made longer and more complicated. Step Three is not something that one does with a prayer of surrender as the early AAs apparently did, but something that one works at for a lifetime. In the "Twelve and Twelve," Step Three is described as difficult, but the key, Wilson said, is willingness. As long as one practices willingness one can work Step Three *a little at a time*.

#STEP FOUR: Made a searching and fearless moral inventory of ourselves.

Nowhere is the difference between the "Big Book" and the "Twelve and Twelve" more apparent than in Wilson's discussions of Step Four. In the "Big Book" the emphasis is on resentment, which is called "the number one offender."[41] Wilson suggested that each alcoholic look at his or her own dishonesty, selfishness, self-seeking, and fear in relation to each resentment and that he or she tabulate or write down the people they are resentful of, the cause or reason for it, and how it affects them. For instance, in the example given in the "Big Book," someone is resentful of a Mr. Brown because of the attention Brown pays to the man's wife. This affects his sex relations, self-esteem, and so forth.

The interpretation of this step given in the "Twelve and Twelve" is radically different. Here the root problem is not resentment, but instincts. According to Wilson, "nearly every serious emotional problem can be seen as a case of misdirected instinct."[42] Despite this seemingly psychological foundation, Wilson recommended using religion's Seven Deadly Sins (pride, greed, lust, anger, gluttony, envy, and sloth) as a guide for naming the defects.

In both books, Wilson suggested making the inventory in writing. In the "Twelve and Twelve" he recommended asking and then answering a series of questions. For instance: "When, and how, and in just what instances did my selfish pursuit of the sex relation damage other people and me?"[43] And: "In addition to my drinking problem, what character defects contributed to my financial instability?"[44]

#STEP FIVE: Admitted to God, to ourselves, and to another human being the exact nature of our wrongs.

Step Five is basically about confession. This is one item where the "Big Book" and the "Twelve and Twelve" do not diverge, or diverge very little. Both emphasize the importance of the step and the difficulty of taking it. In the "Big Book," Wilson wrote: "We must be entirely honest with somebody if we are to live long or happily in this world."[45] In the "Twelve and Twelve," Wilson warned: "So intense... is our fear and reluctance to do this, that many AA's at first try to bypass Step Five."[46] In both books, Wilson's main concern was that Step Five be taken – that one's shortcomings and character defects be discussed – and that they be discussed with the right person.

#STEP SIX: Were entirely ready to have God remove all these defects of character.

This step has one of the briefest discussions in the "Big Book." In one or two paragraphs, Wilson described how this step immediately follows Step Five and immediately leads into Step Seven.

In the "Twelve and Twelve," however, the emphasis is different. "'This is the Step that separates the men from the boys,'" Wilson wrote, quoting "a well-loved clergyman who happens to be one of AA's greatest friends."[47]

Once again, Wilson's discussion in the "Twelve and Twelve" is quite a departure. While the "Big Book" leaves the impression that Step Six is something that is done and over with, in the "Twelve and Twelve" it literally becomes a lifetime job. One has to repeatedly work the step, *"without any reservations whatever."*[*][48] Step Six, Wilson explained, is "difficult, but not impossible."[49]

#STEP SEVEN: Humbly asked Him to remove our shortcomings.

The "Big Book" also makes short work of this step. "When ready," Wilson wrote, "We say something like this:

> My Creator, I am now willing that you should have all of me, good and bad. I pray that you now remove from me every single defect of character which stands in the way of my usefulness to you and my fellows. Grant me strength, as I go out from here, to do your bidding. Amen.
>
> Stated Wilson: "We have then completed STEP SEVEN."[50]

That's the "Big Book's" version. Again, in the "Twelve and Twelve," Wilson takes a different approach. In the *Twelve Steps and Twelve Traditions,* Step Seven is about *humility,* and gaining the proper amount of humility, Wilson believed, "takes most of us a

---

[*] Emphasis in the original.

long time."[51] According to Wilson: "It was only by repeated humiliations that we were forced to learn something about humility."[52]

STEP EIGHT: Made a list of all persons we had harmed, and became willing to make amends to them all.

The "Big Book's" discussion of Step Eight is the briefest of all. "We have a list of all persons we have harmed and to whom we are willing to make amends," the "Big Book" says. "We made it when we took inventory."[53] That's it.

The "Twelve and Twelve's" discussion of Step Eight is longer and seems to make it more daunting. "This is a very large order," the "Twelve and Twelve" says. "It is a task which we may perform with increasing skill but never really finish."[54]

STEP NINE: Made direct amends to such people wherever possible, except when to do so would injure them or others.

This step is about making restitutions or amends. Here there is no essential difference between the discussions in the "Big Book" and the "Twelve and Twelve."

It is in this part of the "Big Book" that we find what have become known as the Twelve Promises. As they appear in the "Big Book," the Promises are unnumbered and there is no evidence that Wilson actually counted them. It appears to be coincidental that they can be numbered to make twelve. With the numbers added in brackets, the Twelve Promises are: If we are painstaking about this phase of our development, [1] we will be amazed before we are half way through. [2] We are going to know a new freedom and a new happiness. [3] We will not regret the past nor wish to shut the door on it. [4] We will comprehend the word serenity and we will know peace. [5] No matter how far down the scale we have gone, we will see how our experience can benefit others. [6] That feeling of uselessness and self-pity will disappear. [7] We will lose interest in selfish things and gain interest in our fellows. [8] Self-seeking will slip away. [9]

Our whole attitude and outlook upon life will change. [10] Fear of people and of economic insecurity will leave us. [11] We will intuitively know how to handle situations which used to baffle us. [12] We will suddenly realize that God is doing for us what we could not do for ourselves.[55]

#STEP TEN: Continued to take personal inventory and when we were wrong promptly admitted it.

Step Ten is sometimes called a maintenance step. It is a continuation, on a daily basis, of Steps Four, Five and Nine. It is during the discussion of Step Ten in the "Big Book" that Wilson brings up the idea of daily maintenance. Elsewhere in the "Big Book," Wilson frequently used the word "recovered,"[56] Take, for example, this statement in the Foreword to the First Edition:
"To show other alcoholics PRECISELY HOW WE HAVE RECOVERED is the main purpose of this book."*[57] But when it came to Step Ten, Wilson took back some of this assertion: "We are not cured of alcoholism. What we really have," Wilson said, "is a daily reprieve contingent on the maintenance of our spiritual condition."[58]

The discussion in the "Twelve and Twelve" for this step is longer, but not significantly different. The most important differences are in the previous Steps. Where the "Big Book" gives the impression that many of the Steps can be performed rather quickly, the "Twelve and Twelve" emphasizes that they could take "a long time."

#STEP ELEVEN: Sought through prayer and meditation to improve our conscious contact with God AS WE UNDERSTOOD HIM, praying only for knowledge of His will for us and the power to carry that out.

Step Eleven is about prayer and meditation. No specific method of meditation is taught. In AA, it is often said that prayer is talking

---

* Emphasis in the original.

to God and meditation is listening. The Oxford Groupers called this "two way prayer."[59]

The "Big Book" recommends that time be set aside in the mornings and evenings for prayer and meditation or listening. Without mentioning its author, the "Twelve and Twelve" recommends studying "a really good prayer," which in this case is the prayer of Saint Francis of Assisi. As quoted in the "Twelve and Twelve," the famous prayer of Saint Francis is as follows:

> Lord make me a channel of thy peace – that where there is hatred, I may bring love – that where there is wrong, I may bring the spirit of forgiveness – that where there is discord, I may bring harmony – that where there is error, I may bring truth – that where there is doubt, I may bring faith – that where there is despair, I may bring the hope – that where there are shadows, I may bring light – that where there is sadness, I may bring joy. Lord, grant that I may seek rather to comfort than to be comforted – to understand, than to be understood – to love, than to be loved. For it is by self-forgetting that one finds. It is by forgiving that one is forgiven. It is by dying that one awakens to Eternal Life. Amen.[60]

#STEP TWELVE: Having had a spiritual awakening as the result of these steps, we tried to carry this message to alcoholics, and to practice these principles in all our affairs.

AA's Twelfth Step contains three distinct parts: 1) having a spiritual awakening; 2) carrying the message; and 3) practicing AA's principles.

When this step was first published, AA used the words *spiritual experience* rather than spiritual awakening. This lead many who read the "Big Book" to believe that a specific, profound experience, such as Wilson himself reportedly had, was a necessity for recovery. As Wilson described his experience in the "Big Book":

There was a sense of victory, followed by such a peace and serenity as I had never known. There was utter confidence. I felt lifted up, as though the great clean wind of a mountain top blew through and through. God comes to most men gradually, but His impact on me was sudden and profound.[61]

The misunderstanding was so common and so important that AA changed the wording of the step and added an appendix to the "Big Book," Appendix II, which explains that it is perfectly all right to have an experience of the "educational variety" – that is, a slow and gradual awakening to God or a Higher Power.

The "Big Book" devotes an entire chapter (Chapter Seven, "Working With Others") to the second part of this step. Chapter Seven is loaded with advice on helping others, some of which may have been made obsolete by the passage of time and the emergence of professional treatment providers. Perhaps wisely, the "Twelve and Twelve" avoids this emphasis.

The third part of this step says to "practice these principles in all our affairs." Nowhere does AA itself specifically enumerate what the principles are. Some say they are the Oxford Group's Four Absolutes: honesty, purity, unselfishness and love. Others say they are honesty, open mindedness and willingness (HOW). Still other AA members, other Twelve Step programs, and some professional counselors have different ideas, many of which can be found on the Internet. The principles are apparently not limited to the number twelve. The hindsfoot.org website calls attention to a number of virtues that were taught to early AA members. As published in a short pamphlet named "The Tablemate,"* these are: humility, generosity, simple justice, honest pride in work well done, simplicity, patience, industry, faith, hope, trust, willingness and "so on through a long list."[62]

---

* The official title is "Alcoholics Anonymous: An Interpretation of the Twelve Steps," sometimes called the "Table Leader's Guide," the "Detroit pamphlet," and so on.

AA's Culture and Traditions

Almost everyone has heard of Alcoholics Anonymous, but what is it, exactly? AA's most basic description of itself is designed to briefly describe what AA is and what it is not; this statement is known as "The AA Preamble." It reads as follows:

> Alcoholics Anonymous is a fellowship of men and women who share their experience, strength and hope with each other that they may solve their common problem and help others to recover from alcoholism.
> The only requirement for membership is a desire to stop drinking. There are no dues or fees for AA membership; we are self-supporting through our own contributions. AA is not allied with any sect, denomination, politics, organization or institution; does not wish to engage in any controversy; neither endorses nor opposes any causes. Our primary purpose is to stay sober and help other alcoholics to achieve sobriety.
> Copyright © by The AA Grapevine, Inc.

This description of AA was first used (with some slightly modified wording) in the June 1947 issue of the *AA Grapevine*, AA's official magazine. It appears on page one of every issue of the *Grapevine* and is used as an opening for many AA meetings.

AA meetings are considered by many members to be *the* most important part of AA. "Don't drink, don't think, and go to meetings" is advice that is frequently given to an AA newcomer. For those who are just starting out, many AAs suggest going to a meeting every day for three solid months – "ninety meetings in ninety days."

> AA meetings are often jocular affairs, filled with funny stories that members tell about themselves and their exploits during their drinking days. There are numerous types of meetings and formats, which may not be available in every town or city: speaker

meetings, discussion meetings, closed meetings (for alcoholics only), open meetings (for anyone who is interested) and meetings for special populations such as young people, African-Americans, Hispanics/Latinos, Native-Americans, women only, gays and/or lesbians, doctors, lawyers, airline piolets, pharmacists, veterinarians, and so forth.

Meetings are usually opened with a reading of the Preamble and/or a recitation of The Serenity Prayer:

God, grant us the serenity to accept the things we cannot change, Courage to change the things we can, and wisdom to know the difference.

It is also a standard practice to read the first two and one-half pages of the "Big Book's" Chapter Five, "How it Works." These pages include AA's Twelve Steps. When anyone speaks at an AA meeting, it is customary, if not mandatory, to introduce oneself by saying "My name is _____ and I am an alcoholic." (or "an alcoholic and a drug addict").

Meetings are usually ended by asking everyone to join hands while reciting the Lord's Prayer or, rarely, a less explicitly Christian ceremony may be used. There are no dues or fees for AA membership, but a collection basket is usually passed asking for nominal contributions to defray expenses.

Sponsorship is an increasingly important element of AA. A sponsor is an older member (older in terms of sobriety) who takes a special interest in and counsels a newer member, helping him or her to work the steps. The newer member is called a sponsee. In some groups a newcomer may be assigned a sponsor, but in most cases the sponsee is responsible for asking someone to be his or her sponsor.

As far as most AA members are concerned, AA's governance is accomplished at the group level and is guided by AA's Twelve Traditions. The Traditions were created by Bill Wilson and are designed to keep AA together in spite of differing personalities and views. They have accomplished their purpose admirably since AA has been in existence for well over seventy-five years. The Traditions exist in two forms, a long form, which is how Bill Wilson originally wrote them, and a short form, which was created to make the format of the Traditions more like that of the Steps. The Twelve Traditions of AA (short form) are:

1. Our common welfare should come first; personal recovery depends upon AA unity.

2. For our group purpose there is but one ultimate authority—a loving God as He may express Himself in our group conscience. Our leaders are but trusted servants; they do not govern.

3. The only requirement for AA membership is a desire to stop drinking.

4. Each group should be autonomous except in matters affecting other groups or AA as a whole.

5. Each group has but one primary purpose—to carry its message to the alcoholic who still suffers.

6. An AA group ought never endorse, finance, or lend the AA name to any related facility or outside enterprise, lest problems of money, property, and prestige divert us from our primary purpose.

7. Every AA group ought to be fully self-supporting, declining outside contributions.

8. Alcoholics Anonymous should remain forever non-professional, but our service centers may employ special workers.

9. AA, as such, ought never be organized; but we may create service boards or committees directly responsible to those they serve.

10. Alcoholics Anonymous has no opinion on outside issues; hence the AA name ought never be drawn into public controversy.

11. Our public relations policy is based on attraction rather than promotion; we need always maintain personal anonymity at the level of press, radio, and films.

12. Anonymity is the spiritual foundation of all our traditions, ever reminding us to place principles before personalities.[63]

Programs Patterned after AA

In 1999, Bill Wilson was named one of *Time* magazine's "100 Persons of the Century."[64] If Wilson had done nothing more than co-found Alcoholics Anonymous, he could have deserved such an honor for the impact he had on alcoholism, one of the world's biggest health and social problems. But Wilson's work has extended far beyond problem drinking to address scores of other addictions and mental-health conditions.

It is doubtful that anyone has a 100 percent complete and accurate list of all the Twelve Step or anonymous programs there are or ever have been. Alcoholics Anonymous has been very liberal in allowing others to adopt and use its Steps, Traditions and slogans. Usually only slight modifications are needed to the Steps and Traditions to create a program that is intended to solve some other problem. For instance, for the Narcotics Anonymous program, the wording of Step One is changed from "powerless over alcohol" to "powerless over *our addiction,*" and the wording of Step Twelve is changed from "carry this message to alcoholics," to "carry this message to *addicts.*" [emphasis added]

Below is a partial list and brief description of some of the programs that are patterned after AA. The list is extensive and you may want to skim through it, looking for programs that especially interest you.

Adrenaline Addicts Anonymous -
http://www.adrenalineaddicts.org/
> AAA is a support group for persons who use their own adrenaline as an addictive drug.

Adult Children of Alcoholics -
http://www.adultchildren.org/
> ACA (or ACOA) is an organization for those who had an alcoholic parent, or who grew up in any sort of dysfunctional family or home. It was started in 1978 in New York City.

Al-anon/Alateen –
http://www.al-anon.alateen.org/
> Al-anon is for families and friends of alcoholics. Alateen, an affiliated organization, is for teenage children of alcoholics. Al-anon was founded in 1951 by Lois Wilson and Anne B. It was probably the first program to use the Twelve Steps for something other than alcoholism.

Alcohólicos Anónimos –
http://www.aa.org/lang/sp/subpage.cfm
> Spanish-speaking AA meetings are available in most cities and Spanish speaking communities and there are Spanish language editions of the "Big Book," the "Twelve and Twelve" and other Twelve Step literature.

All Addicts Anonymous –
http://www.alladdictsanonymous.org/
> This program is for those suffering from any sort of addiction. It claims to teach the original way of working the Twelve Steps, the way the earliest AA members did it. The program includes

the Oxford Group's Four Absolutes of honesty, purity, unselfishness and love.

Bettors Anonymous –
http://www.bettorsanonymous.org/home.html

Bettors Anonymous was founded on May 9, 1990 in Stoneham, MA. It is said to be based on the original Twelve Steps and Twelve Traditions of AA. BA's goal is to help its members overcome compulsive gambling.

Changing Attitudes In Recovery –
http://www.cairforyou.com/

C.A.I.R. (pronounced "care") was founded in 1990 by psychologist James O. Henman, PhD. It is a program that treats addictions, along with other problems, and its meetings are free. C.A.I.R. uses many tools for change, including the Twelve Steps. The heart of the program is said to be eight "Fundamental Principles of Healthy Change." These include items such as Principle No. 1: "A growing commitment to being non-judgmental, open and accurate." Henman says that: "These eight Fundamental Principles of Healthy Change are the heart of an esteeming New Program that allows you to nurture your ability to bring healthy perceptions into your life."[65]

Chemically Dependent Anonymous –
http://www.cdaweb.org/

CDA is a Twelve Step program for those with any drug problem or combination of drug problems, including alcohol. It was started in Annapolis, Maryland in 1980.

Cocaine Anonymous –
http://www.ca.org/

CA is for those who are addicted to cocaine. It was founded in Los Angeles in 1982. To utilize CA, it is not necessary to identify yourself as a cocaine addict. The affiliate or auxiliary program for family members is Co-Anon.

Compulsive Eaters Anonymous – H.O.W. –
http://www.ceahow.org/ -
> CEA-HOW's roots go back to 1979 but it was not incorporated until 1998. It is a fellowship whose purpose is to help individuals overcome compulsive eating. All groups are sugar and flower abstinent and committed to weighing and measuring the food they eat.

Crystal Meth Anonymous –
http://www.crystalmeth.org/
> CMA is for those who are recovering or trying to recover from an addiction to methamphetamine. It was founded in 1994 in California. Since methamphetamine use is popular in gay communities, many meetings in large cities are designated gay/lesbian.

Debtors Anonymous –
http://www.debtorsanonymous.org/ -
> DA is for those whose lives are unmanageable due to debt, compulsive spending, or under-earning. Debtors Anonymous has existed periodically since 1968. It has been in permanent operation since 1976.

Depressed Anonymous –
http://www.depressedanon.com/
> Depressed Anonymous is a Twelve Step program for those who are depressed. It is headquartered in Louisville, KY.

Double Trouble in Recovery –
http://www.doubletroubleinrecovery.org/
> DTR uses an adaption of the Twelve Steps to help those who are dually diagnosed with addiction and a mental health problem.

Dual Diagnosis Anonymous –
http://ddaws.com/about.htm -
> DDA is a peer support group based on the Twelve Steps of Alcoholics Anonymous plus an additional five steps that focus on Dual Diagnosis. It was founded in 1996.

Dual Recovery Anonymous –
http://draonline.org/
> This program is for those who suffer from chemical dependency and also from one or more mental health disorders. DRA began in Kansas City in 1989.

Emotional Health Anonymous –
http://emotionalhealthanonymous.org/
> According to its preamble: "Emotional Health Anonymous is a fellowship of men and women who share their experience, strength and hope with each other that they may recover from their emotional problems and help others who still suffer to find a new way of life."[66] EHA has face to face meetings, mostly in the greater Los Angeles area, and also hosts a teleconference meeting every Sunday evening.

Emotions Anonymous –
http://www.emotionsanonymous.org/
> EA is a program for those who are suffering from emotional or psychological problems or difficulties. EA requires members to have a desire to become emotionally well. It was incorporated in 1971.

Families Anonymous –
http://www.familiesanonymous.org/
> FA is for families and friends of those who have addiction or behavior problems.

Food Addicts Anonymous –
http://www.foodaddictsanonymous.org/

FAA seeks to help people with what it describes as the biochemical disease of food addiction.

Food Addicts in Recovery Anonymous –
http://www.foodaddicts.org/
This organization was founded in 1998. Its purpose is to help people recover from food addiction or bulimia.

Gamblers Anonymous –
http://www.gamblersanonymous.org/
GA is for compulsive gamblers. It was founded in 1957 in Los Angeles. Gamblers Anonymous has affiliated programs, Gam-Anon and Gam-A-Teen, for the families of problem gamblers.

GreySheeters Anonymous –
http://www.greysheet.org/cms/
This is a fellowship whose members seek to recover from compulsive overeating. It was founded in 1998.

GROW –
http://www.grow.net.au/ -
GROW was founded in 1957 by Father Cornelius Keogh, a Catholic priest, and other former mental patients in Sydney, Australia. Its purpose is to promote mental health recovery and personal growth. GROW uses a rewritten – not just adapted – version of the Twelve Steps. Today there are nearly 600 GROW groups in various English speaking countries, including the United States. The website for GROW in America is: http://www.growinamerica.org/ .

Heroin Anonymous –
http://www.heroin-anonymous.org/haws/index.html
HA is for those who have a heroin addiction problem.

Marijuana Anonymous –
http://www.marijuana-anonymous.org/
>   MA is an adaption of the AA program for those who are addicted to marijuana. It has been in existence since 1989.

Methadone Anonymous –
http://www.methadonesupport.org/
>   Methadone Anonymous is a Twelve Step program for individuals who are in methadone treatment programs.

Moms on Methadone –
http://methadonesupport.org/Pregnancy.html
>   MOM offers support for pregnant women who are on methadone.

Narcotics Anonymous –
http://www.na.org/
>   NA is for those who are addicted to drugs other than alcohol. "The White Booklet," an early NA pamphlet, describes the Narcotics Anonymous program this way:

>>   NA is a nonprofit fellowship or society of men and women for whom drugs had become a major problem. We ... meet regularly to help each other stay clean... We are not interested in what or how much you used... but only in what you want to do about your problem and how we can help.[67]

There were a number of failed attempts and false starts at initiating a program called Narcotics Anonymous. The Narcotics Anonymous program that is available today, however, is very well established. It was started by Jimmy Kinnon and others in 1953. NA is the largest world-wide Twelve Step organization other than AA itself. The related family support program is Nar-Anon.

Nicotine Anonymous –
http://www.nicotine-anonymous.org/
   NicA is for those addicted to nicotine. It was started in California in 1982.

Neurotics Anonymous –
http://neuroticosanonimos.us/index.html*
   According to its website, which is available in English and Spanish: "Neurotics Anonymous is a group of people who are banded together to solve their emotional problems by following the Alcoholics Anonymous Recovery Program."[68]

Online Gamers Anonymous –
http://www.olganon.org/
   OLGA is for those who suffer from excessive video game playing. It was founded by Elizabeth Woolley in 2002.

Overeaters Anonymous –
http://www.oa.org/
   OA is for those who are trying to overcome an eating problem. The headquarters for OA is in Rio Rancho, New Mexico. It was started by Rozanne S. and two others in 1960.

Oxford House –
http://www.oxfordhouse.org/
   An Oxford House is a democratically run, self-supported, alcohol- and drug-free home. Oxford House is not a Twelve Step program per se, though some sort of recovery group meetings or counseling may be required. Oxford Houses are intended to provide a clean and sober environment for those coming out of treatment or detox, but there is no limit to the amount of time a resident in good standing may stay. The first Oxford House was

---

* Another Neurotics Anonymous website can be found at:
http://www.recovery.org/topics/about-the-neurotics-anonymous-12-step-recovery-program/

established in 1975 at Silver Springs, Maryland. Now there may be more than 1,300 Oxford Houses in the U.S., Canada and other countries. There are no co-ed Oxford Houses but there are houses for women and some houses for women with children.

Pills Anonymous –
http://www.pillsanonymous.org/
> PA is for those who have, or have had, an addiction to prescription drugs. The family and friends group is called Pill-Anon

Procrastinators Anonymous –
http://procrastinators-anonymous.org/
> Procrastinators Anonymous is a Twelve Step fellowship for those who suffer from chronic procrastination.

Recoveries Anonymous –
http://www.r-a.org/home.htm
> RA is open to anyone with any type of a problem. It claims to focus on working the Twelve Steps in the way that the original AA pioneers worked them. It was started in 1981.

Recovering Couples Anonymous –
http://www.recovering-couples.org/
> RCA is a fellowship of recovering couples. It was founded in 1988. The only requirement for RCA membership is a desire to stay in a committed relationship.

Rx Anonymous –
http://rxanonymous.org/
> Rx Anonymous was founded by Michael Gibson in Atlanta, GA. It uses the Twelve Step philosophy to help people recover from prescription drug addiction.

Sex Addicts Anonymous –
http://www.sexaa.org/
> SAA is for those addicted to sex. It was founded in 1977. The family auxiliary of SAA is COSA.

Sexaholics Anonymous –
http://www.sa.org/index.php
> SA was founded in 1979. It is a recovery program for those who want to stop their sexually self-destructive thinking and behavior.

Sex and Love Addicts Anonymous –
http://www.slaafws.org/
> SLAA is for those with addictions to sex, love, or both. It was founded in Boston in 1976. COSLAA is the auxiliary for family and friends.

Sexual Compulsives Anonymous –
http://www.sca-recovery.org/
> SCA is for those with sexual compulsions. It is open to all sexual orientations but the majority of members are said to be gay and bisexual men. It was founded in New York City in 1982.

Sexual Recoveries Anonymous –
http://sexualrecovery.org/
> SRA offers a Twelve Step path of recovery from sex addiction.

Spenders Anonymous –
http://www.spenders.org/
> Spenders Anonymous is a Twelve Step program based on the principles of AA. Its members admit they are "powerless over spending and money."

Survivors of Incest Anonymous –
http://www.siawso.org/
SIA is a program for survivors of childhood sexual abuse. It was started in 1982.

Teen Addiction Anonymous –
http://www.teenaddictionanonymous.org/
Teen AA was created by teens, for teens. It addresses all addictive behaviors such as eating disorders, smoking, drinking, bullying, poor attendance, poor coping skills, cutting, etc. In order to make Teen AA acceptable in public schools, the program uses a somewhat secularized and rewritten version of the Twelve Steps. Adult facilitators who have been trained by Teen AA oversee the program.

Underearners Anonymous –
http://www.underearnersanonymous.org/index.html
UA is a Twelve Step program for those who are under-achieving.

Workaholics Anonymous –
http://www.workaholics-anonymous.org/
WA is a Twelve Step program for compulsive workers. It was stated in 1983 in New York City. The related fellowship for friends and family of workaholics is Work-Anon.

Young and Recovering –
http://www.youngandrecovering.com/index.html
Young and Recovering was founded in 1999. It is a Twelve Step program for people age 18 - 24. It is for young adults who have an addiction problem and also for those who have an addicted friend or family member.

In addition to the various programs described above, there are a number of organizations for members of certain professions who are involved in AA.[*] These include:

- Anesthetists in Recovery - (http://groups.yahoo.com/neo/groups/airforsobriety/info)
- Birds of a Feather (Pilots in AA) - (http://www.boaf.org/)
- Clergy Recovery Network - (http://www.clergyrecovery.com/)
- Fellowship of Recovering Lutheran Clergy - (http://frlc.org/)
- Intercongregational Addictions Program (For women in religious orders)
- International Doctors in Alcoholics Anonymous - (http://www.idaa.org)
- International Lawyers in Alcoholics Anonymous - (http://www.ilaa.org)
- International Ministers and Pastors in Recovery
- International Pharmacists Anonymous - (http://home.comcast.net/~mitchfields/ipa/ipapage.htm)
- Nurses in Recovery
- Psychologists Helping Psychologists
- Realtors Helping Realtors
- Recovered Alcoholic Clergy Association (For Episcopal clergy) (http://racapecusa.org/)
- Social Workers Helping Social Workers
- Therapists in Recovery[69]

Taking These Roads

If you find yourself attracted to Alcoholics Anonymous, Narcotics Anonymous, or any of the Twelve Step programs, you are

---

[*] For updates, phone numbers and physical addresses of these groups see:
http://www.facesandvoicesofrecovery.org/resources/support/occupational_groups.htm

in luck. Twelve Step programs are by far the most available form of peer-based support to be found anywhere. The same is true if you are a loved one, friend or family member of an alcoholic, addict, or any sort of addicted person. Family support programs such as Al-anon and its sister organizations far outnumber any other mode of support for family members and friends.

Twelve Step programs vary not just in the problems that they address, but also in their approach and adherence to the Twelve Steps. Some rely heavily on the Steps and attempt to work them exactly according to the "Big Book" and other instructions from the pioneers of AA. Other organizations may make relatively little use of the steps. Some programs may use other methods and literature in addition to the Twelve Steps, Traditions, etc. Direct personal experience is probably the only way of telling which Twelve Step program, if any, is right for you. No doubt there are many people who attend meetings of two or more different Twelve Step organizations.

My own experience with Twelve Step meetings was some years ago in several different cities and towns (mostly a good-sized prairie town). At that time smoking was universal and meeting rooms were almost always clouded with smoke. Since then, non-smoking meetings have found their way into the culture and such meetings are often available for those who want them.

While this chapter's section on the Twelve Steps and the differences between the "Big Book" and the "Twelve and Twelve" is not a criticism of the program or of either book, it is suggesting that if you are confused about working the steps, as I once was, it may be that you are trying to follow two sets of instructions at the same time. Some Twelve Steppers recommend working the steps with the "Twelve and Twelve" and the "Big Book" side by side, but others may find this confusing. Talk to your sponsor, if you have one, or pick one of the two AA books to go by. Perhaps you will want to go through the steps twice: once according to the "Big Book" and once according to the "Twelve and Twelve." These days there are many other books, workbooks and guidelines that give suggestions on working the steps; you and your sponsor may choose to follow one or more of them.

The web addresses for many Twelve Step or anonymous groups are included in the discussions given above. Meeting places and times, or how to find meetings, are usually listed on the websites that are given. Some of these organizations merit special notice. *Narcotics Anonymous* is the largest world-wide Twelve Step organization other than AA itself. At the group level, NA is often considered to be the equal of AA. Strictly speaking, the *Oxford House* movement is not a Twelve Step program but a unique institution for providing clean and sober housing. It has been in existence for about forty years and has a fine reputation. A list of houses and vacancies can be found on the Oxford House website.

The geographic availability of some of these Twelve Step groups may be limited, but in the United States, the availability of AA is virtually unlimited. To get in touch with AA, first check your local phone directory. The mailing address for AA's national headquarters is P.O. Box 459, Grand Central Station, New York, NY 10163; the phone number is (212) 870-3400. AA's web address is http://www.aa.org/

If you find that the Twelve Step programs do not appeal to you, this book is especially for you because it gives more alternatives than any other source. But if you do like the Twelve Step program and its philosophy, count yourself lucky – you won't be alone. On page 164, the last page of the first section of the "Big Book," Bill Wilson wrote: "Abandon yourself to God as you understand God. Admit your faults to Him and to your fellows. Clear away the wreckage of your past. Give freely of what you find and join us." Literally millions of people have taken him up on that; and Wilson closed with: "May God bless you and keep you – until then."[70]

Chapter Endnotes

1. Sinclair, Upton (April 28, 1914) "Socialist writer Upton Sinclair's open letter to Rockefeller,"quoted in Public

Broadcasting Service's "*The Ludlow Massacre*" (n.d.). Retrieved 11/16/2010 from: http://www.pbs.org/wgbh/amex/rockefellers/sfeature/sf_8.html

2. "The Ludlow Massacre" (2001, 2006). *Industrial Relations Counselors, Inc.* Retrieved 11/16/2010 from: http://www.ircounselors.org/history/history02.html
3. *New York Times*, (May 4, 1914) "I.W.W. Pickets Pen Rockefellers"
4. Chernow, Ron (1998) *Titan: The Life of John D. Rockefeller, Sr.*, London: Warner Books, page 586.
5. Kurtz, Ernest (1979) *Not-God: A History of Alcoholics Anonymous*, Center City, MN: Hazelden Educational Services, page 94.
6. Burwell, Jim, (n.d.) *The Evolution of Alcoholics Anonymous*. Retrieved 5/24/2010 from: http://www.barefootsworld.net/aa-jb-evolution.html And Haverstick, John (Aug 27, 1955) "'The Big Book': Bible for Alcoholics," *Saturday Review*.
7. Hunter, T. Willard (July 1978) "The Oxford Group's Frank Buchman," unpublished manuscript quoted in B., Dick (1998) *The Oxford Group and Alcoholics Anonymous: A Design for Living that Works*, page 127.
8. [Wilson, Bill, et al.] (1955) *Alcoholics Anonymous*, 2nd Edition, New York: Alcoholics Anonymous World Services, Inc., pages 59-60.
9. B., Dick (1998) *The Oxford Group and Alcoholics Anonymous: A Design for Living that Works*, Kihei, Maui, HI: Paradise Research Publications, Inc., page 109.
10. [Wilson, Bill] (1957) *Alcoholics Anonymous Comes of Age*, New York: Alcoholics Anonymous World Service, Inc., page 39.
11. Anonymous (1984) *Pass It On*, New York: AAWS, Inc., pages 386-387.
12. B., Dick (1998) page 28.
13. Clapp, Charles, Jr. (1938) *The Big Bender*, New York: Harper & Brothers, page 113.

14. Clapp (1938) page 124.
15. Clapp (1938) page 127.
16. Clapp (1938) pages 129-130.
17. Clapp (1938) page 152.
18. Clapp (1938) page 159.
19. Foot, Stephen (1935) *Life Began Yesterday,* New York: Harper & Brothers, page ten.
20. Foot (1935) page 10.
21. Foot (1935) page 11.
22. Kitchen, V.C. (1934) *I Was a Pagan,* New York: Harper & Brothers, page 74.
23. Kitchen (1934) page 67. 24. Kitchen (1934) page 65.
25. Kitchen (1934) page 73.
26. Kitchen (1934) page 120.
27. Kitchen (1934) page 158.
28. Shoemaker, Sam (1953) *How to Become a Christian,* New York: Harper & Brothers, page 56.
29. Kitchen (1934) page 89.
30. B., Dick (1998) page 131.
31. [Wilson, Bill] (1952, 1953) *Twelve Steps and Twelve Traditions,* New York: Alcoholics Anonymous World Service, Inc., page 17.
32. [Wilson, et al.] (1955) pages 20-21.
33. [Wilson, et al.] (1955) page 31. And [Wilson] (1952, 1953) page 23.
34. [Wilson, et al.] (1955) page 51.
35. [Wilson, et al.] (1955) pages 48-49.
36. [Wilson] (1952, 1953) page 27.
37. [Wilson] (1952, 1953) page 109.
38. [Wilson, et al.] (1955) page 60.
39. [Wilson, et al.] (1955) page 62.
40. [Wilson, et al.] (1955) page 63.
41. [Wilson, et al.] (1955) page 64.
42. [Wilson] (1952, 1953) page 42.
43. [Wilson] (1952, 1953) page 50.
44. [Wilson] (1952, 1953) page 51.

45. [Wilson, et al.] (1955) pages 73-74.
46. [Wilson] (1952, 1953) page 55.
47. [Wilson] (1952, 1953) page 63.
48. [Wilson] (1952, 1953) page 63.
49. [Wilson] (1952, 1953) page 65.
50. [Wilson, et al.] (1955) page 76.
51. [Wilson] (1952, 1953) page 73.
52. [Wilson] (1952, 1953) page 72.
53. [Wilson, et al.] (1955) page 76.
54. [Wilson] (1952, 1953) page 77.
55. [Wilson, et al.] (1955) pages 83 - 84.
56. [Wilson, et al.] (1955) pages 17, 20, 29, 45, 90, 96, 113, 132, 133, 146.
57. [Wilson, et al.] (1955) page xiii.
58. [Wilson, et al.] (1955) page 85.
59. B., Dick (1998) page 68
60. [Wilson] (1952, 1953) page 99.
61. [Wilson, et al.] (1955) page 14.
62. "The Tablemate" (n.d.) Retrieved 6/25/2013 from: http://hindsfoot.org/archives.html. And "Discussion No. 3, Inventory & Restitution" (n.d.) Retrieved 6/27/2013 from: http://hindsfoot.org/Detr3.html
63. [Wilson, et al.] (1955) page 564.
64. *Time* (June 14, 1999) "TIME 100 Persons Of The Century."
65. Henman, James O. (2003) *Who's Really Driving Your Bus,* Modesto, CA: Psychological Associates Press, page 5.
66. The Emotional Health Anonymous Fellowship (2012). Retrieved 12/8/2013 from: http://emotionalhealthanonymous.org/.
67. "Information about NA" (n.d.). Retrieved 9/18/2013 from: http://www.na.org/admin/include/spaw2/uploads/pdf/PR/Information_about_NA.pdf
68. Neurotics Anonymous (n.d.). Retrieved 12/8/2013 from: http://neuroticosanonimos.us/neurotics.html.
69. *Faces and Voices of Recovery* (n.d.) "Occupational Recovery..." Retrieved 1/5/2014 from:

http://www.facesandvoicesofrecovery.org/resources/support/occupational_groups.htm
70. [Wilson, et al.] (1955) page 164.

CHAPTER III:
The McGoldrick Method and Bridge House:
A Forgotten Treasure

Ed McGoldrick wasn't your typical ex-drunk. He wasn't your typical young attorney either. It was 1943 when he turned down an appointment with the New York City Corporation Counsel's Office. "A post whose prestige and opportunities were not to be dismissed lightly by a young lawyer still in his thirties," he said.[1]

But he just didn't want it. He hoped instead for an unlikely opportunity that would certainly bring him less in the way of material benefits and rewards. He dreamed of a city bureau for alcoholism therapy, an addiction treatment program that would be the first such undertaking in the country to be sponsored by a municipality.

The fate of McGoldrick's unusual proposition lay in the hands of Fiorello La Guardia, New York City's powerful mayor. McGoldrick had entered the Mayor's office to refuse the Corporation Counsel's offer. He stayed to lobby for the municipal alcohol treatment unit. It didn't take long. La Guardia decided the issue on the spot. "Go ahead," he said. "It's something we need badly – every community does."[2]

However, there was one condition. The mayor pledged McGoldrick to secrecy. Not until a year later, May 10, 1944, did *The New York Times* report: "Edward McGoldrick, formerly a practicing attorney in Manhattan, has been devoting all his time for a year as a city employee operating a bureau to help alcoholics regain control of themselves… His efforts, with the aid and encouragement of Mayor La Guardia, have achieved results sufficiently successful to cause the Mayor to approve plans to house his bureau in a building of its own."[3]

Thus, the founding of *Bridge House,* an official agency in the New York City Department of Welfare, a prototype facility for the modern treatment of addictions, and the home of the *McGoldrick Method* for treating alcoholics.

Edward J. McGoldrick, Jr. – The Man Behind the Method

Ed McGoldrick was described by a sympathetic journalist as "tall, lean, [and] likable."[4] The son of a former New York State Supreme Court Judge, and a Fordham University Law School graduate himself, he was the proverbial man who had, or might have had, almost anything.

But McGoldrick's youth was marred by an extreme sense of shyness. "The fear of blushing followed me through high school and into college," he said.[5] It was during those early years that McGoldrick made a common and sometimes disastrous discovery: "that liquor put me at ease no matter how small or great the issue to be faced."[6]

By the age of twenty-seven McGoldrick was taking morning-after drinks to ease the pain of hangovers. Yet, he admitted, "[t]here still lurked in the back of my mind the reservation that some day I could drink moderately and 'handle it right.' So the merry-go-round continued with countless plunges off the wagon, alternating with 'drying-out' spells followed by brief periods of comparative sobriety."[7]

"[He] will tell you frankly that he is an alcoholic himself, that for fifteen years straight he was periodically in and out of sanitariums," an independent source affirmed.[8] The reality of McGoldrick's profound drinking problem cannot be doubted.

Finally, and hesitantly, he decided to enter a private sanitarium. After several weeks of treatment, he was discharged only to go off on yet another alcoholic spree. His second visit to a sanitarium lasted for seven months, the third lasted for eight. These were followed by a period at Bellevue Hospital's alcoholic ward, succeeded by an eight-week convalescence in Rockland State Hospital.

After achieving a stable sobriety, and determined to uncover the reasons for his drinking, McGoldrick became a pupil of Dr. Menas Gregory, the head of Bellevue Hospital's psychiatric division. He was even allowed to help with some of Dr. Gregory's more stubborn cases. Following this apprenticeship, McGoldrick went down to the Bowery, then New York's slum area of cheap hotels, brothels and skid row bums. He spent several months there with the drunkards and derelicts, learning to relate to alcoholics from all levels and walks of life. He dressed like them, slept in flophouses, ate handouts, and talked with those who were not too besotted by booze or other drugs.

By 1943 McGoldrick had decided to devote himself full-time to the work of helping alcoholics. When the mayor of New York offered him employment with the city, he asked for and received the position of alcoholism therapist with the New York City Department of Welfare. Then for the remainder of his life – nearly a quarter of a century – he devoted himself entirely to his career as a lay-therapist, the ingenious method of therapy that he developed, and his job as the director of Bridge House.

Bridge House: A Treatment Center Before Its Time

"There's no other place in the world quite like Bridge House," Meyer Berger, a *New York Times* feature writer penned in 1954. "The other day, within an hour after city cops started handing out pamphlets on agencies that try to help alcoholics, Bridge House on the south margin of Bronx Park had a stream of new applicants at its quiet doors… The sad thing about that is that low-budgeted Bridge House will be able to take in only a few of the hundreds who learned about the place from police literature. The three-story old tan-painted dwelling has only eighteen beds and they're always taken."[9]

Berger went on to describe Bridge House as a frame dwelling that was kept "almost squeakingly clean and tidy." But, he added, "it somehow manages to escape the institutional atmosphere." According to Berger, Bridge House wasn't welcome in the neighborhood when it first opened. The residents were harassed and a few bricks were thrown at the windows. But that all ended in just a few weeks. After that, Berger said, the Bridge House students were accepted and they "walked with dignity."[10]

Bridge House was fittingly named, some say by McGoldrick himself, some say by Mayor La Guardia, to symbolize the crossing from "wet land" to "dry land." Its approach to treatment was decidedly educational. Those receiving help at Bridge House were called students. They attended lectures and discussion groups. They studied the Bridge House philosophy and psychology – and they were given written and oral examinations that they were expected to pass.

There were actually two programs at Bridge House, a residential course and a nonresidential program. The residential treatment lasted three to four weeks. For the next year, though, the students spent a minimum of three hours a week at Bridge House receiving further instructions. Before any student could graduate, he or she had to complete one year's absolute sobriety and show proficiency in the principles of recovery that were taught at Bridge House.

Those whose circumstances made residential treatment impossible could enroll directly in the nonresidential program. Only the nonresidential program was open to women. McGoldrick never succeeded in getting coeducational residential treatment.

From time to time, investigations were made into the effectiveness of the Bridge House program. In 1949, a report noted that for five years the program had maintained an approximate 66 percent effectiveness of non-alcoholism in individuals for at least one year.[11] In 1953, McGoldrick claimed to be graduating 66.4 percent of the students, most of whom, he said, "had come to Bridge House after trying other means of therapy, including Alcoholics Anonymous and psychiatric care."[12] At about the same time, a re-survey of 100 Bridge House men who had been sober for at least twelve months was conducted. The survey showed fifty-six still abstinent; eleven who had died but who had been abstinent until death; eighteen who had resumed drinking; and fifteen who were lost to follow-up.[13] In 1966, probably the last formal accounting of the program, the founder cited numbers which indicated that – over the years – about 41 percent of the alcoholics who were treated at Bridge House had been freed from their addictions.[14]

A success rate of 41 percent is well beyond what most treatments can offer today and rates of +66 percent or more are truly outstanding. In comparison, a three-year follow-up of Project MATCH, the largest and most expensive clinical study ever conducted, found abstinence rates that ranged from 24 percent to 36 percent and averaged about 29 percent for three highly regarded treatment methods.[15]

Managing the Mind: The Program Theory

Ed McGoldrick's recovery theories were founded upon a belief in the intrinsic dignity of all humanity. "This much I long ago learned," McGoldrick declared, "there is no one who does not see within himself something far better than the world sees, a promise infinitely greater than what has been realized... I learned this first in my own life. There were times when, trembling, fitful, violently ill after a spree, I knew myself to be something less than human. There was never a time when I did not feel myself something more."[16]

Such perceptiveness into the human condition is uncommon in anyone, but McGoldrick wanted more. He wanted to know how to reach that better self: "How to bridge that formidable gap? There were crossings that served others in my plight, and serve still," he wrote. "I tried them all; some left me stranded as before, others led me part way across, and there left me to flounder and turn back; none enabled me to complete the journey."[17]

So he set about finding his own way. In addition to his apprenticeship at Bellevue Hospital and his Bowery experience, he read anything that looked like it might help solve his problem and he talked to anyone that he thought might be able to help. He found that: "The most difficult part of the search was unflinching self-scrutiny, bringing myself to face and recognize myself as I was." It was only after this honest self-examination revealed nothing as terrible as he feared that he found himself on the right path. "From that point on," McGoldrick declared, "I developed the therapy that eventually cured me."[18]

The therapy McGoldrick developed is based on a profound though actually quite simple psychology that seems to be somewhat esoteric in origin. If the sources are not partly esoteric, they are at least obscure for McGoldrick generally avoided citing credits. "In developing this therapy I have not made any distinction between the insights of others and those which arose in my own mind," he wrote, "for the simple reason that I am totally unable to make this distinction. In my desire to discover a technique to cure myself, I did all that I could externally, then I simply allowed my mind to work on its own. When you let it function in this way – without any preconceived or set ideas – your mind is free to work constructively. It goes to work on those insights and assembles them like the pieces of a jigsaw puzzle... This process," he explained, "makes it utterly impossible to distinguish between what you receive from others and what you created yourself."[19]

McGoldrick's Diagram of the Mind

McGoldrick did not believe that alcoholics had a disease that made them physically different from others, and neither did he believe them to be mentally ill in the sense of having minds that functioned abnormally. "Granted that your conduct as an alcoholic is deplorable and destructive..." McGoldrick explained, "[but] your mind is still working perfectly. It creates and forms your habit patterns faultlessly...[and] the effect – your drinking conduct – is but the playback of your own thoughts, both conscious and subconscious. Had you thought correctly, those very same principles in operation would have effected a similarly perfect movement of your mind but with *constructive* not destructive results."[20]

To illustrate this, McGoldrick constructed a helpful little diagram to portray the workings of the mind. The diagram used here is based on McGoldrick's 1954 book, *Management of the Mind: How to Conquer Alcohol and Other Blocks to Successful Living*, page 27.

In the diagram on your left, the circle represents the mind. The area above the horizontal line is labeled *"Conscious Mind,"* representing that part of the mental process of which we are aware. The area below the horizontal line is labeled *"Subconscious Mind,"* indicating the mental processes that go on outside of conscious awareness. The diagram is not to be regarded as showing the existence of *two* minds, however; the *one* circle divided approximately in half demonstrates the fact that we have *one mind* — one mind which, from our conscious point of view anyway, seems to operate in two different ways.

At the lower left of the area labeled *"Subconscious Mind"* are the initials "DHP," standing for *Destructive Habit Patterns*; at the lower right are the initials "CHP," for *Constructive Habit Patterns*.

Above the circle, the words *"External Stimulus"* illustrate the point that thoughts frequently arise as a result of external influences. The words *"Internal Stimulus"* at the bottom of the circle indicate that the mind is also stimulated to think by internal stimuli.

Two arrows, one originating from "DHP" and the other from "CHP," point in different directions, but to the same word: *"Action."* This shows that both DHPs, *Destructive Habit Patterns*, and CHPs, *Constructive Habit Patterns*, are capable of manifesting as external events. The objective, it should be needless to say, is to increase the circumstances generated by CHPs and to reduce those rooted in DHPs.

But how is this to be accomplished? McGoldrick's answer was that the solution is to be found in certain laws of the mind. "We do not know everything about our minds… far from it," McGoldrick wrote, "but we know from study and observation that there are certain provable and demonstrable principles or laws upon which we can rely and by which we can act to achieve expected results… Set your thought in motion, which is *cause*, and your conduct will be in the nature of your thought. That conduct is *effect*."[21]

"If you really want to change your habit of excessive drinking into a habit of not drinking," McGoldrick advised, "you must, no matter what else you do, eliminate the kind of thinking that makes you indulge in your kind of drinking."[22]

The Conscious Mind and the Subconscious Mind

Also important to an understanding of McGoldrick's method is an understanding of the conscious and subconscious functions of the mind. The conscious mind is the part of one's mind that is aware of itself and its environment. The subconscious operates below the level of conscious awareness.

A major distinction which differentiates the operation of the conscious mind from the subconscious mind lies in the realm of reasoning. The subconscious mind is able to reason *deductively*, but not *inductively*, while the conscious mind can do both.

Deductive reasoning follows the form of a logical syllogism, reasoning from a general premise to a specific application. It confirms that a proposition must be true if certain other propositions are assumed, but it does not probe into the truth or falsity of the initial generalizations. That task lies in the conscious mind's domain of *inductive reasoning*, the mental process that draws conclusions from the observation of a series of facts. In other words, *inductive reasoning* is the process of comparing several separate instances with one another until the common factor behind them all is revealed (you observe the sun rising in the east for a series of days and conclude that the sun rises in the east). *Deductive reasoning* is the process of applying such common factors to other situations (if the sun always rises in the east, it will rise in the east tomorrow). *Induction* proceeds by the comparison of facts; *deduction* by the application of principles.

Do not be put off by the apparently academic nature of this discussion. One reason that it may be confusing at first is that the words themselves are commonly confused in our everyday language. For example, when Sherlock Holmes follows a series of clues leading to the identity of a murderer, he is using *inductive reasoning* – from specific circumstances (clue A, clue B, clue C, etc.) to a general premise that accommodates all of the clues observed (the butler did it). He is not using *deductive reasoning* as he frequently informs – or rather, misinforms – dear Mr. Watson.

In human personality, change is inaugurated by the activity of the conscious mind. The conscious mind initiates change by formulating premises, sometimes referred to as *seed-ideas* (e.g., alcoholics can recover). The subconscious mind accepts these premises as suggestions and elaborates them by the process of *deductive reasoning* (for example, "I can do it too").

This leads to a most important property of the subconscious mind: that it is totally *amenable to suggestion*. Therefore it is always "susceptible, willing, and receptive" to your thoughts.[23] As McGoldrick explained it, your mind in its subconscious aspect is like the soil, which is always willing to receive the seed that is planted in it. "It will not refuse the seed of a rose and fail to bring it to flower because it prefers a daisy."[24]

A second important feature of subconsciousness is that it is the *storehouse of memory*. "Your habits are formed largely as the result of influences that become thought impressions on your subconscious…" McGoldrick wrote; "after you have experienced anything, it will be [remembered or] forever inscribed on your subconscious mind."[25]

Although, in his view these "mental-emotional grooves," as he called them, were not erasable, he taught that they did not need to be activated: "Whatever you remove your attention from withers and dies. What you give your attention to flourishes and lives."[26] Consequently, McGoldrick recommended managing the mind by giving and withholding attention.

The third principle of subconsciousness that McGoldrick taught was the relationship of the subconscious to the physical body. The point that McGoldrick wanted to emphasize was the relationship between mental-emotional attitudes and health. "It is *normal* to be healthy," he taught, "[and] it is *abnormal* to be unhealthy."[27] "Your subconsciousness accepts without question the type of thought you plant within it. A result or effect must follow… The thoughts you impress upon your subconscious are therefore of vital concern in the aim to have a sound mind as well as a sound body."[28]

The Laws of Learning

At Bridge House, McGoldrick taught certain universal laws of learning. Briefly, these are: first, the law of *use*, which simply states that the more anything is practiced and repeated, the easier it will be to learn and the longer it will be retained. Second, the law of *disuse*, which states the opposite: if something that was once learned is neglected or not used, it will atrophy or be all but forgotten. The third primary law of learning that McGoldrick addressed is known as the law of *effect*. This is simply the principle that people will repeat actions that have given pleasure or satisfaction, and avoid repeating those that give displeasure or pain.

Besides these three primary laws, McGoldrick instructed his students in certain "secondary laws of learning." These are the law of *primacy,* the common phenomenon that things learned first are apt to be remembered better and longer; the law of *recency*, the fact that things seen recently will linger in the memory; and the law of *vividness*, the principle stating that those things which stand out because of oddity, emotional significance, or another reason, are apt to be remembered.

Finally, McGoldrick explained how these principles were to be put to use. "From this point on," he advised, "you can actually refashion your mental-emotional patterns… You are going to do this by a systematic application of the laws of learning: *use, disuse, effect, primacy, recency,* and *vividness*… Specifically, you are to *use* the principles over and over again… [and] you will not use the erroneous principles that they replace. By *disuse*," McGoldrick taught, "you will allow these mistaken habits of mind to wither and atrophy… Your old habits of thought and action will weaken their hold and your newly acquired ones will be reinforced."[29]

"Soon," McGoldrick promised, "there comes a time when experience no longer shapes your personality… it is your personality that shapes experience."[30]

William James' Rules for Breaking Old Habits

William James, the renowned philosopher and psychologist, established four rules for breaking old habits and forming new ones. McGoldrick thought that they needed little explanation. "You can see from your study… on what principles they are based," he said.[31] They are:

1. Old habits are destroyed by forming new ones. In forming a new habit, launch yourself with as strong and decided an initiative as possible. You must be convinced of the

necessity of replacing the old with the new, sincere in your conviction; and you must make the strongest effort you can summon up.
2. Never suffer an exemption to occur in the formation of a new habit… To allow an exception to occur, to repeat an indulgence just once, is to strengthen the destructive habit pattern and to sabotage the constructive one. You are trying to eliminate the old pattern by disuse; to use it just once is to restore its original strength.
3. Seek the first possible opportunity to act upon a new resolution. Actually, any delay is in itself a demonstration that the sincere conviction of a needed change is absent. Delay is an excuse – the time to start is NOW!
4. Keep the faculty of effort alive in you by little gratuitous exercises daily. You must be constantly aware that you are forming a new habit pattern in order to be able to fight off the unexpected pressure that would hurl you back upon the old… Mere abstention from some action is not enough; there must be positive action…[32]

The Mental Diet: Capsules of Thought

The method of recovery McGoldrick developed "is not a way for hands or feet," he said. "It is based on the use of mental, emotional and psychological techniques."[33] McGoldrick taught that a great deal can be achieved through such things as "positive thinking"; "the power of faith"; "self-reliance"; "constructive outlook"; and similar philosophies popularized under other names. "Actually," he believed, "the whole aim of any kind of psychotherapy is to replace 'negative thinking,' the 'destructive outlook,' [or] a lack of faith in oneself… with more constructive thought patterns."[34] McGoldrick's method of replacing negative thoughts (Destructive Habit Patterns or DHPs, he called them) with more positive modes of thought (Constructive Habit Patterns or

CHPs in his terminology) was a "Mental Diet" of seventeen affirmative thought capsules.

The following discussion of the Mental Diet's seventeen items is based on the version found in McGoldrick's 1966 book, *The Conquest of Alcohol: A Handbook of Self Therapy*, though his 1954 statement, *Management of the Mind: How to Conquer Alcohol and Other Blocks to Successful Living*, was also consulted and quoted.

As they are written, the thought capsules address problems with alcohol. It should be easy to see, however, that they can be adapted to address addictive drug problems and "other blocks to successful living," as the subtitle of McGoldrick's 1954 book phrased it. In that book the statements included a blank for you to insert whatever problem you were having. For example, the statement that is now item ten was written: "I realize that I must be absolutely sincere in my effort to overcome alcoholism (or _____); otherwise no one can help me."[35]

Item One: I know I must abstain from alcohol, not merely for the sake of others, but first and foremost for my own self-esteem. The solution of the problem rests primarily with me.

This first precept might have been taken from a Twelve Step list of slogans. "It's a selfish program," the properly instructed AA member says. And AA's meaning is more or less the same as McGoldrick's: motivation must come from a desire to improve one's *own* life, not that of another.

In his 1954 commentary on this principle, McGoldrick offered yet another of his deeper insights into the human condition: "None of us is to blame for his faults; they are always instilled, driven into us by others, or by circumstances – so we tell ourselves. On the other hand," he observed, "we *do* assume generally that the faults of others grow out of basic defects in their character, usually out of selfishness. That is why, in attempting to reform another, we automatically appeal not to his selfish interests, but to his so-called 'better instincts' – usually his love for something outside himself.

'You must stop this for the sake of your wife and children,' the wastrel is universally told. 'Think of them.'"[36]

And of course, it doesn't work. In effect, this strategy is like telling men and women that they must forego their own preferences and go against their own nature. "The end result," McGoldrick said, "is that the inner turmoil goes on and you keep on drinking."[37]

"Therefore," he advised, "be 'selfish' and think '*self*ishly' if you please, but only about what your sober self really desires. 'Selfishness' of this kind dictates that you choose the best without compromise. But understand that it is not for the sake of anybody but yourself that you must eliminate your bad habit of drinking."[38]

Item Two: I refuse to amuse others with my drinking escapades of the past. My abnormal drinking was pathetic, not funny. I know that fundamentally frustration was the cause of my abnormal drinking. I realize I was seeking to escape from a belief in my inability to express myself as I desired.

Drunkalogs, anyone? None for Ed McGoldrick, thank you. In AA slang, "drunkalogues" are stories of former drinking adventures, and McGoldrick wanted no part of them. "There are sound psychological reasons for refusing to amuse others with your drinking escapades..." he said. "The ideas expressed not only impress others, but they also impress the subconscious mind of the one who gives them expression."[39] Certainly a drunkalog does not *always* lead to a relapse; but the psychological principle McGoldrick described is completely sound. And if indulging in drunkalogs does result in a bender? That, McGoldrick warned, "is indeed very tragic."[40]

Concerning the second and third parts of this capsule *("I know that fundamentally frustration was the cause of my abnormal drinking. I realize I was seeking to escape from a belief in my inability to express myself as I desired")* McGoldrick always thought that frustration was one of the keys to the onset of alcoholism. And he also believed that he had the answer: "changing the image of oneself from an inadequate and inferior person to one of competence and confidence is the way to handle frustration," he said.[41] He believed, too, that he had the answer to deficiencies in the art of expression, real or self-perceived, "learn how to rid yourself of frustration and express yourself as you desire," he said. "Then you can be a credit to yourself, your family and your community."[42]

Item Three: If I pray for help, I don't expect God to perform a miracle. He cannot do for me what can only be done through me. Persistent effort must be made. God will provide the food – He won't cook the dinner.

You don't win by giving up: *"Persistent effort must be made."* It was while discussing this item in 1954 that McGoldrick addressed the faults he perceived in "exhortatory group movements [that] substitute for the figure of Christ a 'Higher Power'"[43]– an obvious reference to Twelve Step programs.

"Alcoholics who have attempted and failed to attain sobriety through mutual confession and exhortation groups frequently come to Bridge House with their pernicious habits actually confirmed," he wrote. "These groups start by telling the drinker that he must admit that he is himself powerless to combat his alcoholism, and that he must therefore rely on a higher power to help him conquer it."[44]

In McGoldrick's view, this doctrine of powerlessness was often seized upon as a perfect rationalization for continuing destructive habits. After exposure to such philosophies, the group alum "is with difficulty re-educated," McGoldrick said, "because he *wants* to believe that he is helpless."[45] But at Bridge House it was also found that, as a rule, former group members "always *know* that the responsibility and the power for their transformation lies wholly *within* them, even when they most seek to deny it."[46]

In his second book, *The Conquest of Alcohol*, McGoldrick expanded upon and clarified this doctrine: "*God will provide the food – but he won't cook the dinner...* means that there *is* a power available to you but you are not to sit around and expect manna to drop from heaven... You must manage your own life by managing your mind."⁴⁷ By doing that, you allow the Power to work *through* your personality, not instead of it.

Item Four: An alcoholic is made, not born. Heredity, therefore, is not the cause of my drinking. Such an excuse is an age-old dodge to avoid the reality of seeing myself as I really am.

As far as the director of Bridge House was concerned, alcoholism was not hereditary. Period. "The idea that heredity is responsible for alcoholism has no foundation in fact," he wrote. "Science has no proof that alcoholism can be transmitted from blood to blood."⁴⁸

Not in McGoldrick's time perhaps, at least no proof that McGoldrick was willing to accept. Since then, however, there have been a number of scientific studies suggesting the possibility of a "genetically transmitted biological predisposition to the development of alcoholism."⁴⁹ But there are also grounds for doubt. As yet, there is no procedure that can discover that there is, or is not, such a "biological predisposition" in any specific individual.⁵⁰ And it is absolutely true that without alcohol, all "predisposing factors" – if such exist – mean absolutely nothing. One can *never* become alcoholic without drinking alcohol.

The truths and falsities of this debate aside, what McGoldrick so adamantly opposed was not *predisposition* (an inclination or tendency) but *predestination* (an inalterable fate). "Don't accept any idea that you are predestined to be anything…" he warned, "much less a drunken failure."⁵¹

Item Five: I know my drinking past has no power over me other than what my present feeling about the past gives it. Therefore, I will avoid thinking about or talking about my former drinking escapades.

McGoldrick understood this fifth recommendation as having to do with the positive experience of *renewing the mind*. "To renew the mind is to discard the old mental content, to decline to give the old a new lease on life, to face forward and pick out some point in the future by which to guide our journey instead of looking backward and stumbling blindly on."[52] And to emphasize the point, he quoted from St. Paul's Letter to the Romans: "Be ye transformed by the renewing of your mind."[53]

Item Six: Regret and despair over yesterday's drinking will only make today a torment, and since tomorrow grows out of today, it will bear the image of today. I will avoid such manner of thinking as it is only living in a rut.

"Regret and despair are the other side of the coin whose face is nostalgia," McGoldrick asserted. "No one can fill himself with regrets and then proceed to act wisely and constructively."[54] Therefore, this was McGoldrick's advice: admit that the past was, by and large, one's own fault, and then entertain no thoughts of regret and despair.

Easier said than done? Perhaps. Rather than advocate that which he considered to be an "excuse," the concept of alcoholism as a disease, McGoldrick championed the more demanding course: take responsibility. Then, he reasoned, "Having earned your dispensation from regret and despair, you can climb out of that rut onto the smooth road of sobriety, equipped to deal with your problems of living."[55]

Item Seven: I know there is danger in being too self-confident because of short-lived sobriety. A sense of exhilaration, as well as one of depression, is an equally good excuse for taking a drink.

As always, McGoldrick related the application of this precept to the basic principles of the mind as he understood them. The struggle is not over upon first attaining sobriety, he taught. "Disaster can result from overconfidence, and this mood represents a danger point in the early sober period of the alcoholic who is attempting to reform."[56] Therefore, McGoldrick taught that daily effort is required as the conscious mind struggles to overcome old patterns associated with drinking and to install new, constructive habit patterns.

Item Eight: I do not need alcohol. Others can do without it, so can I. Any person of average intelligence who is sincere, and honestly exerts an effort over a reasonable length of time, can lead a life without alcohol.

A critic said of this thought capsule: "Many of the thousands and thousands of victims of alcoholism would like very much to follow this advice if they could."[57] But of course it was not intended that this statement, offered as mere advice, would be effective in-and-of-itself. This eighth item needs to be understood within the context of the total program and the laws of psychology taught at Bridge House. "By applying the sound scientific principles of psychology to your problem," McGoldrick counseled, "you are altering and changing the patterns of your thoughts. By changing the direction of your mind's movement, you are freeing yourself of the need for alcohol. Now you can say with conviction, 'Others can do without it, so can I.'"[58]

Item Nine: I know from my own personal experience that drinking never solved a problem for me. As a matter of fact, it only made matters worse.

This ninth statement needs little elaboration. "There is no power in your bad habit of drinking to help you," McGoldrick declared. "The only power the indulgence in alcohol can have is the power of depriving you of the use of your finest means of helping yourself – your mind."[59]

Item Ten: I Realize that I must be absolutely sincere in my effort to overcome the habit of drinking; otherwise no one can help me.

If McGoldrick's tyros had a problem with drinking, or in other areas of life, they were counseled to study and apply the Bridge House principles of psychology. "You must uproot these subconscious mental reservations and change your thought patterns to conform with what you know instinctively to be straightforward, ethical conduct…" McGoldrick advised, "You must teach yourself new habits, which means you must *learn* to be sincere."[60]

Item Eleven: I know that I have put a lot of effort and time into becoming an alcoholic. I know that were I to exert a similar effort and concentrate on doing so, I could successfully achieve that which I want to do, to be, to have.

"You want to change your life and you are going to change your life," McGoldrick admonished. "Get to work!"[61]

"As long as you spend all of your time and effort in staying drunk you are missing the mark. Were you to exert a similar effort in worthwhile pursuits, you could successfully achieve that which you want to be, do, or have, and attain [your] personal goals."[62]

Item Twelve: I know that I cannot do everything that I wish to do in twenty-four hours, but [by] staying sober and working diligently, all things can be handled in due course.

This adage, which appears at first to be merely another overworked corrective for the problem of stress (or perhaps a restatement of the "one day at a time" philosophy of AA) is really the basis for a sophisticated mental technique. "Never let yourself go off to sleep before you have righted in your mind a wrong action of yours during the day," McGoldrick advised. "Revise any experience, any action of yours where you didn't behave credibly. Rewrite it mentally in your imagination and visualize yourself acting in the correct way – in an ideal manner."[63]

Mentally rewriting experiences uses the creative imagination to form positive and constructive images. According to McGoldrick, this technique helps identify those aspects of personality that should be changed, and then actually helps transmute these unwanted patterns into positive tendencies. "Think it over," McGoldrick urged.[64] He might better have advised, don't just think about it – do it!

Item Thirteen: I realize that staying sober is of paramount importance in my life, and that one drink of any form of alcohol, including wine and beer, is sufficient to start me on a spree.

Though McGoldrick was absolutely opposed to the disease doctrine, this thirteenth item shows that he was pretty much in agreement with some of its ideas, particularly the *one drink, one drunk hypothesis* – or the belief that an alcoholic's first drink (more or less) *always* leads to a bender.

McGoldrick differed somewhat from conventional ideas in that, for him, the one drink, one drunk phenomenon was not the "manifestation of an allergy"[65] – as AA's Dr. Silkworth taught – but a result of certain principles of psychology.[66] Once a habit pattern was formed, McGoldrick believed, it would forevermore be subject to reactivation.

As he saw it: "Habit patterns are applicable not only to the alcoholic. They apply to everyone, to all forms of behavior. They are principles of mind. This is the way you are made and designed to function… Staying sober permanently is only the first step. You go on from there to rebuild your life."[67]

Item Fourteen: I know that in abstaining from liquor I am not doing something big for society, but only that which I ought to do.

In certain ways, this is but a restatement of capsule number one *("I know I must abstain from alcohol, not merely for the sake of others, but first and foremost for my own selfesteem...").* The doctrine that one must pursue sobriety out of self-interest, not for the pleasure or approval of others, is the essence of both capsules. "There is a true, not a false compensation for your ego," McGoldrick said, "that will enable you to do in life that which ought to be done – stay sober... you will find satisfaction in your own sense of maturity when you do."[68]

Item Fifteen: I realize that I must not neglect my physical health.

"This, the shortest item on the Mental Diet, needs no prolonged discussion," McGoldrick wrote. "Your common sense tells you that you should take care of yourself physically."[69] By this, McGoldrick did not intend that rigorous workouts or uncompromising diets were a necessity, "daily exercise such as morning and evening calisthenics, care in the choice of food in quality and quantity, and regular sleep will work wonders in creating in you a feeling of well-being," he advised.[70]

McGoldrick recognized that one of the perils of accentuating the potency of the mind is that it may lead to a disregard of the body. "Whatever the mental condition to be changed," he said, "it can be accomplished more easily with the combined power of both mind and body."[71]

Item Sixteen: I know that my abnormal drinking has retarded maturity. I therefore realize that what I need is a change of thought, and that a change of thought is only a normal perception of values that were distorted during my drinking career.

"It is impossible for excessive drinkers to be mature because their very conduct retards it," the Bridge House founder said.[72] His opinion was based upon the clear-eyed observation that alcohol was, and is, a powerful drug. A drug that robs habitual users of the ability to exercise the higher faculties of the mind and heart. "Is it not true that, being drugged by alcohol, you didn't go through life gathering wisdom in order to live adequately," McGoldrick challenged, "[but] that life passed you by and you were not really living?"[73]

Item Seventeen: I realize that it is necessary to abstain from alcohol, but my ultimate goal is to attain peace of mind in an active, industrious and constructive life.

"Sobriety in itself is not sufficiently attractive to lure any drunkard to reformation," McGoldrick thought. "To induce him to exert the necessary effort to reform, there must be promise of an end of frustration and futility, and of a greater reward than he can find in drunkenness."[74] So, by "peace of mind," McGoldrick did not mean apathy, indifference, or even the relatively passive concept of serenity. He meant the peace that comes with having fulfilled desires. "Why have you been unable to find peace of mind thus far?" McGoldrick asked.

"Because, as an alcoholic, you failed to understand the meaning of your dominate desires. Instead of their satisfaction being the open sesame to an active, industrious, and constructive life, it was the means through which you became a prisoner locked up behind walls of frustration."[75]

"Your desires are the key to what you actually are," McGoldrick declared. "If you are growing and changing psychologically by altering your mental attitude, no longer thinking like an alcoholic, you will be ready to meet life anew with informed action. Then you can consider that you are indeed something more today than you were yesterday… [and] you will find that precious gift – 'the peace that passeth understanding.'"[76]

Absorbing the Mental Diet: From Theory to Practice

McGoldrick readily acknowledged that the seventeen thought capsules "are but different facets of the same truth," and that the central idea of the Mental Diet can be stated in a single sentence: *"You are what you make yourself."*[77] Why then the need for seventeen items? Because, McGoldrick taught, the mind must be nourished too, "much as we feed the body."[78]

But there was another factor that he considered to be even more important. "The Mental Diet is designed as a tool, to be worked with in fashioning your daily life," he wrote. "Each of the principles is designed to bring home the application of the central truth to some problem of daily life that many alcoholics find too great to bear."[79]

McGoldrick wisely advised that the process of "digestion" – assimilating the healthful patterns of the Mental Diet – would not always be easy. "But," he urged, "you can do it… because you are going to do it systemically and scientifically, in accordance with what psychology has taught us are the laws of the functioning of the mind."[80]

Primarily, the McGoldrick Method was intended to be executed during a three or four week residential stay at Bridge House. (Followed for the next year by a minimum of three hours a week spent receiving further instructions.) However, the program was also presented on a nonresidential basis, and both of McGoldrick's books suggest that the method may be used as a self-therapy program for combating alcoholic drinking or other problems.

Whether in the form of residential treatment, outpatient treatment, or self-therapy, the Mental Diet was to be absorbed through a series of exercises to be performed for each of the thought capsules. These basic exercises are briefly described here:

Exercise one: *Learn the principles of the Mental Diet.*

McGoldrick suggested copying them onto cards to be carried in a pocket or purse. His 1966 book, *The Conquest of Alcohol,* included such cards already printed with the Mental Diet's seventeen statements. "Carry these cards with you everywhere for the next three weeks," he instructed.[81]

Exercise two: *Ask yourself, "What is it that you most want to be? To do? To have? What would give you the greatest, most enduring happiness?"*[82]

This exercise was to be performed the first day if possible. "Bear in mind," McGoldrick cautioned, "that the answer does not lie in the realm of fantastic daydreams. It is not possible for [everyone to] become Chief Justice of the United States. Start from what you are in terms of education, training, background, the highest level of intelligence and ability that you have demonstrated."[83]

This is not to say, either, that career or monetary rewards must be everyone's primary objective. "Remember that security, money, thrills, power, luxury, all the goals most persons set for themselves do not in themselves bring happiness," McGoldrick counseled. "What you are aiming at, above all, is the role, the function, the station and manner of life that you believe will bring you the most peace of mind."[84]

Exercise three: *This recommended practice is the creation of a mental movie, "to see yourself actually doing in imagination what you most want to do."*[85]

This exercise is preceded by relaxation. "First, lie down and get comfortable." McGoldrick instructed. "Don't fold your arms don't cross your legs… Now you're going to direct every muscle, every nerve, every ligament, every organ in your body to relax – relax – relax."[86] This is followed by detailed instructions on relaxing the body, "beginning with the toes."[87]

Once relaxed, McGoldrick directed that you: "Picture in your mind a blank screen, as in a motion-picture theater. You are going to cast upon this screen a movie in which you are the star… You are going to project your future on this screen."[88] Picture yourself as you would like to be: sober, successful, contented, happy – doing what you want to do, having what you want to have, being who you want to be.

McGoldrick received recognition for this technique from a highly popular contemporary writer, Dr. Maxwell Maltz, who wrote extensively on the importance of a positive self-image. In his book *Psycho-Cybernetics,* Maltz recognized the significance and importance of McGoldrick's work:

Edward McGoldrick uses this [visualization] technique in helping alcoholics cross the "bridge" from the old self to the new self. Each day, he has his "students" close their eyes, relax the body as much as possible, and create a "mental motion picture" of themselves as sober, responsible persons. They see themselves actually *enjoying* life without liquor. This is not the only technique used by McGoldrick, but it is one of the basic methods used at "Bridge House" which has a higher record of cure for alcoholics than any other organization in the country.[89]

Exercise four: Review the day's item of the Mental Diet. This requires reading the pages which discuss the item in one or the other of McGoldrick's books.

Exercise five: Write out the essentials that you learned from the reading.

Exercise six: This exercise is performed in four steps to be taken in the evening.

1. briefly review the Mental Diet principle studied
2. congratulate yourself on your achievement
3. tell yourself that your first thoughts upon awakening will be of the Mental Diet and the mental-movie exercise
4. run your mental motion picture

In working this program, you are to review these four steps just before going to bed. Then turn out the lights, perform the steps – and go to sleep.

For the second day onward through the seventeenth day, you are to start the day with the mental motion picture and a brief review of the previous day's mental diet principle. Next, think about positive actions that can be taken towards making the mental image a reality. After discarding the negative habit of insobriety, what is the next move? Education? Finding work? Increasing your attractiveness to the opposite sex? Whatever your goal, plan or take the first steps.

Following that, for each of the first seventeen days, find some time to relax and rerun the mental movie. You should also take time to read the notes taken on the previous day's Mental Diet principle and to study today's principle while taking notes. At bedtime, repeat the nighttime exercises described above, substituting that day's Mental Diet item for the previous one.

Beginning with the *eighteenth day,* McGoldrick recommended rereading parts of the program literature and reviewing the *Diagram of the Mind.* By the *twentieth day*, McGoldrick advocated trying to write out, from memory, all seventeen of the Mental Diet items.

On the *twenty-first day,* he recommended jotting down all of the difficulties that must be addressed during the next month. "Put each problem at the top of a sheet of paper," he said, then "think about what concrete steps you will take to solve them."[90] For each problem, write down the actions that can be taken to solve it – or to better the situation associated with it.

The Bridge House Twenty-one Day Course of Treatment ended on that problem-solving note, thought the mental movie exercises were to continue. Students who attended the residential course at Bridge House were to return for two evenings a week for a full year before they graduated. "I would suggest that two evenings a week for a full year is a minimum for you, too…" McGoldrick advised, addressing himself to those who used this as a method of self-therapy.[91]

In closing, McGoldrick predicted that the journey to stable sobriety was not necessarily complete. At some future date, a time of crisis, the old habits could launch a final assault. But, having already defeated them once, the weapons needed for the final conquest are at hand. "Stand your ground;" McGoldrick urged, "defeat them once and for all time. You will find the experience the most exhilarating of your life!... the conquest of alcohol is yours," he proclaimed, "and it is certain."[92]

Taking This Road

McGoldrick subtitled his last book "a handbook of *self-therapy*." (Emphasis added.) Perhaps it was a premonition. About a year after its publication, on November 21, 1967, Edward McGoldrick, Jr. died of a heart attack. He was 62. Bridge House seems to have carried on for a while without its founder and then quietly closed its doors. Ever since, the only availability of the McGoldrick Method has been as a self-help program or *self-therapy*. It's a shame. If the McGoldrick Method were but better known, it could be more popular today than ever.

I wish I had found the McGoldrick Method earlier in my sobriety. As it was, I got and applied some of the same principles by reading Maxwell Maltz's *Psycho-Cybernetics,* which was a big seller at the time. Maltz taught the importance of a new self-image and a version of McGoldrick's "mental motion picture" technique – "Mental-picturing the desired end result," Maltz called it.[93] *Psycho-Cybernetics* was published in 1960 and it is still in print, as are numerous other books that Maltz wrote on the same subject. There are also newer versions of Maltz's classic: *Psycho-Cybernetics 2000* (1993) and *The New Psycho-Cybernetics* (2001).

Although working the McGoldrick Method will have to have an element of self-therapy, those who are in tune with the New Age culture of today may find some support from the emerging New Age recovery groups and programs discussed in Chapter X. However, don't take this to mean that McGoldrick or his method were necessarily New Age. In one of his books McGoldrick actually pooh-poohed the idea of astrology.[94]

Another possible source of support could be the various New Thought churches such as Unity, Divine Science, Science of Mind and Spirit and so forth. Again, this needn't be taken to mean that the McGoldrick Method is necessarily religious.

Further, it may be possible to work the McGoldrick program while attending AA or NA meetings. Although McGoldrick had his criticisms of Twelve Step groups, he sometimes identified himself as an AA member.[95]

If you decide to work the McGoldrick Method as self-therapy, you may want to rewrite one or two of the thought capsules to bring them into line with modern research. Personally, the only one I would change is item number four: "An alcoholic is made, not born. Heredity, therefore, is not the cause of my drinking..." I would change capsule four to read something like this: "Although science has discovered the possibility of a genetically transmitted predisposition to develop alcoholism, I refuse to use this as an excuse." On the other hand, I might substitute this capsule from McGoldrick's 1954 book: "I know that alcoholism (or ____) is the product of pernicious thought. I know how to nip destructive thought in the bud, and I shall bring the full power of my mind to bear in keeping my thoughts constructive."[96]

McGoldrick's two books *Management of the Mind: How to Conquer Alcohol and Other Blocks to Successful Living* and *The Conquest of Alcohol: A Handbook of Self-therapy* are both out-of-print, but used copies can be found for sale on the Internet, and many libraries have a copy of at least one; or they can obtain one or both through the interlibrary loan program. If you are really lucky you may find one of these books in a used bookstore as I did, but don't count on it. The two books are very similar so it is not really necessary to have them both.

Finally, if you are a self-starter, you may want to start a McGoldrick Group in your own community. If you decide to do this, I would like to hear from you. Whatever way you choose to work the McGoldrick Method, self-therapy or with the aid of whatever support groups you can muster, I wish you the very best.

Chapter Endnotes

1. McGoldrick, Edward J., Jr. (1945) "Help for Alcoholics," *The American Mercury,* Vol. LX, No. 254, February, page 226.
2. McGoldrick (1945) page 226.
3. *New York Times* (May 10, 1944) "Secret City Bureau Cures Alcoholics," Page 21 Column 1.
4. Worden, Helen (1944) "Maybe I Can Do it Too," *Reader's Digest* (condensed from *Argosy*), October, page 115.
5. McGoldrick (1945) page 226.
6. McGoldrick (1945) page 227.
7. McGoldrick (1945) page 227.
8. Worden (1944) page 115.
9. Berger, Meyer (1954) "About New York: Store Finds it Owns an Orphan Street Lamp –Applicants Swamp School for Alcoholics," *New York Times*, October 15, page 25, Column 2.
10. Ibid.
11. *New York Times* (February 6, 1949) "Therapist Scores Alcoholic 'Alibis,'" Page 19 Column 1.
12. *New York Times* (March 9, 1954) "New Plan to Aid Alcoholics," Page 29 Column 6.
13. *New York Times* (March 16, 1953) "Aid to Alcoholics Sharply Limited," Page 23 Column 2.
14. McGoldrick, Edward J., Jr. (1966) *The Conquest of Alcohol: A Handbook of Self-Therapy*, New York: Delacorte Press, page x.
15. Butler Center for Research (June 2010) "Project MATCH: A Study of Alcoholism Treatment Approaches." Retrieved 9/11/2013 from: http://www.hazelden.org/web/public/researchupdates.
16. McGoldrick (1966) pages viii.
17. McGoldrick (1966) pages viii - ix.
18. McGoldrick (1966) page ix.
19. McGoldrick (1966) page xiv.
20. McGoldrick (1966) page 56.

21. McGoldrick (1966) page 41.
22. McGoldrick (1966) page 47.
23. McGoldrick (1966) page 48.
24. McGoldrick (1966) page 49.
25. McGoldrick (1966) page 56-62.
26. McGoldrick (1966) page 62.
27. McGoldrick (1966) page 65.
28. McGoldrick (1966) page 66.
29. McGoldrick (1966) page 69-70.
30. McGoldrick (1966) page 69.
31. McGoldrick (1966) page 128.
32. McGoldrick (1966) page 128.
33. McGoldrick (1966) page 91.
34. McGoldrick, Edward J., Jr. (1954) *Management of the Mind: How to Conquer Alcohol and Other Blocks to Successful Living,* Boston: Houghton Mifflin Company, page 66.
35. McGoldrick (1954) page 71.
36. McGoldrick (1954) page 77.
37. McGoldrick (1966) page 77.
38. McGoldrick (1966) page 78.
39. McGoldrick (1966) page 79.
40. McGoldrick (1966) page 80.
41. McGoldrick (1966) page 81.
42. McGoldrick (1966) page 81.
43. McGoldrick (1954) page 170.
44. McGoldrick (1954) page 172.
45. McGoldrick (1954) pages 173.
46. McGoldrick (1954) pages 173.
47. McGoldrick (1966) page 84.
48. McGoldrick (1966) page 87.
49. Goodyear, Brian (1989) "Unresolved Questions about Alcoholism: The Debate (War?) Goes on – Is a Resolution Possible?" *Alcoholism Treatment Quarterly*, Vol. 6 (2), page 6.
50. Goodyear (1989) page 6.
51. McGoldrick (1966) page 88.

52. McGoldrick (1954) page 184.
53. McGoldrick (1954) page 184.
54. McGoldrick (1954) pages 189-190.
55. McGoldrick (1966) page 93.
56. McGoldrick (1966) page 94.
57. Nossen, Herbert L. (1949) "Therapy for Alcoholics Urged," *New York Times*, February 19, Page 14 Column 7.
58. McGoldrick (1966) page 98.
59. McGoldrick (1966) page 102.
60. McGoldrick (1966) page 104.
61. McGoldrick (1966) page 108.
62. McGoldrick (1966) page 106.
63. McGoldrick (1966) page 110.
64. McGoldrick (1966) pages 110-111.
65. AA World Service, Inc. (1976) *Alcoholics Anonymous* (third edition), New York: Alcoholics Anonymous World Services, Inc., page xxvi.
66. McGoldrick (1966) page 114.
67. McGoldrick (1966) page 114.
68. McGoldrick (1966) page 116.
69. McGoldrick (1966) page 117.
70. McGoldrick (1966) page 117.
71. McGoldrick (1966) page 118.
72. McGoldrick (1966) page 119.
73. McGoldrick (1966) page 120.
74. McGoldrick (1954) page 215.
75. McGoldrick (1966) page 122.
76. McGoldrick (1966) page 123.
77. McGoldrick (1954) page 230.
78. McGoldrick (1966) page 127.
79. McGoldrick (1966) page 127.
80. McGoldrick (1966) page 127.
81. McGoldrick (1966) page 130.
82. McGoldrick (1966) page 130.
83. McGoldrick (1966) page 130.
84. McGoldrick (1966) page 131.

85. McGoldrick (1966) page 131.
86. McGoldrick (1966) page 133.
87. Ibid.
88. McGoldrick (1966) page 131-136.
89. Maltz, Maxwell (1960) *Psycho-Cybernetics,* New York: Pocket Books, page 42.
90. McGoldrick (1966) page 143.
91. McGoldrick (1966) page 144.
92. McGoldrick (1966) page 145.
93. Maltz (1960) page 41.
94. McGoldrick (1954) pages 37-38.
95. "Help for Drunkards" (1944) *Time Magazine,* October 23.
96. McGoldrick (1954) page 72.

CHAPTER IV:
Synanon:
The Rise, The Fall and The Legacy

Chuck Dederich had failed at everything.

He was overweight, deformed, loud-mouthed and unemployed. He lived in a tiny apartment in the slums of Ocean Park, California, subsisting on $33 a month in unemployment benefits. He called himself "a rube from Ohio." Others called him "fatso."

But he was one hell of an AA member. And starting in 1958, in less than three decades he would parlay his AA experience into a multimillion-dollar drug rehabilitation program, utopian commune, business corporation and faux religion, all of which went by the name of *Synanon*.

In addition to "fatso," in the process of building and then destroying his empire, Dederich would acquire many more colorful nicknames. Among other titles, he was called a "master hoodwinker," a "megalomaniac nut," an "ill-mannered boorish Midwestern creep," an "outrageous showman," a "lusty iconoclast," a "wrecking ball from outer space," a "herd of one elephant," an "earthquake of a man," "the funniest man I ever knew," and "Mr. Synanon."

Born March 22, 1913 in Toledo, Ohio, Charles Edwin Dederich led a checkered life. Even his friends conceded: "Chuck made a failure of his business career, made a failure of his marriages, made a failure of himself with his addiction to alcohol and Benzedrine."[1]

Dederich's mother was a music teacher; his father, a "drunken promoter" who was killed in an automobile accident when Dederich was only four. Dying in an automobile wreck was "something which could not have been easy in 1917,"[2] Dederich once remarked, a little ruefully perhaps since his mother later married a man Dederich hated.

Dederich attended the University of Notre Dame, flunked out, and tried the University of Toledo where he flunked again. Despite his academic failures and the long-lasting Great Depression of the 1930s, family connections enabled him to land a minor white-collar job at Gulf Oil's Toledo Office. In nine years at Gulf he progressed through the ranks modestly enough to become a traveling sales representative. He married, had a son, and hung out with dedicated Communist Party members, becoming in his own words a "parlor pinko."[3]

In 1944 Dederich suffered an attack of meningitis. He was comatose for two weeks and might have died except that he was selected for an experimental treatment with spinal injections of penicillin. Even though he recovered, the meningitis left half his face paralyzed and destroyed the hearing in one ear. Another operation – some say it was brain surgery – resulted in the widening of the ear canal on that paralyzed right side of his face, leaving a sizeable hole. The result, in the words of admirer Guy Endore, was "the head of a later day Socrates: ugly and wise, complex and simple. A face that repels and attracts, refusing to leave you indifferent."[4]

Even after recovering from meningitis, Dederich was still certain that he would die and he wanted to see California before that happened. So he left Ohio for the Golden State. Once there, he settled in Los Angeles, divorced his first wife, remarried, had a daughter, and found sporadic work as a salesman, promoter, and factory machinist.

And he drank. A bar-fly and a pill-head at the same time, he used chemicals to put himself to sleep and other chemicals to wake himself up. He used still a third kind of pill to keep him smart, or at least that was what he imagined. But, Dederich claimed he wasn't an alcoholic. By his account, a man wasn't an alcoholic so long as the milk bill was paid before the liquor bill. His second wife called AA anyway.

Now in those days, AA did most of its own recruiting work so the proselytizer who showed up was probably a real honest-to-goodness AA member. But he got nowhere with the "non-alcoholic"

Dederich. Three years later Dederich made the call himself and, as luck will sometimes have it, he got hold of the very same sponsor, or so he said. "Fatso," the sponsor told him, "if you don't go to a meeting every goddamn day, you'll die."[5]

"I became a very, very fanatical Alcoholics Anonymous fellow," Dederich bragged. "I lived it, I breathed it, I slept it, I ate it. For weeks I did nothing else but AA work. And then, when I needed money badly, I went out and got myself a job as a pattern-maker at Curtis-Wright, but without changing my schedule any more than I damn well had to."[6] As for his wife, she had had enough. Once it was fairly certain that Dederich was on his feet in AA, they divorced. "We divided everything equally," Dederich joked. "She took the inside of the house and I took the outside."[7]

This chapter will describe the outcome of Dederich's efforts: Synanon, the drug addiction recovery organization he founded, and its rise and fall under his powerful, charismatic leadership.

The TLC Club and Synanon I: How it Started

In January of 1958, or thereabouts, Dederich decided to devote himself to the work of sobering up drunks: "I had no job, two cents in my pocket, and was living off unemployment benefits, in a small apartment near the beach in Ocean Park, California," he said.

> With some friends from AA, I had set up a Wednesday night 'free association' discussion group. The group was set up to explore 'a line of no line' [whatever that means]. The meetings were loud and boisterous. Attack of one another was a keynote of the sessions, with everyone joining in. I could detect considerable lying and self-deception in the group. I began to attack viciously – partly out of my own irritations and at times to defend myself. The group would join in, and we would let the air out of pompously inflated egos, including my own. The

sessions soon became the highpoint of everyone's week.[8]

For a time, Dederich and his cronies continued to attend AA meetings, but as "Dederich's faction." They also held long discussions on philosophical issues such as Ralph Waldo Emerson's essay on "Self-Reliance," a work which Dederich regarded as a very profound manual for practical living.

Those first little meetings seemingly had nothing. No clubhouse, no program, no structure, no name – but as a man who participated in those early discussions later recalled, their power was apparently enormous:

> [O]ur first little group of AA members got together in order to probe deeper into ourselves for the source of our urge to obliterate our rational minds with alcohol. And you know how Chuck, with his grasp of Emersonian philosophy, gave us our basic axioms: that only truth, the unadulterated truth, could set us free, and that anything that was good for us must be good for all. That's all we had to start with: just those two ideas.
>
> And now picture us in the grip of this all-consuming faith that caused us all to shed every vestige of selfishness, with everyone's purse open to everyone else, freely stripping ourselves down to our most hidden moments, the most intimate and secret details of our lives, and pitching into each other with verbal weapons that loving friends had never before used against each other, in order to compel ourselves to this state. Who needed alcohol: I tell you … we were drunk with ideas. Drunk with the possibilities that this method was opening up on every side.[9]

One possibility was that the method might work for drug addicts as well as alcoholics. The first addict was brought to the group by Grey Thompson, an AA member and lavish admirer of Dederich. "Grey brought Whitey into my little bit of a room," Dederich said. "When you pulled out the slide out bed with the couch and a big chair, the room was full. Grey brought him in this night, and... He said, 'I want you to meet an old friend of mine – Whitey. We knew each other since boyhood and blah, blah, blah. Let's try to straighten him out. I want you to talk to him.'"[10] The talking somehow worked and "Whitey" (not his real name) started staying sober and straight.

In July of 1958, still broke and living off unemployment checks, Dederich rented a nearby storefront and announced the formation of the "Tender Loving Care [TLC] Club.'" The following month he pulled his faction out of the AA. Eventually, in about September of 1958, Synanon would come to concentrate exclusively on drug addicts to the exclusion of alcoholics. As Dederich himself put it: "I became the champion of the addicts, chucked the alcoholics out, and Synanon was then fully launched for the addicts."[11]

"Because most of the people had some psychoanalytic orientation," Dederich confided, "the early sessions were focused around sexual problems."[12] Early discussions enthusiastically addressed the basic needs of men and women, whether it was TLC, tender loving care, or DVO, deep vaginal orgasms. Both sets of abbreviations were actually painted on the window of the Tender Loving Care Club's storefront – to the profound puzzlement, I suppose, of strangers who were passing by.

Somehow Dederich found a way to provide more than just meetings for his addicts. He provided room and board. The members lived together, ate together, and attended meetings together. In providing this live-in framework, Dederich pioneered the first modern Therapeutic Community, or TC, run by ex-addicts.

Synanon would eventually devolve from a legitimate therapeutic community, to a commune that was open to anyone, to a "new religion" that *Time* magazine characterized as a "kooky cult." But according to historian William L. White, in the beginning Synanon made at least three significant and lasting contributions to addiction treatment:

1. Synanon was the first to use ex-addicts as therapists or counselors.
2. Key individuals who left Synanon went on to found other successful therapeutic communities.
3. Synanon pioneered a method that was able to move the addict from the "culture of addiction" to a "culture of Recovery."[13]

Three Synanons

There have been various schemes to categorize the changes that Synanon went through during its three decades. Harvard trained psychologist Steven Simon called Synanon's first decade "Synanon I" and the period after 1968 "Synanon II."[14] Sociologist Richard Ofshe thought that Synanon went through four stages of development. Before Simon's Synanon I, there was a "voluntary association of former alcoholics." This was the time when Dederich and his friends were still attending Alcoholics Anonymous meetings. The second phase (1958-68) was the generally well-thought-of therapeutic community that concentrated on drug rehabilitation.

Synanon's third stage (1969-75) was its attempt to create an alternative society that included "squares" (people who had never been addicted) in addition to addicts, or what Synanon called its "dope fiends." Stage four (from 1975 onward) was Synanon's attempt to remake itself as a recognized religion.[15] This fourth phase was the period of Synanon's greatest excesses that lead to its downfall. Most scholars now combine Ofshe's stages one and two to create a view of three Synanons: I, II and III.

The Synanon Game

The Game was central to the Synanon experience. It was to Synanon what meetings are to AA. Although it evolved into something dramatically different, the Game started as an adaption of AA meetings. Where the AA meetings are generally supportive, however, the Synanon Games were highly confrontational.

The Game usually opened with a reading of the Synanon philosophy, a short, awkwardly written document that was continually revised and expanded by Dederich. What may be the final version of the Philosophy is given in Rod Janzen's book *The Rise and Fall of Synanon: A California Utopia:*

> The Synanon Philosophy is based on the belief that there comes a time in everyone's life when he arrives at the conviction that envy is ignorance; that imitation is suicide; that he must accept himself for better or worse as his portion; that though the wide universe is full of good, no kernel of nourishing corn can come to him but through his toil bestowed on that plot of ground which is given to him to till. The power which resides in him is new in nature, and none but he knows what it is that he can do, nor does he know until he has tried. Bravely let him speak the utmost syllable of his conviction. God will not have his work made manifest by cowards.
>
> A man is relieved and gay [happy] when he has put his heart into his work and done his best; but what he has said or done otherwise shall give him no peace. As long as he willingly accepts himself, he will continue to grow and develop his potentialities. As long as he does not accept himself, much of his energies will be used to defend rather than to explore and actualize himself.

No one can force a person towards permanent and creative learning. He will learn only if he wills to. Any other type of learning is temporary and inconsistent with the self and will disappear as soon as the threat is removed. Learning is possible in an environment that provides information, the setting, resources, and by his being there. God helps those who help themselves.[16]

The Game was usually played by about a dozen people who sat in chairs arranged in a circle. Discussions might be started by questions such as "What really pissed you off this week?" or "Who is the most boring person in this group?"

An important part of playing the Game was the *indictment* where one player brutally criticized another for some real or perceived shortcoming. Other players were expected to *back the play,* which usually meant that the entire group would join in the criticism, which appeared to be brutal, loud and profane. Especially in the beginning, the Game was democratic so that everyone, even Dederich himself, had a turn at being *indicted.* (Eventually, however, it became off limits to *indict* Dederich and other top Synanon leaders.)

The idea of the Game was to expose a persons' shortcomings or character defects. It was also thought to toughen a person so that he or she would be more able to deal with life. Of course, this sort of "attack therapy" was, and still is, highly controversial. But those who played the Game attributed to it almost magical healing powers, much as AA members do with their meetings.

The Game was usually ended with a recitation of the Synanon Prayer. Thus, the Game retained at least two characteristics of AA meetings by opening with a reading and ending with a prayer. The prayer read:

Please let me first and always examine myself.
Let me be honest and truthful,
Let me seek and assume responsibility,

Let me understand rather than be understood,
Let me trust and have faith in myself and my fellow man,
Let me love rather than be loved,
Let me give rather than receive.[17]

The Fall of Synanon

You have probably heard it said that "power corrupts and absolute power corrupts absolutely." This was certainly the case with Charles E. Dederich. The beginning of Synanon's demise may be traced to an event that happened in 1973. Dederich became upset with a member who was dominating a Game and poured a bottle of Dad's Root Beer over her head. While this may be considered merely boorish behavior, it violated – if only symbolically – Synanon's cardinal rule against violence of any kind (or even the threat of violence). Dederich first apologized for his actions but then reversed himself and maintained that this mild act of violence was right and proper. The entire community of Synanon was shocked.

Synanon III eventually endorsed violence to the extent that it supplied itself with a cache of weapons and gave beatings to several people who were at odds with it over one issue or another.

As the decade progressed, Synanon became increasingly weird in the eyes of America's main-stream society. Two highly controversial policies were the mandating of vasectomies for all adult males who had been in the community over five years (Dederich himself excepted) and forced abortions for some females. In a move that alienated almost everyone outside of Synanon, Dederich decreed that everyone "change partners," that is, divorce their present spouse and marry another. *Time* magazine looked at these practices and labeled Synanon a "kooky cult."[18]

The event that most alarmed the American public was Synanon's attempt to murder lawyer Paul Morantz by placing a live rattlesnake in his mailbox. In 1980 Dederich, along with two Synanon members, were convicted of this crime. The two members served short prison terms while Dederich avoided prison due to his poor health.

What the public did not know, for the most part, was that Dederich's health issues were partly, or perhaps largely, due to the fact that he had resumed drinking. According to some reports, he drank as much as two quarts of expensive scotch whiskey every day. Many members were alarmed when Synanon abandoned its policy against alcoholic beverages in 1978, and those forebodings proved to be correct.

In the end, the fall of Synanon was brought about by the Internal Revenue Service, which contested Synanon's tax exempt status because the Dederich family was enriching itself with the profits from Synanon's various businesses. To be fair, Synanon did continue to do some charity and drug rehabilitation work, but it also paid Dederich, his son and daughter some princely salaries and bonuses. In September 1989, Synanon lost its battle to reinstate its tax-exempt status. The result was a tax assessment of $17 million, which forced Synanon into bankruptcy and led to the dissolution of the Synanon corporation in 1991.

Largely as the result of Dederich's megalomania, the first successful therapeutic community to be run and staffed by ex-addicts was no more. Despite his positive contributions to drug rehabilitation, *Time* magazine's March 17, 1997 obituary of Dederich referred to him as the "'power-mad founder' of Synanon"[19]

Taking These Roads

If you visit the Synanon website today (www.synanon.org) you will find a note that says Synanon is no longer in operation. It refers those who need help to other TCs that are or were staffed by former Synanon residents. These include:

- Delancey Street (http://www.delanceystreetfoundation.org/wwa.php)
- Samaritan Village (http://www.samvill.org/)

- Amity Foundation (http://www.amityfdn.org/)
- Marvins Corner (http://www.marvinscornertherapeuticcommunity.org/)
- Phoenix House (http://www.phoenixhouse.com/)

There are many other TCs, not all of which use Synanon's methods (and those that do may have modified certain features considerably, most notably the Game). There's a website for the Therapeutic Communities of America: (http://www.therapeutic communitiesofamerica. org/main/). This site gives the names, addresses, and Internet sites for numerous TCs that are members of that organization. There is also an Internet site for the World Federation of Therapeutic Communities (http://www.wftc.org/). There is still a therapeutic community named Synanon in Germany (http://www.synanon-aktuell.de/)* but I don't know if it uses Dederich's methods or not.

According to the National Institute on Drug Abuse, "TCs are drug-free residential settings that use a hierarchical model with treatment stages that reflect increased levels of personal and social responsibility."[20] This means that at first, along with treatment, you would probably be given low-level jobs such as washing dishes, mopping floors, or cleaning restrooms. But you would quickly be given a chance to work your way up and would eventually become nearly equal to the staff. Some community members may even become members of the staff after successfully completing their treatment.

TCs differ from other forms of therapy in length and intensity of treatment. Due mostly to funding limitations, the recommended stay at a TC has gradually decreased from 15-24 months to 9-15 months.[21]

According to George DeLeon, PhD: "The typical day in a TC is highly structured. It begins at 7:00 A.M. and ends at 11 P.M. During this time, residents participate in a variety of meetings, encounter

---

* The website is in German.

and other therapeutic groups and recreational activities; perform job functions (work therapy); and receive individual counseling."[22]

Therapeutic Communities serve those with the most severe substance abuse and social deviancy problems. Therefore it is appropriate that TCs are the most demanding of all treatments. While critics have charged that "the success rate in Synanon imitators was no better than ... the dismal statistics of Synanon itself,"[23] TCs do sometimes work when other methods fail. They are the Synanon legacy.

Chapter Endnotes

1. Endore, Guy (1967, 1968) *Synanon,* Garden City, New York: Doubleday & Company, Inc. page 124.
2. Gerstel, David U. (1982) *Paradise Incorporated: Synanon,* Novato, CA: Presosio Press, page 33.
3. Gerstel (1982) page 34.
4. Endore (1967, 1968) page 18.
5. Gerstel (1982) page 35.
6. Gerstel (1982) page 180.
7. Gerstel (1982) page 35.
8. Yablonsky, Lewis (1965) *The Tunnel Back: Synanon,* New York: The Macmillan Company, page 49.
9. Endore (1967, 1968) page 65.
10. Yablonsky (1965) page 51. 11. Yablonsky (1965) page 55.
12. Yablonsky (1965) page 49.
13. White, William L., (1998) *Slaying the Dragon,* Bloomington, IL: Chestnut Health Systems/Lighthouse Institute, page 244.
14. Janzen, Rod, (2001) *The Rise and Fall of Synanon: A California Utopia,* Baltimore: John Hopkins University Press, page 56.
15. Ofshe, Richard (Summer 1980) "The Social Development of the Synanon Cult: The Managerial Strategy of Organizational Transformation," *Sociological Analysis,* Vol. 41, No. 2.
16. Janzen (2001) page 247.

17. Janzen (2001) page 12.
18. *Time* (December 26, 1977) "Life at Synanon is Swinging: A Once Respected Drug Program Turns Into a Kooky Cult."
19. Janzen (2001) page 6.
20. National Institute on Drug Abuse Research Report Series (August 2002) "Therapeutic Community." Retrieved 5/11/2010 from: http://drugabuse.gov/ResearchReports/Therapeutic/Therapeutic2.html
21. DeLeon, George (2008) "Therapeutic Communities" in *Textbook of Substance Abuse Treatment,* 4th Edition, Washington: American Psychiatric Publishing, Inc., page 459.
22. DeLeon (2008) page 465.
23. Morantz, Paul (Nov 2012) "Aftermath – the Synanon legacy." Retrieved 7/12/2013 from: http://www.paulmorantz.com/the_synanon_story/aftermath-the-synanon-legacy/

CHAPTER V:
Women's Recovery Programs:
By Women, Primarily *for* Women – and Men Use Them Too

Jean Kirkpatrick[*] was an AA member.

With the emphasis on *"was."* She attended AA meetings for about three years in the 1950s and, although she didn't disclose much about her AA experience, she may have been an up-and-comer. Kirkpatrick wrote that she was well acquainted with Marty Mann, who was the first successful woman in AA and the high-profile founder of the National Council on Alcoholism. She planned on going to work for Mann after earning her PhD, "but," she lamented, "I blew it all by drinking."[1]

According to the Women For Sobriety website, Kirkpatrick drank because she "couldn't cope with the fact that she was the first woman to receive the Fels Fellowship award at the University of Pennsylvania."[2] According to Kirkpatrick herself, the explanation was a little less politically correct. His name was Jim.

The two met on what AA calls a "twelfth step call" – members going to see active drinkers in the hope that they too will give up alcohol and join the fellowship. But instead of Jim getting sober and joining AA, Jean got drunk and quit. "We used each other, we destroyed each other, and – finally," she confessed, "we got drunk together."[3]

The lengthy affair ended when Jim committed suicide. "[P]art of me grieved. But part of me felt relieved," Jean wrote. "At last I was emotionally free to begin the long road to recovery."[4]

---

[*] Not to be confused with Jeane (ending with an "e") Kirkpatrick, who served as Ambassador to the United Nations during the Reagan presidency.

Kirkpatrick returned to AA but found that, for her, it wasn't the same. The second time around she quickly gave up on the venerable program. Forsaking AA, she decided that she would find a new way to recover. That turned out to be a great idea because it led to the founding of Women For Sobriety (WFS) in 1975.

Kirkpatrick wasn't the only woman to found an addiction recovery program. In 1989 Gail Unterberger created "Twelve Steps for Women Alcoholics" and in 1992 Charlotte Kasl launched a feminist recovery model to serve women and minorities. She calls it "Sixteen Steps for Discovery and Empowerment." And in 2005 another woman, "Roberta Jewell," (not her real name) started a program called "My Way Out." Although My Way Out (MWO) was not designed to be exclusively for women, 80 percent of the visitors to its website are female.[5] It is so popular with them that it merits inclusion in this chapter.

These four women, their programs, and their efforts to help men too, will be discussed in this chapter, as will the struggles and successes of women in AA.

Women in AA: Long Road to Success

Kirkpatrick, Unterberger, Kasl and Jewell weren't the first women to have problems with the Twelve Steps of AA. In fact, the first women to have difficulty in AA *were* the first women in AA. Only three of the first 100 AA members were women and none of those pioneers fared well.[6] The first woman seeking Twelve Step recovery got drunk, like Kirkpatrick, with the help of a male prospect. This was followed by a string of failures that included some apparently high-class characters such as Sylvia K. a glamorous divorcee known only as Jane, "the wife of a wealthy industrialist, and Lelia M. who was reportedly an heiress

The first woman to have any success at all in AA was Florence R., who managed a year of sobriety. Her story, "A Feminine Victory," appeared in the first edition of *Alcoholics Anonymous,* AA's beloved "Big Book."

"To my lot falls the rather doubtful distinction of being the only 'lady' alcoholic in our particular section," Florence R. wrote.[8] (Apparently she – or an editor – placed "lady" in quotes because it was thought that a female alcoholic couldn't be one.)

As the only successful woman in AA, Florence R. was lonely. "Perhaps," she bemoaned, "it is because of a desire for a 'supporting cast' of my own sex that I am praying for inspiration to tell my story in a manner that may give other women who have this problem the courage to see it in its true light and seek the help that has given me a new lease on life."[9] And she went on to tell the story of how she was helped by "B---" (AA co-founder Bill Wilson) and "L---" (Wilson's wife, Lois).

"I know that my victory is none of my human doing," Florence concluded with an abundance of humility. "I know that I must keep myself worthy of Divine help. And the glorious thing is this: I am free, I am happy, and perhaps I am going to have the blessed opportunity of 'passing it on.' I say in all reverence – Amen."[10]

The opportunity didn't arrive in time. A 1939 letter from AA pioneer Fitz Mayo to Bill Wilson contained this racy message about Florence: "She is in love with a hellion 15 years younger than she who feeds her beer – so says her landlady."[11] In her autobiography, Lois Wilson explained the matter more tactfully: Florence "made an unfortunate second marriage and started drinking again."[12] In April of 1943 Florence R. was found dead of an apparent suicide.

Not until the arrival of Marty Mann did any woman manage to change her life permanently by working the Twelve Steps. And Mann's recovery program also had its failings. She relapsed three times before 1941 and again, "some time between 1959 and 1964."[13] These later dates are vague because Mann's drinking was hushed up amongst AA members. It was an "undirected conspiracy of silence," as Mann's biographers diplomatically phrased it.[14] No doubt it was disappointing, shocking and probably more than a little frightening that the most famous woman in AA could have a slip or relapse after twenty (more or less) years of sobriety. Nobody wanted to talk about it; maybe not even think about it.

But despite these few drinking episodes, Mann did make remarkable changes and achieved a great deal in her life. Sober, she became one of the most important figures in the modern alcoholism movement. It is no coincidence that after Marty Mann arrived at AA, articles expressing concern about women alcoholics began to appear in AA's official magazine, the *AA Grapevine*. Mann was one of the magazine's founders.

A 1945 article written by Marty M. (almost certainly Mann herself) proclaimed by its title: "Women Alcoholics Have a Tougher Fight." The article estimated that women in AA were "one in ten of our total membership," and it emphasized the apparent fact that women alcoholics were more likely to use tranquilizers in addition to alcohol. "We need perhaps a little more help," Mann concluded, "a little more tolerance, a little more time…"[15]

A *Grapevine* article published the following year did little to promote such tolerance. It was penned by Grace O. of Manhattan, who described herself as: "just one woman AA sticking her neck out." Stick the neck out she did. While her message was no doubt written with the best of intentions, she rather ruthlessly critiqued AA's women, their faults and foibles. The Grace O. article listed no less than eleven "female frailties," including complaints such as: "The percentage of women who stay in AA is low"; "Women talk too much"; "Few women can think in the abstract"; "Too many women don't like women"; and "Women's feelings get hurt too often."[16] As historian and author William L. White observed, the article was "filled with the kinds of stereotypes that women were likely to encounter in the AA of this period."[17]

One positive feature of the Grace O. article may have been the endorsement of meetings just for women, tepid though it was by today's standards: "Women's groups are working out successfully in many cities," Grace O. acknowledged, "though fundamentally segregation is somewhat contrary to AA principles."[18]

This may have been all the encouragement female AAs needed. Soon, announcements concerning meetings for women were appearing regularly in the *Grapevine*.[19] Today, depending on where you live, there may be an abundance of women's meetings for those women who prefer them. And there are other resources for women: on-line women's discussion groups, pamphlets published by AA, and books written by, for and about women alcoholics.

In the 1940s, according to Mann's estimate, the percentage of women in AA was just 10 percent. In the 1950s, the percentage of females rose to 15 percent and by 1968 it was up to 22 percent.[20] A mid-1970s study of Hazelden, a famous Twelve Step based treatment center, found that 67 percent of its women graduates were frequent attenders of AA, compared to just 56 percent of the men.[21] These and other data seemed to indicate that conditions for women in AA were changing for the better. The percentage of women in AA continued to grow during the 1970s and 1980s, reaching 35 percent in 1989 and then stabilizing at about that level.[22]

The status of women in AA is still a matter of some controversy, with various experts expressing differing opinions. William L. White, who researched the problems women had in early AA but remains a strong supporter of the fellowship, wrote:

> One must be careful in assuming that, because women were not well represented within the early years when AA's program of recovery was being formulated, this program is not inclusive enough to meet the needs of women or that [it] has not evolved to meet the needs of women.[23]

Marian Sandmaier, who wrote *The Invisible Alcoholics: Women and Alcohol* – and who apparently has no bias for or against Alcoholics Anonymous – says:

> for all its strengths, AA is still primarily a "male club" to which some women find difficulty relating. Some women feel their special issues are not always adequately dealt with at meetings, or feel hesitant about bringing up certain sensitive topics in a primarily male group.[24]

And Stephanie S. Covington, the author of *A Woman's Way Through the Twelve Steps,* and a recovered alcoholic herself, offered this assessment:

> In many ways, Twelve Step recovery programs are based on a feminine model of support and healing. Although the languages and practices may not always follow this feminine model, the spirit of the Steps and the structure of Twelve Step programs offer an opportunity for us to explore both our recovery from addiction and our empowerment as women.[25]

The last word on the matter, of course, belongs to you, the individual woman (or man) seeking recovery. If AA or some other Anonymous group seems right for you, it probably is; if it doesn't, other programs may be better.

Women For Sobriety: The First Alternative

Sometime in the early 1970s Jean Kirkpatrick achieved permanent sobriety. At about the same time, she finished her doctorate degree in sociology, which she had been working on for many years. More or less concurrently with all this, she lost her job. She would have been about 50 years old, over-educated with a very thin résumé.

She had tried working at "a hundred things," she believed, "and never mastered any."[26] At her age, with her education, mismatched with her lack of experience, Dr. Kirkpatrick was virtually unemployable. Drinking had consumed her life. It was the only thing she had stuck with, and now she didn't do that anymore. She hadn't had a drink in "four or five years, depending on when you count from," she said.[27] Which is an odd way to measure sobriety, but the point was that she had gotten sober, and she had done it without AA.

"How to recover without AA. That's what you're an expert in," she told herself. It was a revelation. Finally, her future was clear: she would dedicate herself to helping female alcoholics, "those for whom AA didn't work."[28]

The way Kirkpatrick had gotten herself sober relied heavily on the philosophies of Ralph Waldo Emerson and the Unity Church. Emerson (1803 - 1882) was a leader of the American transcendentalism movement. The transcendentalists greatly influenced the fledgling New Thought movement of the 1800s and out of this movement grew several churches and religious organizations including Unity, which was founded in 1889 by Charles and Myrtle Fillmore. A fundamental tenet of all these philosophies – Emerson, New Thought, and Unity – is that humans create their experiences through their thinking. "If I had learned anything from Emerson," Kirkpatrick said, "it was that thought… our thoughts… make or break us. And that had become my key to sobriety."[29]

The WFS "New Life" Acceptance Program

When the time came for Kirkpatrick to create her program of recovery for women, she didn't think in terms of confessing past errors or making amends. She looked at ways of changing the negative *thoughts* underlying the damaging behavior. She didn't use "steps." She wrote affirmations: "Thirteen Statements of Acceptance," which form the heart of the WFS program.

These affirmations have been subject to some minor editing over the years. For example, the thirteenth statement used to read: "I am responsible for myself and my sisters" – apparently a declaration of feminist solidarity. It now reads: "I am responsible for myself and for my *actions*." At some point what might be called the secondary statements, shown below in italics, were added. These are usually, but not always, included with the statements. Here are the WFS "Statements of Acceptance" as they are found on the WFS website:

1. **I have a life-threatening problem that once had me.** *I now take charge of my life and my disease. I accept the responsibility.*
2. **Negative thoughts destroy only myself.** *My first conscious sober act must be to remove negativity from my life.*
3. **Happiness is a habit I will develop.** *Happiness is created, not waited for.*
4. **Problems bother me only to the degree I permit them to.** *I now better understand my problems and do not permit problems to overwhelm me.*
5. **I am what I think.** *I am a capable, competent, caring, compassionate woman.*
6. **Life can be ordinary or it can be great.** *Greatness is mine by a conscious effort.*
7. **Love can change the course of my world.** *Caring becomes all important.*
8. **The fundamental object of life is emotional and spiritual growth.** *Daily I put my life into a proper order, knowing which are the priorities.*
9. **The past is gone forever.** *No longer will I be victimized by the past, I am a new person.*
10. **All love given returns.** *I will learn to know that others love me.*
11. **Enthusiasm is my daily exercise.** *I treasure all moments of my new life.*
12. **I am a competent woman and have much to give life.** *This is what I am and I shall know it always.*
13. **I am responsible for myself and for my actions.** *I am in charge of my mind, my thoughts, and my life.*[30]

To use this program and make it effective, Kirkpatrick recommended that each morning you arise early to go over the affirmations. Then think about each statement by itself. Next, take one affirmation in particular and use it consciously all day. At the end of the day, review the use of that affirmation and the effect that it had for you and your actions.[31]

WFS and AA

Jean Kirkpatrick often contrasted Women For Sobriety with the AA program, usually in the context of what she felt was right for women as opposed to the Twelve Steps being right for men. "I believe the WFS Program provides more help for women alcoholics," she wrote, "because it was developed from a woman's experience, while the AA program was the result of a man's experience."[32]

But WFS and AA do agree on some important points. In particular, they agree that alcohol or drug addiction is a disease or illness. But they disagree on the psychology of addiction and on the best approach for recovery. A significant difference, for many, could be that WFS doesn't pressure members to introduce themselves as alcoholics or drug addicts. Instead of proclaiming "My name is Jean and I am an alcoholic," WFS members say: "My name is _____ and I'm a competent woman." Women For Sobriety also urges members to not dwell on the past and to practice healthy habits such as taking vitamin supplements and limiting the intake of coffee and sweets.

In a pamphlet published in 1994, Dr. Kirkpatrick summarized what she believed were the major differences between her program and AA:

Alcoholics Anonymous	Women For Sobriety
1. Philosophy is to "Turn over" our will and our lives.	1. We take charge of "Our bodies ourselves."
2. Higher Power concept.	2. Emotional and spiritual growth are fundamental.
3. Emphasis on alcoholism. "My name is Jean and I am an alcoholic."	3. Emphasis on recovery. "My name is Jean and I'm a competent woman."
4. Keep past vibrant in order to stay sober.	4. Put past behind us to stay sober.
5. AA Program based on Oxford Group religion that recommends: a) admitting powerlessness; b) moral inventories; c) confessing short-comings; d) prayer and helping others.	5. WFS Program based upon metaphysical philosophy – our thoughts create our world.
6. A meeting a week for a lifetime or you will be drinking.	6. Once we learn how to cope with the problems of life, we won't need a group any longer.
7. Emphasis on humility and dampening down the ego.	7. We must overcome humility and learn to find ego strengths.
8. Not opposed to coffee.	8. Opposed to coffee in excess of one or two cups a day.
9. Often urge members to eat candy when wanting to drink.	9. Sugar detrimental to alcoholics. Urge use of vitamins and learning about nutrition.[33]

Lee Kaskutas, who was an intern with the Marian Institute for the Prevention of Alcohol and Other Drug Problems, also offered an analysis of WFS contrasted with AA: "In WFS, women 'think their way into good actions,'" she wrote, "while AA members 'act their way into good thinking.'" She also thought that for WFS members, *"Sobriety is inside the mind,"* and thus they are able to directly affirm sobriety. For AA members, however, *"Sobriety is outside the self."* Therefore they rely on externals such as perpetual heavy attendance at AA meetings. While both AA and WFS recognize loss of control as a mark of addiction, Kaskutas observed that AA members *surrender* to loss of control in order to gain outside assistance while WFS women strive to *regain control* or to take charge.[34]

These significant differences notwithstanding, for the most part WFS allows AA its greatness. In fact, Women For Sobriety members often attend AA or some other Twelve Step group in addition to their women's program. Occasionally, however, the WFS founder expressed frustration with the much larger and more powerful Anonymous group movement, and with what she saw as interference by some of its over-zealous members. Discernibly, the frustrations seemed to grow over time:

> *1977* – "[T]he AA program has not met the needs of everyone, especially not women. Fewer than 10 percent of all alcoholics are in AA and fewer than 3 percent of [all] women alcoholics. Surely women need something more."[35]
>
> *1981* – "In those early years I did not know the amount of resistance I would encounter from alcoholics who were members of AA. Nor did I ever think about feelings they might have that "New Life" was a direct challenge to the authority of the AA program. ... Although I knew I'd meet some resistance, never did I believe it would be this strong."[36]
>
> *1990* – "Many AA members are filled with rage, nastiness, and are very immature. Their immaturity

is such that they cannot permit themselves to listen to what we are saying.[37] AA women who take the trouble to come hear me speak are often present only to give me a hard time. Twelve years of this is beginning to get to me."[38]

"Needless to say, my fight for these ideas has been an uphill battle," Kirkpatrick lamented in her last major book. "As time goes on, the validity of what I am preaching will be totally accepted but I won't be here to witness it."[39] On June 19, 2000, Jean Kirkpatrick passed away at the age of 77.

Kudos for WFS

There's no question that Women For Sobriety works for some women. It is now around 40 years old, having outlived its founder by more than a decade. Along the way it has accumulated a good number of supportive testimonials. Testimonials don't mean that something works for everyone. WFS doesn't claim that it does. Testimonials do mean that it works for *somebody* and if it works for somebody – anybody – it might work for you, particularly if what those successful people have to say about it resonates or strikes a chord in you. The testimonials from women who have been helped by WFS are impressive. Some are briefly quoted here:

- [U]sing the WFS program really helped change my way of thinking – from totally negative to a positive attitude about everything … I used those statements like I never used anything all day long, and I mean all day long… I realized that it worked. It was incredible for me.[40] ~ Rita
- That need that I had felt for something religious was working for me in WFS. I found that I was growing.[41] ~ Denise
- We have a lot of women who have gotten sober in Women For Sobriety and haven't done anything else.[42] ~ Sandy
- Everyone needs Women For Sobriety. And it certainly doesn't have to exclude AA. There isn't a woman alive, regardless of her status with substance problems, who can't

get this program to work for her. It is a recovery program. It's a self esteem building program, and it works.[43] ~ Kathryn
- They were sober and happy! I liked the humor and lightness I saw there. Could I really feel that way sober?... I wanted what these women had. Badly.[44] ~ Deb

Men For Sobriety: Men Suffer Too

When Women For Sobriety was founded in the mid1970s, it was the first national alternative to AA in about 40 years. At the time, it was probably not possible for any program to challenge AA directly, head to head. AA was just too big, too well known and too powerful. Successful alternatives had to settle for niche markets. The niche Dr. Kirkpatrick went after was the female alcoholic. She was content to leave all the men to AA, while her program, she believed, was for the women.

Not everyone who supported WFS agreed. "One of my biggest conflicts with WFS is Jean's feeling that AA is for men," a successful WFS member was quoted as saying. "That's hogwash. Real hogwash."[45]

Eventually, WFS decided to accommodate men with a separate program: Men For Sobriety (MFS), which is something of a little brother to the women's program. MFS is a virtual clone of WFS, with masculine or neuter words being substituted for feminine ones. Thus the Men For Sobriety members say, for example, "I am a competent *man* and have much to give life."[46]

Dr. Kirkpatrick was adamantly opposed to co-ed meetings. In a note to me dated December 1993, she explained: "The reason I believe in separate groups [for women and men] is because studies have shown that men tend to dominate conversations in groups. Moreover, men's and women's problems are quite, quite different."[47]

The segregated programs are a nearly unique feature of WFS and MFS. Some women and men may find this to their liking, others not. But segregated or not, Jerry Dorsman, who is an expert on recovery without using AA, said this: "The WFS program works for men too... men find the thirteen statements of acceptance to be strong esteem-boosters and, like women, can use them as helpful building blocks to a successful recovery."[48] Men who are interested in a positive thinking alternative to the Twelve Steps of AA have a ready-made program in MFS.

Twelve Steps for Women Alcoholics: AA's Steps Blended with Kirkpatrick's Statements

A decade and a half after Kirkpatrick founded Women For Sobriety, Gail Unterberger, a pastoral counselor, wrote an article titled "Twelve Steps for Women Alcoholics," which was published in the December 6, 1989 issue of *Christian Century* magazine.

"Some people dislike the spiritual nature of the [traditional Twelve Step] recovery program," Unterberger believed. "And some women find that A.A. is overly masculine in approach and its form of spirituality. While certain A.A. groups have addressed the former problem by identifying themselves as pagan or agnostic, few have responded to the latter complaint."[49]

She continued: "Many pastoral counselors routinely recommend – or even require – that their alcohol-dependent counselees attend Alcoholics Anonymous meetings. However, a substantial number of people drop out of A.A., and some data suggest that half of A.A.'s new participants do not continue after 90 days."[50]

On the other hand, as a mainstream pastoral counselor Unterberger felt that some of Jean Kirkpatrick's statements were "too much orientated toward positive thinking or New Age spirituality for mainline church people."[51] To correct this apparent problem, Unterberger created her own twelve steps. In doing so, she claimed to have "adapted the Twelve Steps to reflect women's spirituality."[52] It's clear, however, that her Twelve Steps for Women Alcoholics were influenced by both AA's Twelve Steps *and* Kirkpatrick's Thirteen Statements. Her steps are:

1. We have a drinking problem that once had us.
2. We realized we needed to turn to others for help.
3. We turn to our community of sisters and our spiritual resources to validate ourselves as worthwhile people, capable of creativity, care and responsibility.
4. We have taken a hard look at our patriarchal society and acknowledge those ways in which we have participated in our own oppression, particularly the ways we have devalued or escaped from our own feelings and needs for community and affirmation.
5. We realize that our high expectations for ourselves have led us either to avoid responsibility and/or to overinvest ourselves in others' needs. We ask our sisters to help us discern how and when this happens.
6. Life can be wondrous or ordinary, enjoyable or traumatic, danced with or fought with, and survived. In our community we seek to live in the present with its wonder and hope.
7. The more we value ourselves, the more we can trust others and accept how that helps us. We are discerning and caring.
8. We affirm our gifts and strengths and acknowledge our weaknesses. We are especially aware of those who depend on us and of our influence on them.
9. We will discuss our illness with our children, family, friends and colleagues. We will make it clear to them (particularly our children) that what our alcoholism caused in the past was not their fault.
10. As we are learning to trust our feelings and perceptions, we will continue to check them carefully with our community, which we will ask to help us discern the problems we may not yet be aware of. We celebrate our progress toward wholeness individually and in community.
11. Drawing upon the resources of our faith, we affirm our competence and confidence. We seek to follow through on our positive convictions with the support of our community and the love of God.

12. Having had a spiritual awakening as the result of these steps, we are more able to draw upon the wisdom inherent in us, knowing we are competent women who have much to offer others.

Notice that the emphasis in these steps is on the community, as opposed to AA's more individualistic approach. John J. McNeill, author of *Freedom, Glorious Freedom,* commented on this:

Gail Unterberger finds that A.A.'s twelve steps insinuate a hierarchical, domination-submission model of the individual's relationship to God. In traditional groups, God is always referred to as male, and God's activities are described in stereotypically masculine terms. Furthermore, the spirituality described in the steps can be seen as exclusively individualistic. A.A. portrays the individual in a one-to-one relationship with God, before whom the individual person must admit total powerlessness. The alcoholic comes to "believe in"... a God to whom one must surrender one's will...

Adult women can find the image of a paternalistic and domineering God harmful; it hinders the development of the mature sense of self that addicted women lack. The call for submission can all too easily blend with other unhealthy demands to submit that are destructive to women's self-image.[53]

For those who feel likewise, Unterberger's Twelve Steps for Women Alcoholics may be a better path.

Sixteen Steps for Discovery and Empowerment: Saying No to Patriarchy

In the mid-1980s, Charlotte Kasl decided that she couldn't say the Twelve Steps anymore. They didn't feel right to her. She was (or is) – as she described herself then – a "middle class, white, female, single mother, bi-sexual woman from Missoula, Montana, who has lived in seven different cities and towns."[54]

She didn't mention that she is also a Doctor of Psychology (PhD) and the author of several books. In one such book, she wrote: "The wisdom underlying the steps... is profound in its understanding of the process of healing."[55] But perhaps she didn't believe that anymore. What she did believe, evidently, is what she wrote next: "The wording of the steps... carries a definite patriarchal Christian tone, using the image of an all-powerful, external male God."[56]

To her, the Twelve Steps of AA were patriarchal and supportive of a social hierarchy based on gender and race. "Bill Wilson based the steps and the Big Book [*Alcoholics Anonymous*, AA's basic text] on experiences of a hundred white men and one woman," Kasl observed. "He also based his definition of an alcoholic personality – egocentric, arrogant, resentful, controlling, or violent – on these people."[57] Kasl rightly points out that there are many people who have these personality traits who are not alcoholic, just as there are "countless people who are passive, afraid, and lacking a sense of self who are alcoholic and drug addicted."[58]

Kasl also explored some of the alternatives to AA, most notably Women For Sobriety. While she liked some parts of that program, she had "mixed feelings" about other parts.[59] The psychology of affirmations – affirming something until it becomes real for you – didn't seem to appeal to her. To her, it felt as if she was "being told how to be, how to feel, [and] how to think."[60] In the end, Kasl decided to create her own program from her own perspective as a feminist, social activist, and therapist with a special interest in co-dependency.

Charlotte Kasl's Sixteen Steps:

1. We affirm we have the power to take charge of our lives and stop being dependent on substances or other people for our self-esteem and security.

    Alternative: We admit/acknowledge we are out of control with/powerless over _____ yet have the power

to take charge of our lives and stop being dependent on substances or other people for our self-esteem and security.
2. We come to believe that God/Goddess/Universe/Great Spirit/Higher Power awakens the healing wisdom within us when we open ourselves to the power.
3. We make a decision to become our authentic selves and trust in the healing power of the truth.
4. We examine our beliefs, addictions and dependent behavior in the context of living in a hierarchical, patriarchal culture.
5. We share with another person and the Universe all those things inside of us for which we feel shame and guilt.
6. We affirm and enjoy our intelligence, strengths and creativity, remembering not to hide these qualities from ourselves and others.
7. We become willing to let go of shame, guilt, and any behavior that keeps us from loving ourselves and others.
8. We make a list of people we have harmed and people who have harmed us, and take steps to clear out negative energy by making amends and sharing our grievances in a respectful way.
9. We express love and gratitude to others and increasingly appreciate the wonder of life and the blessings we do have.
10. We learn to trust our reality and daily affirm that we see what we see, we know what we know and we feel what we feel.
11. We promptly admit to mistakes and make amends when appropriate, but we do not say we are sorry for things we have not done and we do not cover up, analyze, or take responsibility for the shortcomings of others.
12. We seek out situations, jobs, and people who affirm our intelligence, perceptions and self-worth and avoid situations or people who are hurtful, harmful, or demeaning to us.
13. We take steps to heal our physical bodies, organize our lives, reduce stress, and have fun.
14. We seek to find our inward calling, and develop the will and wisdom to follow it.

15. We accept the ups and downs of life as natural events that can be used as lessons for our growth.
16. We grow in awareness that we are sacred beings, interrelated with all living things, and we contribute to restoring peace and balance on the planet.[61]

Dr. Kasl says that her work is for all, "but essentially positioned from the perspective of women and minorities."[62] She promises that her program is not designed to place onuses upon anyone: "My reworking of the steps is not intended to set women apart from men," she wrote. "On the contrary, it is intended to help us move closer to an integrated, nonviolent balance between men and women which will benefit us all. It is the system I oppose, not individuals."[63]

And having reworked the Twelve Steps herself, she allows others the same privilege with her program. The Sixteen Steps For Discovery and Empowerment, she says, "are only suggestions; change them in any way you like so they feel true to your heart."[64]

Kudos for Sixteen Steps
- I think the 16 steps are wonderful! They give us a guideline to follow on the road to realizing the "power" within. ~ An incarcerated woman
- The 16-step program encourages the voice inside of me to speak... I can choose whatever I want to do. I don't have to mouth words from the 1930s. ~ Adam W.*
- The 12-step program told me what I shouldn't do, the 16-step program tells me what I can do. The results are amazing. ~ Anne
- For 15 years... When I tried to speak out on political issues or abusive relationships, I was always treated as if I was wrong... I like the 16-step meeting I'm going to – it's a place to talk about whatever I want, to experiment, to be wrong, to take chances. ~ Nancy

---

*Kasl's program is for men, particularly minority men, as well as for women.

- *Stressing "powerlessness" to victims… does little to help our healing and keeps us in the cycle of abuse.* ~ Man from Minnesota[65] [emphasized in the original]

My Way Out: A Four Step Program

"Roberta Jewell" (a pseudonym) believes she had a drinking problem because, "I was issued a receptor gene on a region of chromosome 15 that involves the activity of a brain chemical called GABRG3, which happened to increase my likelihood for an addiction to alcohol."[66] Although not a doctor nor a scientist, she was able to develop this apparently very scientific theory because, by her own account, she's "a proficient researcher – particularly when it comes to medical matters" (a skill she developed while trying desperately to find treatments "beyond ineffective standard medical procedures" for one of her children).[67]

During the course of her research, she happened upon an article that discussed the off label[*] use of a certain drug for the treatment of alcoholism.[68] The drug was topiramate, which is marketed primarily for the treatment of epilepsy and migraine headaches under the brand name Topamax.®

Thus, prescription drugs became one part of Roberta Jewell's four step program. The original prescription drug, the one Jewell used to achieve her own recovery, was Topamax.® Other drugs such as Campral, Baclofen, and oral and injectable forms of the drug naltrexone can also be used, and some people choose to work the My Way Out program without *any* prescription drugs.

The other three parts of the four-step program are nutritional supplements, hypnosis CDs, and light exercise. Altogether, the four steps of the My Way Out program are:

---

[*] "Off-label prescribing allows physicians to provide medications to patients suffering from conditions other than those the medication was specifically tested for in clinical trials. It is a common and accepted practice." (Roberta Jewell, *My Way Out,* page 28.)

1. Six weeks of a combined vitamin, mineral, amino acid, and herb therapy, including kudzu, an herb that the Chinese call "the drunkenness dispeller."
2. One month daily behavior modification hypnotherapy sessions delivered via CD's that you can play at home.
3. Twelve weeks or longer of anti-addiction drug administration.
4. A regime of 15 to 20 minute exercise sessions performed three times per week.[69]

My Way Out was founded around 2005 and in its brief existence it has been remarkably successful. The MyWayOut.org website is one of the highest trafficked alternative recovery sites on the Internet.[70] Concerning this, Jewell says: "I am very proud to be part of a movement in which problem drinkers and alcoholics are given entirely new choices and are issued the respect they deserve when they begin their important journey on the road to recovery."[71]

Kudos for MWO

The message boards at the MWO website list a number of testimonials. Some of the more interesting of these are repeated here.

- I wanted to write and tell you THANK YOU THANK YOU THANK YOU for this program... It has been a lifesaver, literally. It is really something, the difference over these past four months... It's truly a blessing.
- I'm glad AA works for other people. I'm just not one of them. Thank goodness options are finally available for those of us who wish to pursue other methods. Incidentally, I opted out [of] taking any medication but committed myself to all other elements of this programme (sic) and am delighted with the outcome.
- For me, the hypnotism is the key that brings it all together. I don't know if it's the same for everybody but it has really helped me... Plus, the vitamins are a trip in themselves.

- This program is phenomenal. As someone who 'got in early,' it's (sic) been fun watching it take off... I knew it was just a matter of time. I am a whole new person, and I know others will have the same results.
- Everything my doctor has been complaining about for the last few years is getting better and I have only the MWO program to thank for getting me back into a lifestyle that may enable me to live long enough to see my children and my grandchildren grow up; [and] a chance for my wife[*] and me to be happy again!
- For anyone new to the program, I can honestly say this DOES work. I was a mess 6 months ago and will forever remain grateful for MWO.[72]

Taking These Roads

The first thing to be said about ***Women in AA*** is that about one-third of AA's members are women, and most of them seem to be OK with being a regular part of that fellowship. My own AA experience was mostly in a fair-sized prairie town some years ago. At that time and place, there were no women's meetings, nor was there any thought that women's meetings might be needed. That then, and times may have changed. If you are a woman working a Twelve Step program now, there may be legitimate concerns for your safety and comfort that you might want to consider when deciding whether to attend the regular Anonymous meetings or seek out meetings that are more closely supervised (such as church sponsored meetings) and/or especially for women.

The language at some Twelve Step meetings can be crude, which may or may not make you uncomfortable. It also seems that the practice of Thirteenth Stepping (men trying to date female members) is embedded in AA's culture. Again, this may or may not

---

[*] Although women account for 80 percent of its website visitations, MWO is also used by men.

be a disadvantage depending on your situation. This book is about choice, *your choice,* so if you like the Twelve Steps, but not the regular Anonymous group meetings, you may want to look for women's meetings or possibly explore some of the faith-based Twelve Step programs that are described in Chapter VII. To find women's AA meetings, try contacting your local central office or intergroup. Go to the AA website (http://www.aa.org) and search for meetings. You may not find "women's groups" specifically, but you will have a listing of local offices that should be able to help you.

Perhaps you prefer, or want to include, Jean Kirkpatrick's program, **Women For Sobriety,** which has an estimated 150 to 300 groups.[73] To find or start a WFS meeting, contact Women For Sobriety through their website: http://www.womenforsobriety.org/; by telephone: 215-536-8026; by fax: 215-538-9026; or by mail: P.O. Box 618, Quakertown, PA 18951. To start and lead a group you must be a Certified Moderator, which requires, among other things, that you "have good sobriety and be thoroughly acquainted with the WFS program and its philosophy."[74]

Jean Kirkpatrick's four books are all at least partly autobiographical. In addition to telling and retelling her story, the two that, in my opinion, do the best job of explaining the WFS program are*: Turnabout: New Help For The Woman Alcoholic* and *Goodbye Hangovers, Hello Life.* Both of these are available on the Internet and from the WFS website: http://www.wfscatalog.org/.

Unfortunately, there seems to be a real scarcity of **Men For Sobriety** meetings at the present time. If you are a man, I imagine you would be welcome to become certified and start one if you are so inclined.

One reason that the men's program lags behind may be that there isn't much MFS literature. Kirkpatrick's books, with their long passages about herself, can be interesting and entertaining but for a man they can also be a bit discomforting, almost like reading your sister's diary. The one piece of literature that is specifically for the men's program is *The MFS Program Booklet.* It is available from: http://www.wfscatalog.org/Booklets_c3.htm. But even this little book follows the *WFS Program Booklet* very closely.

MFS does not have a website. To find Men For Sobriety's presence on the Internet, you have to go to the Women For Sobriety website: http://www.womenforsobriety.org/. The mailing address and phone numbers for MFS are the same as those for WFS.

Whether supported by a group or not, the Women/Men For Sobriety affirmations make excellent self-help tools. The recommended procedure is to take one affirmation each day, study it in the morning and use it throughout the day. Then in the evening, review your day looking for the positive thoughts, feelings and experiences that have come from using the affirmation.

Gail Unterberger's *Twelve Steps for Women Alcoholics* may be used individually or perhaps some women's groups may want to adopt them. Unterberger's article can be found on (at least) two locations on the Internet:
http://www.silkworth.net/religion_clergy/01090.html and
http://www.religion-online.org/showarticle.asp?title=923.

Charlotte Kasl's *Sixteen Steps for Discovery and Empowerment* seem to be especially intended for those with a strong political or social consciousness, particularly women and minorities. Given that Kasl describes herself as bisexual, this surely must include sexual orientation and gender identity issues. If you feel discriminated against or put-down at your regular meetings, or if you are just frustrated with traditional groups that lack any hint of a social consciousness, then you may want to try Kasl's groups. For some, political or social activism of any persuasion could be just the thing to replace the excitement of a bar or club scene. It goes without saying that Kasl's political ideas are somewhat left-of-center, which wouldn't be appropriate for everyone and may, or may not, be appropriate for you.

According to Kasl's website, there are 200-300 groups that are using the Sixteen Steps. Kasl's two books about her program are *Many Roads, One Journey: Moving Beyond the 12 Steps* and *Yes You Can! A Guide to Empowerment Groups*. Both are available from her website and elsewhere on the Internet. Her website address is: http://www.charlottekasl.com/

The ***My Way Out*** program is Internet based. There are no face-to-face meetings for *My Way Out* followers. Mutual help and support come from a very active Internet website at http://www.mywayout.org/. Although the vast majority of visitors to this site are women, *My Way Out* is for men as well as for women. The *My Way Out* book has occupied the number one spot for alternative recovery books on the huge bookseller website, Amazon.com. And founder Roberta Jewell says she has sold just as many copies as a downloadable PDF file from the MyWayOut.org website.[75]

MWO supports both abstinence and moderation goals. Because it is Internet based, with separate threads for those seeking moderation and abstinence, there doesn't seem to be much conflict between the two groups. Jewell herself started with a goal of moderation and then switched to abstinence.[76] A number of MWO community members have done the same and the majority choose abstinence as their goal right from the start.[77]

Like most mutual-help groups, the *My Way Out* program requires an investment in books and other resources in order to fully implement the program. Jewell estimates the cost for the six week program initiation to be approximately $130, considerably less than the cost of drinking.[78] Depending on your insurance, additional costs may be involved if you choose to use prescription medications (as most MWO followers apparently do). Although Jewell herself got her first prescription via the Internet, *My Way Out* strongly recommends that you consult with a qualified healthcare provider (usually your doctor) prior to taking prescription drugs.[79] These drugs *do* have side effects, which your healthcare provider would explain and he or she can help determine your proper dosage.

In closing, Roberta Jewell had something interesting to say: "if Alcoholics Anonymous or another fellowship-based option is right for you, I'm confident this [My Way Out] program will help ensure your success when used concurrently."[80] To a greater or lesser extent, the same could be said of the other programs discussed in this chapter. Whatever way or ways you choose, success and good luck to you!

Chapter Endnotes

1. Kirkpatrick, Jean (1981) *A Fresh Start,* self-published, page 99.
2. "Profile of Jean Kirkpatrick, PhD," (n.d.). Retrieved 9/5/2013 from: http://womenforsobriety.org/wfs_jean.html
3. Kirkpatrick, Jean (1986) *Goodbye Hangovers, Hello Life: Self-help for Women,* New York: Ballentine Books, page 19.
4. Kirkpatrick (1986) page 27.
5. PRWeb (Oct 12, 2006) "As Seasonal Drinking Increases, Closet Alcoholics Find Hope in NewTreatments."Retrieved9/14/2013from:http://www.prweb.com/releases/alcoholism/recovery/prweb450124.htm
6. White, William L. (1998) *Slaying the Dragon: The History of Addiction Treatment and Recovery in America,* Bloomington, IL: Chestnut Health Systems/Lighthouse Institute, page 361.
7. White (1998) page 158.
8. AA World Services, Inc. (1939) *Alcoholics Anonymous*, first edition (war time printing), New York: Alcoholics Anonymous World Services, Inc., page 217.
9. AA World Services, Inc. (1939) page 217.
10. AA World Services, Inc. (1939) page 225.
11. Anonymous (2007) "Found: Burial Place of Florence R., One of First Women Sober.," *Markings,* Vol. in A.A 27, No. 1.
12. W[ilson], Lois (1979) *Lois Remembers: Memoirs of the co-founder of Al-Anon and wife of the co-founder of Alcoholics Anonymous,* New York: Al-Anon Family Group Headquarters, Inc., page 107.
13. Brown, Sally and David R. Brown (2001) *A Biography of Mrs. Marty Mann: The First Lady of Alcoholics Anonymous,* Center City, MN: Hazelden, page 262.
14. Brown and Brown (2001) pages 263, 348.
15. M., Marty (1945) "Women Alcoholics Have a Tougher Fight," *AA Grapevine,* 1(12):3, May.
16. O., Grace (1946) "Women's Meetings," *AA Grapevine,* 3(5):1,6 October.

17. White (1998) page 159.
18. O., Grace (1946)
19. White (1998) page 160.
20. White (1998) page 161.
21. White (1998) page 161.
22. AA World Services, Inc. (2006) "AA Survey Shows Key Role of Health Caregivers," AAPress Release, March 1.
23. White (1998) page 161.
24. Sandmaier, Marian. (1992) *The Invisible Alcoholics: Women and Alcohol* (second edition), Blue Ridge Summit, PA: Tab Books, page 243.
25. Covington, Stephanie (1994) *A Woman's Way through the Twelve Steps,* Center City, Minn: Hazelden, page 4-5.
26. Kirkpatrick, Jean (1977) *Turnabout: New Help for the Woman Alcoholic,* New York: Bantam Books, page 143.
27. Kirkpatrick (1977) page 143.
28. Kirkpatrick (1977) page 143.
29. Kirkpatrick (1981) page 15.
30. "NewLife'acceptanceProgram"(n.d.). Retrieve 10/2009 from:http://www.womenforsobriety.org/wfs_program.html
31. Kirkpatrick (1981) page 163.
32. Kirkpatrick (1986) page 277.
33. Kirkpatrick, Jean, (1994) *W.F.S. & A.A.*, Quakertown, PA: Women For Sobriety, Inc. page 10.
34. Kaskutas, Lee (1989) "Women for Sobriety: a qualitative analysis," *Contemporary Drug Problems,* Vol. 16, No. 2.
35. Kirkpatrick (1977) Preface.
36. Kirkpatrick (1981) page 66.
37. Kirkpatrick, Jean (1990) *On The Road to Sell Recovery,* self-published, page 34.
38. Kirkpatrick (1990) page 105.
39. Kirkpatrick (1990) page 5.
40. Kirkpatrick (1986) page 253.
41. Hafner, Sarah. (1992) *Nice Girls Don't Drink: Stories of Recovery,* New York: Bergin & Garvey, page 36.
42. Hafner (1992) page 138.

43. Hafner (1992) page 177.
44. Canfield, Jack, et al. (2004) *Chicken Soup for the Recovering Soul,* Deerfield Beach, Fla: Health Communications, page 37.
45. Hafner (1992) page 145.
46. Kirkpatrick, Jean (n.d.) *The Program Booklet: Men for Sobriety,* Women For Sobriety, Inc., page 38.
47. Kirkpatrick (1993) Personal communication with the author, December 28.
48. Dorsman, Jerry (1994) *How to Quit Drinking Without AA: A Complete Self-Help Guide,* Rocklin, CA: Prima, page 224.
49. Unterberger, Gail (1989) "Twelve Steps for Women Alcoholics," *Christian Century,* December 6. Retrieved 9/27/2013 from: http://www.silkworth.net/religion_clergy/01090.html 50. Ibid. 51. Ibid.
52. Ibid.
53. McNiell, John J. (1995) *Freedom, Glorious Freedom,* Boston: Beacon Press, pages 118119. Also see Unterberger (1989).
54. Kasl, Charlotte (1992) *Many Roads, One Journey: Moving Beyond the 12 Steps,* New York: Harper Perennial, page 365.
55. Kasl, Charlotte (1989) *Women, Sex, and Addiction: A Search for Love and Power,* New York: Harper & Row, page 17.
56. Ibid.
57. Kasl (1992) page 5.
58. Kasl (1992) page 5.
59. Kasl (1992) page 168.
60. Kasl (1992) page 169.
61. "16 Step Program" (n.d.) Retrieved 9/5/2013 from: http://charlottekasl.com/16-step-program/
62. Kasl (1992) page xiii.
63. Kasl (1992) page 336.
64. Kasl (1992) page 337.
65. Kasl, Charlotte (1994) *Yes You Can! A Guide to Empowerment for Individuals and Groups,* Lolo, MT: Many Roads, One Journey, pages 1-3.

66. Jewell, Roberta [pen name] (2005) *My Way Out,* Anchorage, AK: Capalo Press, page 9
67. Jewell (2005) page 27.
68. Apparently the article referred to is Johnson, B. A., et al. (2003) "Oral topiramate for treatment of alcohol dependence: a randomized controlled trial," *The Lancet,* May 17;361(9370):1677-85.
69. Based on Jewell (2005) pages 87-88.
70. Ibid.
71. Ibid.
72. My Way Out Testimonials (n.d.) Retrieved 9/15/2013 from: http://www.mywayout.org/testimonials.htm
73. Humphreys, Keith (2004) *Circles of Recovery: Self-Help Organizations for Addictions,* Cambridge, UK: Cambridge University Press, page 90.
74. "'New Life' Acceptance Program" (n.d.). Retrieved 9/20/2013 from: http://www.womenforsobriety.org/wfs_program.html
75. PRWeb (Jan 2, 2008) "'My Way Out' Earns Number One Spot on Amazon for Alternative Recovery." Retrieved 9/6/2013 from:http://www.prweb.com/releases/amazon/recovery/prweb595951.htm
76. Jewell, Roberta (Dec 29, 2007) *SoberRecovery* website. Retrieved 9/6/2013 from: http://www.soberrecovery.com/forums/alcoholism/140379-anyone-read-one.html.Important program updates (March 2006). Retrieved 9/6/2013 from http://www.mywayout.org/important-program-updates.htm. And Jewell (Dec 29, 2007)
78. My Way Out FAQ (n.d.) Retrieved 9/6/2013 from: http://www.mywayout.org/community/f7/my-way-out-faq-3968.html
79. Jewell (2005) pages 29 and 42.
80. Jewell (2005) page 44.

CHAPTER VI:
Secular and Rational Programs:
Believe It or Not

James Christopher was raised a Baptist and for a while at least, he was a believer. At some point, however, his belief changed to skepticism. His lack of a faith created a dilemma for him when he developed a serious drinking problem relatively early in life, but Christopher dealt with his addiction as best he could with the aid of Alcoholics Anonymous (AA). In 1978, while attending AA, he stopped drinking permanently. Christopher described his sobriety moment this way:

> At the age of 35 on April 24, 1978, I had what I think of as my "epiphany" – a strong, out-of-the-blue spiritual, emotional, intellectual, and visceral experience all fused together. It was sort of a flash neon reality of, "What is this? This isn't a life. This is a horror." I later came to think of this experience as "cognitive, visceral, synchronization." It was this mind-gut fusion where you actually see the connection between the euphoria of drinking and its later consequences. Some might call this a "spiritual experience." Some might call it an emotional breakthrough. But more than anything, it is this deep realization that alcohol equals pain...[1]

Despite having had this unusual experience, Christopher was never comfortable with AA's spiritual elements. The program's spiritual – some say religious – approach is evident to anyone right from the start. Alcoholics Anonymous and other Twelve Step meetings are usually opened and closed with prayers to God and fully half of the program's Twelve Steps mention the Deity: twice as "God" (Steps 5 and 6) twice as "God AS WE UNDERSTOOD HIM"

(Steps 3 and 11) once by the pronoun "Him" (Step 7) and once as "a Power greater than ourselves" (Step 2). Another one of the steps (Step 12) calls for "a spiritual awakening." All of this made Christopher uncomfortable. He never came to believe and didn't want to. Nevertheless, he stayed sober.

With six or seven years of sobriety under his belt, Christopher wrote an article titled "Sobriety Without Superstition," which described his experiences as a free thinker in AA. The article was published in the Summer 1985 issue of *Free Inquiry,* a magazine for humanists, freethought advocates, and the like. The response to this article so impressed Christopher that he decided to start a secular recovery program, soon to be called SOS.

Christopher was not the only person who saw the need for a secular alternative to AA. Before SOS, there was AAARG (American Atheist Addiction Recovery Group), which was started in 1983. The AAARG lasted but a few years and never expanded beyond its home base in Denver. Then, according to Vince Fox, a writer on alternative recovery programs, it "folded in 1988 due to lack of acceptance, effective administration, and funds."[2]

Shortly after Christopher founded his group in 1985, Jack Trimpey founded Rational Recovery (RR), a group that quickly achieved national recognition and considerable coverage in the press. Eventually, both RR and SOS both split, creating two new secular programs: SMART Recovery and LifeRing Secular Recovery (LSR). Other secular programs exist that may be useful for addiction recovery and still others have been created by recovered individuals, professional addiction counselors, and psychologists, so the options for secular recovery are abundant.

This chapter will examine the secular and rational recovery programs that have been created to meet the needs of addicts and alcoholics who may be atheists, agnostics, humanists, and so forth – or theists who may have other reasons for preferring a secular alternative. As Rational Recovery founder Jack Trimpey wrote in his first major publication, *The Small Book:* Other alcoholics are less concerned that AA requires spirituality than that it makes them feel powerless, or that it means they will have to attend meetings for the rest of their lives, all the while endlessly repeating the story of their alcohol dependence. Many of these people believe in themselves and want to move on with their lives.[3]

Much of this book is for those who fit that description and this chapter, in particular, is for anyone who is looking for secular recovery.

SOS: Making Sobriety Your Priority

At first, this organization was called Secular Sobriety Groups (SSG), but the name was soon changed to SOS, which stands for both Secular Organizations for Sobriety *and* Save Our Selves. According to addiction counselor and historian William L. White: "If one imagined support groups that operate much like AA, but without references to [a] Higher Power, God, or prayer, one would be very close to a picture of the SOS milieu."[4] This is roughly true, but there are also some significant differences.

There are a number of secular versions of the Twelve Steps, but SOS didn't use anyone's secular steps, neither did it create its own steps. The heart of the SOS program is its six Suggested Guidelines for Sobriety. These were published in Christopher's first book, *How to Stay Sober: Recovery Without Religion*. The original version of the guidelines has been slightly rewritten to accommodate drug users as well as alcoholics. The current SOS Suggested Guidelines are:

- To break the cycle of denial and achieve sobriety, we first acknowledge that we are alcoholics or addicts.
- We reaffirm this truth daily and accept without reservation the fact that, as clean and sober individuals, we can not and do not drink or use, no matter what.
- Since drinking or using is not an option for us, we take whatever steps are necessary to continue our Sobriety Priority lifelong.

- A quality of life – "the good life" – can be achieved. However, life is also filled with uncertainties. Therefore, we do not drink or use regardless of feelings, circumstances, or conflicts.
- We share in confidence with each other our thoughts and feelings as sober, clean individuals.
- Sobriety is our Priority, and we are each responsible for our lives and our sobriety.[5]

Notice that there is nothing in the Guidelines about making amends or improving one's character; nothing about confessing past sins or wrongdoings. Said Christopher:

> [There's] a big difference between [the SOS] approach and the twelve-step package deal. Other programs connect recovery to "spiritual" or emotional "growth," or to becoming a purer, more ethical person. Becoming a better person *is* wonderful – of course it is. But it does not necessarily have anything to do with becoming sober. Similarly, you didn't become an addict because you were scum; the "alcoholic personality" conception of addiction has fostered moralism, not progress; consequently, it has promoted not empowerment, but low self-esteem.[6]

In SOS, the emphasis is simply to *stay sober no matter what*. SOS calls this its Sobriety Priority. It counsels that staying sober and free of illicit drugs should be the *number one priority* in every recovered alcoholic's or addict's life.

SOS views addiction primarily as a physiological problem at the cellular level. The cells themselves become accustomed to alcohol or other drugs. Christopher wrote that he compensated for the craving, or selective memory of pleasure at the cellular level, by constantly reminding himself that, for him, alcohol or drugs equals *pain*.[7] Thus, in a nutshell, the SOS recovery program is complete abstinence: *don't drink or use no matter what*.

If you have other problems, SOS supports finding appropriate help. It doesn't claim to have all the answers for everyone's way of life. "[I]f you have a problem that demands some work, some therapy, whatever it is, then you go out and you find your appropriate source, and you get your needs met..." an SOS member said. "If that means some kind of counseling, then you go to that kind of counseling."[8] The member contrasted this with AA, where the Twelve Steps are sometimes looked upon as the universal answer for every problem.

But in many ways, SOS meetings *are* like Twelve Step meetings, with the attendees telling their stories or discussing some problem that is of particular concern. Of course, at SOS meetings there are no prayers. Meetings are opened with a standard secular reading and closed with all the attendees giving themselves a round of applause.

One of Christopher's books, *SOS Sobriety: The Proven Alternative to 12-Step Programs,* contains transcripts of a typical SOS meeting. Here is a sample of some things you might hear at SOS meetings:

- I like SOS because they tell us it's OK to have a good self-image. We aren't supposed to be constantly beating our breasts and derogating ourselves.[9]
- Instead of being told that we're nothing – that we're just a step away from a drink ...we're told that we're terrific, that we're wonderful. This is so necessary, especially for women who have low self-esteem. We don't need a program designed to create humility when we cannot think of one good thing to say about ourselves.[10]
- The more I saw that dissenting views were tolerated in SOS – and indeed were viewed as intellectually stimulating, actually encouraged – the more at home I felt.[11]
- No sacred cows are safe, no information is withheld or suppressed, all opinions are welcome. One gray area seems to need frequent negotiation: the assumption that all members are atheists. It is often forgotten or overlooked that

many people who end up in SOS are not atheists... Being neither a theist nor an atheist, the "God" and "no God" arguments have no bearing on my reasons for being a member.[12]

Yes, SOS does indeed have a *milieu* (social environment) with elements that are clearly from AA – elements like recognizing or admitting that one is an alcoholic or an addict – and elements like doing things "one day at a time" – but it also has its own social environment and its own philosophy of recovery. SOS stands for Secular Organizations for Sobriety and Save Our Selves. It might also be used to stand for: Something Other-than the Same-old-thing.

Rational Recovery: Defeat the Beast

Jack Trimpey couldn't find a higher power. At AA, he was told that he needed a higher power to keep him sober, but he couldn't find one that did the job. It wasn't that he didn't believe in God, he just couldn't believe that God would do such things. "As a child growing up in the Methodist church," he said, "I learned to worship and pray to God, but not to expect favors from God."[13]

At AA, Trimpey was told that *anything* could be his higher power and – as AA's literature suggests – he was told to try using the AA group itself. "I looked around the room and saw a group of people I would not choose as friends who were willing to pose as my God," the occasionally sardonic Trimpey wrote.[14]

Trimpey tried other AA groups and other higher powers, but nothing seemed to work. For many years he continued drinking. He attended AA meeting "sporadically," he confided, "with the idea that maybe something, either AA or I, might have changed. Neither ever did."[15]

Sometime around 1982, Trimpey decided that he could quit drinking on his own. He picked a date to quit and when that day came, he gave up alcohol forever. Trimpey's task was possibly made easier by the fact that he is a professional social worker who knows a bit of psychology, particularly Rational Emotive Behavior Therapy (a form of rational treatment developed by psychologist Albert Ellis in 1955). He applied Rational Emotive Behavior Therapy (REBT) to himself and his own thinking and, as Trimpey put it, "when push finally came to shove, I was able to become my own rational therapist."[16]

Trimpey found quitting alcohol to be easier than he expected, easier than he had been told at AA. He and his wife, Lois, held long discussions on this issue and concluded that some of the ideas he had gleaned from Twelve Step meetings – such as being *powerless* to quit drinking absent an intervention by a higher power – had actually delayed Trimpey's sobriety.

In his job as a social worker, Trimpey had ample opportunity to meet others who objected to AA. "Certainly many of those who resisted addiction care," Trimpey wrote, "were poorly motivated for any program,"[17] but he also perceived that many of the objections he had heard about AA had some merit. Said Trimpey:

> I also realized that my reasons for rejecting AA were not the only reasons. Others refused because they do not like to talk about themselves in front of a group, because they won't call themselves "alcoholics," because they prefer to pick their own friends, because they don't want to depend on sponsors or groups, because they would prefer to help themselves independently, because they object to the lifetime commitment that the 12 steps require, or because they have conflicting religious views. Still others have no real complaint about AA, but continue to fail despite real, often repeated, efforts to use their 12-step approach. I decided that I would go to bat for those who strike out in AA.[18]

So the Trimpeys started Rational Recovery (RR) as an alternative to Alcoholics Anonymous, Narcotics Anonymous, and all the rest. In the beginning, Rational Recovery was largely based on REBT. Like AA, RR was an organization with an alliterative, two-letter name. Formally, it was made up of two corporations:

Rational Recovery Systems, a for-profit corporation owned by Trimpey, and Rational Recovery Self-Help Network, a non-profit corporation.[19]

In the early 1990s, Trimpey abandoned REBT in favor of other ideas. Chief among these are the Addictive Voice Recognition Technique (AVRT, which may be pronounced "avert") and the Big Plan, which is simply a plan or promise never to drink or use again and never to change one's mind, at least on that matter.

Trimpey based his ideas on what he calls *the structural model of addiction*. According to this view, addictions become seated in the primitive or limbic portion of the brain. According to Trimpey, it is from this area of the brain that thoughts and feelings encouraging the use of alcohol or drugs arise. Trimpey calls these thoughts and feelings the Addictive Voice, which he also labels "the Beast" (because it arises from a primitive, sub-human area of the brain).

RR teaches people to challenge the Addictive Voice or "Beast" and to disassociate it from one's sense of self. It views "the Beast" as an addicted person's mortal enemy. RR maintains that making a Big Plan and learning AVRT are essentially what's needed to overcome an addiction. Matters of physical withdrawal from addictive substances are deemed to be personal responsibilities that may require medical attention.

In 1994, the non-profit arm of Rational Recovery separated from the for-profit organization and became SMART Recovery (discussed below). As a for-profit organization, Trimpey's Rational Recovery program continued more or less unchanged until 1999, when it renounced all self-help or mutual-support groups relating to addictions – including RR groups.[20] According to Trimpey, such groups are not helpful for people with a Big Plan who are using AVRT. Although it no longer holds meetings, RR remains an important part of the alternative recovery movement, offering information, books, CDs and video materials on its website (https://rational.org/) and live AVRT classes.

SMART Recovery: REBT for Everyone

You don't have to be smart to attend SMART recovery. You don't have to be stupid either. SMART is an acronym for S̲elf M̲anagement A̲nd R̲ecovery T̲raining. As mentioned above, SMART got its start when the non-profit and the for-profit corporate parts of Rational Recovery split apart. According to Michael Lemanski, author of *A History of Addiction and Recovery in the United States*, this is how the split happened: "A large majority of the board of directors of the nonprofit corporation ... were professional rational-emotive behavior therapists. Following Trimpey's abandonment of Rational Emotive Behavior Therapy (REBT), the nonprofit corporation began operating as SMART Recovery in 1994."[21]

SMART is an abstinence-based self-help program with both on-line and live, face-to-face group meetings. SMART meetings are free, although donations are accepted. The meetings are led by trained volunteer facilitators. Most, but not all, facilitators are recovered individuals. They may (or may not) be someone who has recovered using SMART. Some may never have suffered from a serious addiction problem, but they still want to perform this community service. In addition to the meeting facilitator, SMART meetings have volunteer advisors. These are professionals in the addictions field who provide advice and consultation to the facilitators. Generally, the volunteer advisors will not attend SMART Recovery meetings.

SMART might be considered a somewhat complex recovery program since it uses a wide assortment of recovery tools based on REBT and other scientifically verified methods. But it organizes it all under a simple, four point program. The four points of the SMART program are:

Point 1: Enhancing and Maintaining Motivation
Point 2: Coping with Urges
Point 3: Problem Solving
Point 4: Lifestyle Balance[22]

Point 1 of the SMART program – enhancing and maintaining motivation – may involve doing a "Cost Benefit Analysis" (comparing the pros and cons of not changing with the pros and cons of quitting an addictive habit). Like many other recovery groups, SMART offers mutual support for believing that it is possible to change. Unlike some groups, SMART rejects labeling oneself an "alcoholic" or "addict." Such labels, SMART believes, are "unnecessary and harmful."[23]

Point 2 – coping with urges – teaches that "you can accept cravings and urges without automatically engaging in the addictive behavior."[24] Among other helpful tools, it teaches a technique called the Destructive Self-talk Awareness and Refusal Method (DiSARM). The technique is to "[p]ersonify or name the urge: 'Destructive self-talk' is not you, it is your 'Enemy.'"[25] (This is similar to RR's AVRT.) Point two also includes learning drink refusal skills and an introduction to Rational Emotive Behavior Therapy.

Among the methods listed under *Point 3* – problem solving – the ABCs of REBT are undoubtedly the most important. The ABCs were developed by psychologist Albert Ellis in the 1950s. In this model, "A" stands for an Activating event, or what's usually viewed as the "cause" of a thought, feeling or behavior (say someone insults you); "B" stands for your Belief about the event (you may believe that the insult is terrible and can't be tolerated or you may believe that it doesn't really matter); and "C" stands for the Consequences, which may be negative or positive (you may be angry and want to fight the person who insults you, or you may just shrug it off).

REBT teaches that "B," your Belief about the Activating event, is more important than the event itself. It teaches people to challenge or dispute what it calls "irrational" beliefs, which are beliefs that do not lead to more happiness and a better life.

In addiction recovery, an "A" may be an opportunity to drink or use and "B" would be your Belief about the event. The Consequences ("C"), are going to depend on "B," your Belief, because there will always be such "A's" that occur from time to time. Some carry the alphabet theme further by saying that the

ABC's include a "D," Dispute the irrational belief, and an "E," Effective new belief and resulting positive consequences.[26]

Point 4 – lifestyle balance – involves creating a lifestyle with a balance of long-term and short-term gratifications. SMART teaches members to practice healthy habits, relax through deep breathing, set goals, prioritize, and plan. SMART encourages having one or more "vital absorbing interests" (other than drinking or drug use, of course). Finally, this point covers relapse prevention strategies.

All this may seem fairly complex, but SMART attendees master the principles over a period of time. Once they are sufficiently mastered, you can keep attending SMART meetings or go on your way. SMART is not intended to be a life-long program, although you may attend for as long as you want (or quit any time that you want). The highest authority for SMART Recovery is science.

LifeRing Secular Recovery: Sobriety, Secularity and Self-Help

In the late 1990s, a large SOS group in Northern California experienced some legal problems over the use of its name (SOS, Secular Organizations for Sobriety, or Save Our Selves). Apparently, there was an organization with a similar name that objected. As a result, in 1999, the SOS name in Northern California was changed to LifeRing Secular Recovery (LSR).[27] Somewhere along the line, LSR completely separated from SOS and now, according to the LSR website: "LifeRing is an independent, free-standing organization, not affiliated with any other."[28] LifeRing is based on what it calls its three "S" philosophy. These are: Sobriety, Secularity, and Self-help:

Sobriety in LifeRing means complete abstinence from alcohol and drugs.

Secularity means that religious discussions (belief or unbelief) are off topic at LifeRing meetings. As is the case with many other activities in America, at LifeRing believers and nonbelievers meet together to do something that does not involve religion. According to a 2005 poll, about 40 percent of LifeRing members attend some sort of religious service, at least sporadically. Martin Nicolaus, who wrote a book about LifeRing's approach to recovery, says this is about the same as America's national average.[29]

In LifeRing, *Self-help* means that the emphasis is on the self, not the group or a program.

According to the LSR website:

> Self-help in LifeRing means that the key to recovery is the individual's own motivation and effort. The main purpose of the group process is to reinforce the individual's own inner strivings to stay clean and sober. LifeRing is a permanent workshop where individuals can build their own Personal Recovery Plans. LifeRing does not prescribe any particular "steps" other than abstinence and is not a vehicle for any particular therapeutic doctrine. LifeRing participation is compatible with a wide variety of abstinence-based therapeutic or counseling programs.[30]

Personal Recovery Plans (PRPs) may occur naturally, as a consequence of attending LSR meetings, or more formally. There is a *Recovery by Choice* workbook (available at http://lifering.org) to help you with creating your own Personal Recovery Plan. According to Martin Nicolaus, the author of the workbook, making a formal PRP may not be for everyone. PRPs, he says, are "for that special population that tends to be anti-authoritarian and insists on figuring things out for themselves – in short," he opines, "the typical alcoholic or addict and the average American."[31]

IACT: The International Association for Clear Thinking, Inc.

"Less than 20 percent of America's 20+ million alcoholics accept AA," wrote psychiatrist Maxie C. Maultsby, Jr. in 1978.

"Obviously, therefore," he added, "we need other types of selfhelp treatment methods that are as effective as AA."[32] To help meet this need and address other mental health issues, Maultsby founded IACT, the International Association for Clear Thinking.

IACT is designed to deal with many types of emotional stress, including substance misuse and abuse. It uses Rational Behavior Therapy, a near relative of Rational Emotive Behavior Therapy (REBT), a technique discussed above. In Rational Behavior Therapy, A stands for an *event;* B represents the *self talk* arising from that event; and C stands for the *feelings* that the self talk creates. As with REBT, people are taught to challenge B (the *self talk*) in order to experience a different C (*feelings*).

The IACT program also teaches other self-help methods, including a visualization technique to help manage the emotions. Maultsby recommends medical treatment for alcohol withdrawal and any alcohol-induced illnesses.[33] Presumably, the same applies when drugs other than alcohol are the problem.

YES Recovery and the YES Recovery Document

"Recovery Without Mythology," is a slogan of the YES Recovery movement, a fairly new and little-known mutual-help recovery system. YES is not an acronym but, according to its founder, "a symbol of positivity and the value of choosing a positive attitude."[34] The program originated in 2000 with the YES Recovery Document being posted on the Internet. Meetings can be face-to-face or on the web.

YES Recovery has 48 Precepts in the form of 12 Steps, 12 Traditions, 12 Suggestions, and 12 Principles. It was started by an anonymous long-time clean and sober addict as a reaction against the multi-million dollar publishing houses that have become attached to some Twelve Step programs and treatment centers. There are: "No fees, no rules, no head office, no books, [and] no permissions needed... Simply copy [the] YES Recovery Document [which is available on the Internet], commit to personal recovery, start a group, connect with others, and pass it on."[35]

Of the 48 precepts, the Steps are a fairly routine secularized version of the Twelve Steps; the Suggestions give some pointers on staying clean and sober; the Principles list some basic truths about clean and sober living (such as Principle 4: "Respect… because we are worthy of giving and receiving it") and the Traditions shed considerable light on the program and its organization. For the purpose of sharing this light and providing a brief and accurate description of the YES Recovery movement, the 12 Traditions (with some minor spelling errors corrected) are presented here:

1. The newcomer who desires to stop using fulfils the only requirement for membership and is our most important member. Any adult is welcome. Belief in any deity or deities is not necessary in this program, but is not an impediment nor disapproved of. We are people of many faiths.
2. Self-reliance is the foundation of our personal and group goals, so we decline external support. We have no fees to pay beyond gratitude donations, nor rules to obey, beyond a commitment to principled behavior.
3. We have no leaders but each group may elect trusted servants.
4. Mentors commit themselves to assisting the recovering addict. Members may change mentors freely.
5. In order to avoid the pitfalls of commercialism, ego and cultism, our public relations policy is to avoid publicity. Groups may place plain and truthful advertisements to spread our message.
6. Each group is autonomous, making democratic decisions according to the consciences of the members. Failure or bad behavior by any group does not reflect on any other group, and we do not litigate against each other.
7. Our aim is to help suffering addicts, not to create dogmas, politics, corporations or publishing houses. Having faith in the right and ability of addicts to manage their own

recoveries and groups, we have no office, employees, property, surplus funds, bureaucracy, text book, scriptures, rules, permanent bank accounts, sponsorships, grants, copyrights, trademarks, hierarchy, nor publications except meetings lists and [the] YES Recovery Document of which we encourage free copying. Temporary bank accounts may be operated in order to organize conventions.
8. Any gathering of two or more people that follows and displays [the] YES Recovery Document alone, unaltered and in full is deemed to constitute a YES Recovery group.
9. YES Recovery groups have no opinion publicly on any matter except that we believe that addicts need not be powerless over addiction nor their lives.
10. We encourage solidarity and try to tame our egos in case our primary purposes are hampered.
11. We may belong to any other group and practice any way of life we choose.
12. We respect anonymity and confidentiality.[36]

Pathways to Sobriety: A Workbook for Change

When Bill Fleeman was a child, his father abandoned him and his mother. "I can remember feeling angry at my father for walking out of my life," Fleeman wrote. Then he added:

> I also remember wishing he would come back. He never did, and soon I stopped thinking about him so much. But I never got over how I felt about his leaving. I felt worthless and defective, unloved and unwanted, angry and rejected. My father's leaving led me to believe you can't trust people to stick by you. If your own father leaves you, who can you trust? Nobody – period. That's what I came to believe.[37]

Fleeman had his first drink when he was only thirteen and he experienced his first blackout (loss of memory due to intoxication) before he was sixteen. Formerly a straight-A student, he was expelled from school in the ninth grade and soon thereafter participated in a robbery and assault. He spent the rest of his teens in a reformatory and on probation. He spent the rest of his youth and early adulthood moving around the country, abusing alcohol and other drugs. Eventually, Fleeman found help in AA, although the emphasis on prayer to open and close meetings made him uncomfortable. "I was an atheist," he said, "and resented what felt to me like a strong religious atmosphere."[38]

After recovery, Fleeman managed to get some education and found a job as a counselor at an alcohol and drug rehabilitation clinic. He still had anger management issues, however, and he changed jobs frequently. "I ultimately discovered," Fleeman admitted, "that I was addicted to anger in the same way I'd been addicted to alcohol and other drugs. I used anger and rage like a drug to change feelings such as anxiety, depression, and fear into a feeling of power."[39]

Fleeman wrote a book on anger, which led to the development of "Pathways to Peace," a self-help program for anger management. The next year he wrote *The Pathways to Sobriety Workbook,* which sets out an addiction recovery program of eight principles. "I couldn't have stayed alive without the fellowship of AA and NA," Fleeman said. "Yet even after ten years I felt on the brink of relapse most of the time – if not relapse back into active use of alcohol and other drugs, then relapse back into the old self-destructive behaviors."[40] He continued:

> I read literally hundreds of books searching for that elusive state called "contented sobriety." I read all the twelve-step program literature. I read books on psychology, including ones written by Jung, Freud, Adler, even B. F. Skinner. I read pop psychology and New-Age self-help books. I read books on philosophy by Bertrand Russell, Jean Paul Sartre, Albert Camus, and others. I read the *Koran* and the *Bible*...

I talked to hundreds of people who, like me, were recovering from an addiction to alcohol or other drugs. Out of all that printed matter and out of all those conversations came the self-help program Pathways to Sobriety.[41]

The Pathways to Sobriety self-help program has eight Principles, which stand in place of the Steps, Guidelines, or Points used by other programs. The Eight Principles of the Pathways to Sobriety program are:

First Principle: We admit we have abused or have been addicted to alcohol or other drugs. We have stopped using all nonprescribed drugs, including alcohol, and now accept responsibility for our addictions.

Second Principle: We understand that our environment can either support our recovery or work against it. Whenever possible, we choose people, places, and things that support our recovery.

Third Principle: As people recovering from addiction, we now know we can never justify using alcohol or other drugs, or other addictive behaviors, to change how we feel.

Fourth Principle: We are now learning new clean and sober techniques that help us to manage our emotions.

Fifth Principle: We discovered that the negative beliefs and values that helped support our addiction were counterproductive. Now we discard those negative beliefs and values and are discovering new, positive beliefs and values that support our recovery.

Sixth Principle: When we were addicted, we lacked meaningful goals. Now we set and move toward meaningful goals that reflect our new, positive values and beliefs.

Seventh Principle: We have discovered, or have chosen to believe, that our lives have a special purpose that can be fulfilled only if we remain clean and sober.

Eighth Principle: Being fully committed to remaining abstinent from alcohol and all nonprescribed drugs, we now choose to live according to a set of beliefs, values, and goals that supports our recovery, and to help others find their pathways to sobriety.[42]

An interesting and possibly unique feature of the Pathways to Sobriety program is the self-agreement, which is a statement to be signed and witnessed, stipulating that (among other things) the signer agrees to stop using alcohol and other drugs and to complete *The Pathways to Sobriety Workbook*.[43]

The Pathways to Sobriety program is new, only a few years old. It's good to remember that at a similar point in its history, AA itself was largely unknown.

Recovery International: A Mental Health Program for Recovery

Recovery International is primarily a program for dealing with mental health issues. It was started in 1937 by Abraham Low, MD, a neuropsychiatrist. In those days it was called Recovery, Inc. In 2007 Recovery, Inc. was reorganized and renamed Recovery International. Some experts consider the Recovery International method to be the first example of cognitive* behavioral therapy.[44] In this sense, it has things in common with REBT (Rational Emotive Behavior Therapy) which is taught by SMART Recovery and other secular programs. Although it is secular and focuses on training (not surrendering) the will, Recovery International is said to be "twelve-step friendly."[45] Surely it would also be "friendly" with the various secular programs.

Working the Recovery International program involves three steps:

1. Attending Recovery International meetings and giving four-part examples.

---

* Pertaining to thought

2. Reading Dr. Low's books
3. Practicing the recovery International tools in daily life.[46]

In addition to reading Low's books and practicing Recovery tools in daily life, Recovery International members attend meetings where Dr. Low's methods are discussed. Although the method is based on the teachings of a neuropsychiatrist, most Recovery International meetings are led by nonprofessionals.

Meetings are structured and often include such things as "spotting" (the practice identifying and reacting appropriately to distressing thoughts or symptoms); "reframing language" (rethinking defeatists thoughts); "self-endorsement" (congratulating oneself for every effort made to use Recovery methods); and "creating examples."

Creating examples provides a structure for story telling that is somewhat similar to AA's "what we were like, what happened, and what we are like now." The Recovery International story telling format, however, has four parts. These are:

1. Details of an event that caused distress.
2. The symptoms and discomfort that the event aroused.
3. How Recovery principles were utilized to cope with the event.
4. How you would have behaved in response to the event before joining Recovery International.[47]

For what it is worth, Recovery International has been praised by none other than William Griffith Wilson, the co-founder of AA. He said: "I have always looked with great sympathy upon Recovery, Inc. [now Recovery International]… In many cases their results have been extraordinary… Altogether I have the highest opinion of that outfit."[48]

Secular Psychologists: Self Help Guidance From the Pros

There have been a number of secular books written by addiction professionals and counselors describing their own ideas or treatment methods in terms suitable for individual (or group) self-help. Sometimes these programs have been or are used at professional treatment centers, other times they are used in the professional counseling practices of their writers.

Among the most well-known of these programs is The Life Process Program described in *The Truth About Addiction and Recovery: The Life Process Program for Outgrowing Destructive Habits* by Stanton Peele and Archie Brodsky. This book is said to be based on how people actually change – not on disease theory or theology.

Peele is one of America's most vocal critics of AA and the Twelve Step movement. In his work, much is made of the idea that addictions of all kinds are *not* diseases. The Life Process Program is designed to harness the natural process of maturing to help overcome addictions. As Peele and Brodsky wrote: "The Life Process Program draws on those strengths and personal resources the addict retains."[49] And: *"The key to fighting addiction is to enhance your natural life experiences."*[50] (Emphasis in the original.)

According to Vince Fox, the Life Process Program is "a tool kit which will enable you to:

"A.   Access where you stand in life and what a particular habit means to you ...
"B.   Set realistic goals for change ...
"C.   Strengthen your life as you strive to change your habits, and create environments that make addiction both unnecessary and undesirable."[51]

Another approach was developed by Gary Blanchard in his book *Building and Maintaining Recovery: A Success-Centered Approach to Addiction Recovery*. He calls it "Positive Path Recovery." Like the Pathways to Sobriety program described above, Positive Path Recovery also has eight principles. They are:

1. Admit that the substance has taken control and commit to a path of recovery.
2. Redefine and rebuild the sense of self. (The true self.)
3. Take responsibility and accept forgiveness for past actions.
4. Learn to identify and express feelings.
5. Improve communication with others.
6. Restore connection with significant people and make connection with others who can support recovery.
7. Identify barriers to recovery and plan to overcome them.
8. Let Go![52]

By "Let Go," Blanchard means letting go of feelings of guilt and shame; letting go of the need to control; letting go of judgments; and letting go of identifying yourself with your addictions.

Yet another rational program was presented by Kenneth Peiser and Martin Sandry. It's in their book, *Beat Your Addiction: A Complete Program for Overcoming Any Addiction*. Their approach adapts the Twelve Steps to Rational Emotive Behavior Therapy. It is based on their Twelve Rational Emotive Behavior Steps to Recovery, which are:

1. I admit that I have lost control of my addiction and that my life is becoming unmanageable.
2. I believe that a rational attitude about my life can restore me to sanity.
3. I shall let rational thinking help me.
4. I shall make a searching and fearless inventory of my past decisions and actions.
5. I shall admit to myself and another human being the exact nature of my wrongs.
6. I am entirely ready to have rational thinking remove all of my shortcomings.
7. I shall apply rational thinking to remove my shortcomings.

8. I shall make a list of all the persons I have harmed, and determine to make amends to them.
9. I shall make amends, wherever possible, except when doing so would injure someone.
10. I shall continue to take my inventory, and when I act wrongly, promptly admit it.
11. I shall seek to improve my conscious contact with reality, striving for the knowledge of what is rational and for the determination to act upon it.
12. Having an increased awareness as a result of what I have accomplished with these steps, I shall practice these principles in all of my affairs, and I will carry this message to others.[53]

Quite obviously, these steps are closely patterned after AA, but with REBT and rational thought substituted for a higher power. They may be useful for secular groups or for those whose only choice is AA or NA, but who are uncomfortable with God or the group as a higher power.

Perhaps the most famous secular version of the Twelve Steps was written by psychologist B. F. Skinner. Skinner's humanistic alternative to the steps is as follows:

1. We accept the fact that all our efforts to stop drinking have failed.
2. We believe that we must turn elsewhere for help.
3. We turn to our fellow men and women, particularly those who have struggled with the same problem.
4. We have made a list of the situations in which we are most likely to drink.
5. We ask our friends to help us avoid these situations.
6. We are ready to accept the help they give us.
7. We earnestly hope that they will help.
8. We have made a list of the persons we have harmed and to whom we hope to make amends.

9. We shall do all we can to make amends, in any way that will not cause further harm.
10. We will continue to make such lists and revise them as needed.
11. We appreciate what our friends have done and are doing to help us.
12. We, in turn, are ready to help others who may come to us in the same way.[54]

Skinner offered this humanistic version of the steps to Alcoholics Anonymous for use by its nonreligious members. AA declined the offer.[55] Along with various other secular versions of the Twelve Steps, Skinner's steps may be useful to anyone who finds such revisions helpful.

Finally, if you are into self-recovery by biblio-therapy (reading), there are many books that could be helpful. Two that I recommend are *How to Quit Drinking Without AA* and *How to Quit Drugs for Good,* both by Jerry Dorsman, a professional counselor. The books describe what may be called The Dorsman Method, a unique and effective approach to recovering from addictions. The Dorsman Method provides numerous worksheets and checklists that allow you to decide what programs, methods and helpful techniques you want to use. As with any of the secular approaches, The Dorsman Method can also be used by theists.

Taking These Roads

First of all, let it be said that there are AA meetings for atheists and agnostics. According to an article in the *New York Times,* there may be about 150 such groups operating nation-wide.[56] You may be able to find a partial list of these meetings by searching the Internet for "atheists and agnostics in AA" or some similar set of keywords. A good secular, AA-friendly website is http://aaagnostica.org/.

Just exactly how non-spiritual meetings work probably varies a lot from group to group, but such adaptions of the AA program do exist. They may not exist in your area, however, or you may not be interested in them.

Second, it *is* possible to be an atheist, humanist, or agnostic in regular AA. I have known a few of these myself. Honestly, though, I need to add that they were not necessarily the happiest campers I ever met in the program. And just because something is possible doesn't mean that it's for you.

Third, if you believe you are being unwillingly coerced into attending any Twelve Step program or treatment by a court or any governmental authority, you may have legal options. In recent years, the use of the powers of the state to force Twelve Step activities upon unwilling participants has been found to be improper by no less than eight high state and federal courts.[57] The compromise typically arrived at is that if government agencies or courts are going to order or coerce attendance at programs such as Alcoholics Anonymous, they must also offer a secular alternative for those who object to the spiritual content of the Twelve Step philosophy.

If you find yourself being coerced into attending Twelve Step meetings, you may want to seek legal advice. You may also want to bring your situation to the attention of some of the secular programs such as Rational Recovery or LifeRing Secular Recovery.

Getting back to the programs, not too long ago ***SOS*** celebrated its twenty-fifth anniversary, so it should be well established. In addition to being the oldest secular organization, it also claims to be the largest. If you are interested in SOS meetings, the websites are: www.cfiwest.org/sos/ and http://www.sossobriety.org/. SOS's mailing address is: Center for Inquiry-Los Angeles (and the Steve Allen Theater), 4773 Hollywood Blvd., Hollywood, CA 90027. The phone number is (323) 666-4295, fax number: (323) 666-4271. The e-mail: sos@cfiwest.org.

For a brief time when I lived in the Southwest, I attended some SOS meetings. In fact, I was one of the group's founders. It was refreshing to have a change from the Twelve Steps, but we did find that for some reason it was hard to keep the group's discussions off the topic of religion verses no religion. Of course, this was just my limited personal experience. Your experience could be different.

Each SOS group is autonomous and the SOS website says: "While many of us are atheists, agnostics, and secular humanists, many others are theists of one form or another who simply want a secular recovery environment – separation of church and recovery."[58] Full disclosure: SOS is a subcommittee of the Council for Secular Humanism. The SOS clearinghouse, however, is autonomously administered by Jim Christopher.[59]

Rational Recovery is no longer a mutual-support program. There are no RR meetings, but it is still an important organization. Expect to pay for most of RR's materials and services except the free portion of their website, which still has a lot of material. The website address for RR is: https://rational.org/. The mailing address is P.O. Box 800, Lotus, CA 95651. The telephone numbers are: 530-621-2667 and 530-621-4374. Rational Recovery's website has a form for you to contact RR by email.

SMART Recovery is headquartered at: 7304 Mentor Avenue, Suite F, Mentor, OH 44060. They have a toll free telephone number: 1-866-951-5357 and a regular number: 440-951-5357. The fax number is: 440-951-5358. The SMART web address is www.smartrecovery.org/. The website has a place to click to send them an email.

At its highest levels, SMART is largely an organization run by professionals. Although it is an abstinence program, some of the professionals may themselves be open to the idea of moderation. As far as I know, however, discussions of moderation verses abstinence do not occur at SMART Recovery group meetings.

The *LifeRing Secular Recovery* program is new but appears to be growing. LifeRing's website is: http://lifering.org/. Its postal address is: LifeRing Service Center, 1440 Broadway, Suite 312, Oakland, CA 94612. The toll-free telephone number is 1-800-811-4142. The fax number is 510-763-1513. To contact LifeRing by email: service@lifering.org .

IACT (International Association for Clear Thinking) is an Internet-based program and a self-help program in the strictest sense of the word. Although there have been *IACT* groups in the past, the program is currently designed only for individual online delivery.[60]

For this reason *IACT* may work best when combined with another program that does provide meetings and fellowship – unless of course, you are looking for a strictly SELF-help method. *IACT's* Internet address is: http://www.iactforyou.org/. The physical address is: 140 West Main Street, Suite B, P. O. Box 455, Winneconne, WI 54986-0455. And the email address is help@iactforyou.org.

Complimenting the website, which addresses all sorts of emotional issues including recovery, are some books Maxwell Maultsby wrote that specifically address addiction. One such book is *Stay Sober and Straight* (previously published as: *The Rational Behavioral Alcoholic Relapse Prevention Treatment Method*); another is *A Million Dollars for Your Hangover*, which appears to be out-of-print. It is very similar to *Stay Sober and Straight* anyway, except for a chapter written by Paul Knipping titled "Rational Self-Counseling to Prevent Alcohol Abuse."

YES Recovery suffered a setback a few years ago when the wikisource.org website deleted its document; and since *YES Recovery* has no head office, it is impossible to know how many *YES* meetings there are, or where they are located. If you want one, the best thing may be to start one. You can find the *YES Recovery Document* by searching for those words on the Internet. Find it, print it, find at least one other person (live or on the Internet) and you've got a meeting!

So far, the **Pathways to Sobriety** program exists mostly as a workbook. There are no meetings that I know of. However, if you also have anger management problems, there are a few Pathways to Peace meetings in the US and Canada. Pathways to Peace has a website: www.pathwaystopeaceinc.com/. This lists the Pathways to Peace meetings that are available.

> If you are interested in starting a Pathways to Sobriety group, the instructions are in *The Pathways to Sobriety Workbook,* or contact William Fleeman, at: PO Box 259, Cassadaga, NY 14718. The phone number is: 1-800-775-4212. The fax number is: 716-

595-3886. To contact Fleeman by email, use: transfrm@netsync.net. Fleeman says that his program is compatible with AA and NA.

Recovery International has a strong Internet presence. You can find it by searching for "recovery international" or "abraham low self-help systems." If you are looking for a meeting, there is an Internet page for that: http://www.lowselfhelpsystems.org/meetings/find-ameeting.asp. Remember that this program is primarily for mental health problems. It may work best for those who are dually diagnosed.

Positive Path Recovery and ***The Twelve Traditional Rational Emotive Behavior Steps to Recovery*** are also said to be workable along with AA or NA meetings (although they may be more compatible with SMART, SOS or LifeRing Secular Recovery). As mentioned above, AA declined to use ***B. F. Skinner's secular alternative*** to the Twelve Steps.

Stanton Peele's ***Life Process Program*** is probably not compatible with any Twelve Step program since Peele is such a forceful and well-known critic of the Twelve Steps. If you check the web you may find one or more addiction treatment centers that say they use the Life Process Program. Stanton Peele's website is at www.peele.net/. It should be noted that Peele is not a strong advocate for abstinence as a solution to addiction. Peele's website tells us that: "Stanton Peele... consults with the Wine Institute and other industry groups on social and cultural aspects of drinking."[61]

And don't forget some of the other programs which may be called secular, but which are described in other chapters. For instance, some consider the *Women For Sobriety* and *Men For Sobriety* programs to be secular and the *My Way Out* program offers no theism. All three of these programs are discussed in Chapter V.

This chapter's list of secular recovery programs is almost certainly more than you will find in any other book. Probably not all of them will be available in your immediate area, but if you are a self-starter, you may be motivated to start a group of your choice. Many of these programs are available on-line as Internet discussion groups. Check out their websites. Except for Skinner's twelve steps, all of these programs are available through books and reading. If you are looking for a secular pathway to recovery, you have many choices. Good luck!

Chapter Endnotes

1. White, William L. (Sept. 1, 2013) "The History of Secular Organizations for Sobriety – Save Our Selves: An Interview with James Christopher." Retrieved 9/22/2013 from: http://aaagnostica.org/2013/09/01/what-is-sos/.
2. Fox, Vince (1993) *Addiction, Change and Choice: The New View of Alcoholism,* Tucson, AZ: See Sharp Press, page 105.
3. Trimpey, Jack (1992) *The Small Book: A Revolutionary Alternative for Overcoming Alcohol and Drug Dependence,* New York: Delacorte Press, page xix.
4. White, William L. (1998) *Slaying the Dragon: The History of Addiction Treatment and Recovery in America,* Bloomington, IL: Chestnut Health Systems/Lighthouse Institute, page 280.
5. "An Overview of SOS" (2000). Retrieved 8/10/2010 from http://www.cfiwest.org/sos/brochures/overview.htm
6. Christopher, James (1989) *Unhooked: Staying Sober and Drug-Free,* Buffalo, NY: Prometheus Books, page 61.
7. Christopher, James (1992) *SOS Sobriety: The Proven Alternative to 12-Step Programs,* Buffalo, NY: Prometheus Books, page 10.
8. Christopher (1992) page 87.
9. Christopher (1992) page 154.
10. Christopher (1992) page 163-164.
11. Christopher (1992) page 169.
12. Christopher (1992) page 197.
13. Trimpey, Jack (1996) *Rational Recovery: The New Cure for Substance Addiction,* New York: Pocket Books, page 7.
14. Trimpey (1996) page 7.
15. Trimpey (1996) page 9.

16. Trimpey (1992) page xxi.
17. Trimpey (1992) page xx.
18. Trimpey (1992) page xx.
19. "Frequently Asked Questions About Smart Recovery" (n.d.). Retrieved 8/13/2010 from http://www.smartrecovery.org/resources/faq.htm#Q. What are the differences between SMART Recovery® and Rational Recovery (RR).
20. Humphreys, Keith (2004) *Circles of Recovery: Self Help Organizations for Addictions,* Cambridge: Cambridge University Press, page 82.
21. Lemanski, Michael (2001) *A History of Addiction and Recovery in the United States,* Tucson, AZ: See Sharp Press, page 134.
22. "Smart Recovery 4-Point Program" (2010). Retrieved 7/13/2010 from: http://www.smartrecovery.org/
23. Steinberger, Henry, editor (2004) *SMART Recovery Handbook,* Mentor, OH: Alcohol and Drug Abuse Self-Help Network, Inc. d.b.a. SMART Recovery, section 3/page 4.
24. Steinberger (2004) section 4/page 2.
25. Steinberger (2004) section 4/page 11.
26. Steinberger (2004) section 5/page 8.
27. Humphreys (2004) page 86.
28. "FAQs" (n.d.). Retrieved 8/15/2010 from http://lifering.org/faqs/
29. Nicolaus, Martin (2009) *Empowering Your Sober Self: The LifeRing Approach to Addiction Recovery,* San Francisco: Jossey-Bass, page 14.
30. "The '3-S' Philosophy" (n.d.). Retrieved 8/15/2010 from: http://lifering.org/the-three-sphilosophy/
31. Nicolaus (2009) pages 101-102.
32. Maultsby, Maxie C. (1978) *The Rational Behavioral Alcoholic-Relapse Prevention Treatment Method,* Lexington, KY: Rational Self-Help Books, page 4.
33. Ibid., page 2.

34. "YES Recovery" (n.d.). Retrieved 9/18/2013 from: http://www.seadict.com/en/en/yes recovery
35. "YES Recovery, Alternative 12 Steps" (n.d.). Retrieved 9/18/2013 from: http://www.addictioninfo.org/articles/88/1/YES-Recovery-Alternative-12-Steps/Page1.html
36. "YES Recovery, Alternative 12 Steps" (n.d.)
37. Fleeman, William (2004) *The Pathways to Sobriety Workbook*, Alameda, CA: Hunter House Inc., pages 14-15. Fleeman (2004) page 41.
38. Fleeman (2004) page 61
39. Fleeman (2004) page 61.
40. Fleeman (2004) page 63.
41. Fleeman (2004) page 63.
42. Fleeman (2004) page 241.
43. Fleeman (2004) page 69.
44. Bell, Carl C., quoted in ""The Original Cognitive Behavioral Therapy" (n.d.) Retrieved 9/19/2013 from: http://www.lowselfhelpsystems.org/system/our-method-about-cbt.asp
45. *Wikipedia* (5 Sept 2013) "Self-help groups for mental health." Retrieved 9/20/2013 from: http://en.wikipedia.org/wiki/Self-help_groups_for_mental_health.
46. "The Recovery International Method" (n.d.) Retrieved 9/10/2013 from: http://www.lowselfhelpsystems.org/system/our-method.asp
47. *Wikipedia* (13 Sept 2011) "Recovery International." Retrieved 11/4/2011 from: http://en.wikipedia.org/wiki/Recovery_International
48. Quoted in: White, William and Ernest Kurtz (2010) "A Message of Tolerance and Celebration: The Portrayal of Multiple Pathways of Recovery in the Writings of Alcoholics Anonymous Co-Founder Bill Wilson." Retrieved 9/20/2013 from: http://www.williamwhitepapers.com/

49. Peele, Stanton and Archie Brodsky (1991) *The Truth About Addiction and Recovery: The Life Process Program for Outgrowing Destructive Habits,* New York: Simon & Schuster, page 161.
50. Peele and Brodsky (1991) page 380.
51. Fox (1993) page 173.
52. Blanchard, Gary (2007) *Building and Maintaining Recovery: A Success-Centered Approach to Addiction Recovery,* Positive Path Press, pages 17-18.
53. Peiser, Kenneth and Martin Sandry (2004) *Beat Your Addiction: A Complete Program for Overcoming Any Addiction* (second edition), Avon, MA: Adams Media, pages 12-13.
54. Skinner, B. F. (July/August 1987) "A Humanist Alternative to AA's Twelve Steps," *The Humanist.* Retrieved 12/1/2010 from http://silkworth.net/magazine_newspaper/humanist_jul_aug_1987.html
55. Skinner (July/August 1987).
56. Freeman, Samuel G. (Feb 21, 2014) "Alcoholics Anonymous, Without Religion," *The New York Times.*
57. Egelko, Bob (Sept. 8, 2007) "Appeals court says requirement to attend AA unconstitutional," *San Francisco Chronicle.* Retrieved 11/28/2010 from http://articles.sfgate.com/2007-09-08/bay-area/17259704
58. "SOS Guidebook for Group Leaders" (2000). Retrieved 8/15/2010 from http://www.cfiwest.org/sos/brochures/leaders.htm
59. "Links"(n.d.). Retrieved 8/15/2010 from http://secularhumanism.org/index.php?section=sos&page=index
60. Personal email 12/21/2013 from "Mary" help@iactforyou.org
61. "Stanton Peele Addiction Website" (2010). Retrieved 8/16/2010 from http://www.peele.net/lib/bottle.html

CHAPTER VII:
Moderation and Controlled Drinking:
An Enduring Quest

Charles Clapp, Jr. was "a friend of Bill W."
Really.
Clapp and AA co-founder Bill Wilson really were friends. Saying someone's "a friend of Bill W." these days is just a cute way of indicating an AA member, but as we saw in Chapter II, Clapp and Wilson really were acquainted.[1] The two met at religious meetings of the Oxford Group in New York City, where both had gone to seek a spiritual solution for their alcohol problems. Wilson had been sober a few months and Clapp was still struggling with his drinking when, as Clapp reported it, "Bill W. turned the 'key' in me and I became 'dry.'"[2]

That was October 1935. Clapp described the scene this way: "we tried to keep ourselves 'dry' and insure ourselves against any return to our former miserable existence. In time the present 12 Steps of the AA program emerged and some of [our] little group went on to form AA."[3] Clapp, apparently, wasn't long among them. In a few years Clapp would become one of the first recovered drunks in the modern era to advocate moderate drinking.

Clapp's adventure ended poorly, as will the stories of some others that are reported here. It can't be denied that some of the founders of moderation programs have had their problems.

Statistically, however, the results of attempted controlled drinking and attempted abstinence may be about the same for drinkers whose problems are not too severe. As the distinguished professor of psychology, William R. Miller, put the matter: "moderation-oriented approaches hold at least as much promise as abstinence-orientated methods in treating less dependent problem drinkers."[4]

In a later work, *Controlling Your Drinking,* Miller along with co-author Ricardo Munoz, urged caution: "It is disturbingly common for authors of self-help books to make extremely optimistic claims," they wrote, "to give pump-you-up promises about how successful you're going to be if you just follow their advice."[5]

Not everyone who tries moderation succeeds. Success at complete moderation is the exception, not the rule. For those wanting an honest measure, Miller and Munoz reported the following more-or-less typical results for a 12 month follow-up:

- Only one in seven (15%) had maintained complete moderation throughout the year ... without any alcohol-related problems or signs of alcohol dependence.
- Another 23% had reduced their drinking substantially ... but continued to experience some alcohol-related problems, at least occasionally.
- A further one in four (24%) had been totally abstinent for at least a year.
- And that left 37% who continued heavy and harmful drinking.*[6]

Providing nothing bad happens along the way, Miller and Munoz say that any of these results may be a happy outcome *if* those who do not experience perfect or at least fairly good moderation learn from the trial and decide to give up drinking.[7]

This chapter tells about some who succeed in moderation and some who failed. With possibly one or two exceptions, none of the lay founders of moderation programs have succeeded by maintaining complete moderation over an extended time (though some of their followers surely have). Beginning with Clapp's debacle – which ultimately resulted in success when he returned to Alcoholics Anonymous – this chapter describes some of the well-

---

* Because of rounding, the sum of these numbers does not equal 100 percent.

known and not-so-well-known self-help and mutual-help moderation programs.

Charles Clapp's Square Pegs: A "Screwy Theory"

After Wilson "turned the key" in him, as described above, Charles Clapp, Jr. remained dry for over four years. Then he happened to spend some time with a professor of psychology who was especially interested in the question of why a seemingly normal person – such as Clapp himself, possibly – becomes an alcoholic. Clapp concluded that it is caused by a failure to find one's proper place in life. He thought that one becomes alcoholic because he or she is a "square peg" trying to fit into a "round hole." Sometime later he concluded that he himself had found his own "square hole" – as a writer rather than a stockbroker – and that therefore he was no longer an alcoholic.

Thus, this friend of Bill Wilson, who was known as "Charly C." in AA circles, became one of the first in the post-prohibition era to take seriously the reasoning that if alcoholism is a disease with uncontrolled drinking as its symptom, then after identifying and removing the root cause of the disease, the symptoms should abate and normal or moderate drinking should follow. According to Clapp's theory, once the alcoholic "square peg" found his or her "square hole," all problems with alcohol would be resolved.

In 1942 Clapp laid out his ideas in a little book titled *Drunks are Square Pegs*. The purpose of this volume, he said, was "to outline what ... steps [are] to be taken after the subject has stopped drinking."[8] These "steps to be taken" included drinking liquor in moderation.

Clapp's analysis partitioned the life of an alcoholic into seven stages, starting with the future drunkard's failure to find the proper place in life and ending with the finding of that "square hole" and thenceforth happily drinking again in moderation. Quoting from Clapp's book, these stages are:

Stage One is the period where the subject is becoming a square peg and driving himself, or being driven, into a round hole.

Stage Two is the period where the subject drinks but seems to be able to handle it… This stage is of indefinite length but is much shorter than the subject will admit: *i.e.,* it has him licked before he admits it.

Stage Three is the period where, admitted or not, the subject is an alcoholic.

Stage Four is the period where the subject admits defeat and seeks a way to get "dry."

Stage Five is the period where the subject becomes "dry," does not drink anything, and is completely released from the desire for, or thoughts of liquor.

Stage Six is the period where the subject does not drink anything and finds his or her SQUARE HOLE.

Stage Seven is the period where the subject has become a normal person, has found the square hole, takes liquor in moderation and has emerged into a beautiful new world.[9]

Clapp tried this theory on himself – with unsatisfactory results. In 1946 he wrote an apology or explanation for AA's official magazine, the *AA Grapevine,* wherein he confessed that the theory "did not work."[10] He said that he had maintained moderation for about 10 months and then drank excessively until May 1945, when he gave it up and rejoined AA.[11]

In his *Grapevine* article Clapp denounced what he called "my screwy theory" and vowed to "write no more books on the subject." Because, he said: "It's all in our AA book."[12] He was a true believer.

But by 1949 he was at it again, writing another book called *Drinking's Not the Problem.*

This work was intended for *potential* alcoholics but it discussed essentially the same theory of "square pegs" being in "round holes." In this revised work, Clapp disavowed the belief that recovered drunks, even if comfortably seated at last in their very own "square holes," could safely drink again.[13]

Whether or not Clapp ever tried to drink alcohol again is unknown. *Drinking's Not the Problem* was apparently Clapp's last work as a writer. After that, like several of the folks we will meet in this chapter, he seems to have disappeared. Other than his final book, possibly one of the last accounts of him came from his old friend Bill Wilson, writing to another old Oxford Group acquaintance, Shep Cornell: "About Charlie Clapp: after having done a swell job in the Army he began to flounder heavily after his discharge. Some months ago he became an ardent AA [member] and his situation looks far better."[14]

Perhaps AA is where this talented but quirky "square peg" finally found his "square hole."

The Society of Seven Sinners: Arthur Cain's "Tragic Fiasco"

Psychologist Arthur H. Cain, PhD, is best known for having penned a couple of very critical magazine articles about AA. In 1963 he wrote "Alcoholics Anonymous: Cult or Cure?" for the popular *Harper's Magazine.*[15] He followed that in 1964 with an article published in the *Saturday Evening Post:* "Alcoholics Can be Cured – Despite AA."[16] And by "cured" he meant nothing less than the resumption of what he supposed to be normal drinking.

Cain developed his ideas in a series of three books published in the 1960s. They were: *Seven Sinners,* adapted from his PhD dissertation and published in 1961 using the pen name "Arthur King"; *The Cured Alcoholic,* which was published in 1964 using his real name; and *Paul King's Rebellion,* the last of Cain's books on alcoholism, published in 1967.

All three books purported to describe a program that had been useful for those who had limited success, or no success at all, with other approaches: "those who had tried Alcoholics Anonymous, psychotherapy, and religious counseling."[17] According to Cain, he not only succeeded with those difficult cases, he returned a significant number of them to normal, problem-free drinking.

Dr. Cain's interest in the matter was more than just professional or academic. Though he was coy about his own drinking most of the time, in *Paul King's Rebellion* Cain finally identified himself as one of the "cured alcoholics."[18] In fact, it is probable that "Paul King," the hard drinking protagonist of *Paul King's Rebellion,* was none other than Arthur Cain himself. They certainly led very similar lives. Both were born in the South at about the same time, both served in the military, both traveled around the world, both attended AA, and both enrolled at Columbia University, where Cain, at least, received his PhD.[19]

In the same book, Cain included a draft charter for incorporating a nonprofit organization to carry on his work. It was to be called *The Society of Seven Sinners, Inc.* In this society, lay members who had "solved their psychological problems," as Cain phrased it, would be full *participating members,* as would psychologists, psychiatrists, physicians, and pastoral counselors.[20] According to Cain, the society had "members in forty-eight of the fifty states and eighteen foreign countries."[21] But despite these auspicious beginnings, and Cain's national reputation, *The Society of Seven Sinners, Inc.* evidently went nowhere.

Seven years later, professor William Madsen, author of *The American Alcoholic,* possibly explained why: "I have learned from the most reliable sources," he confided, "that Cain's venture ended as a tragic fiasco."[22] Just exactly *how* Cain's effort became a fiasco is not known but the *why* can be deduced with some confidence from an analysis of his program, which had some strengths and one glaring weakness.

Cain's program included nine "activities," which were: (1) Physical Training; (2) Educative Counseling; (3) Reading; (4) Organization; (5) Vocational Guidance; (6) Socialization; (7) Aesthetics; (8) Religious Investigation; and (9) Experimentation.

Of these, *Experimentation*, from the point of view of this discussion, is by far the most relevant and certainly the most controversial. Everybody, Cain explained, "was advised that he might be asked, at the end of his course, to be the subject of a controlled alcoholic episode under laboratory conditions."[23] The number of patients actually exposed to Cain's "controlled alcoholic episode" is unclear, but he did definitely assert that some of his patients — or "colleagues" as he called them — had "demonstrated their ability to drink normally."[24]

The main problem with Cain's program seems to be that his math was atrocious. By this I mean his ineptitude at calculating approximate blood alcohol levels and estimating the number of drinks that might be considered "normal." Here is Cain's idea of moderation. A "rough, rule of-thumb description of normal drinking," he called it:

> An *aperitif* before dinner; two glasses of wine with dinner; a liqueur after dinner; a pony of brandy at bedtime. Occasionally, one or two whiskey-and-sodas between dinner and bedtime. On rare special occasions, two or three additional drinks, exceeding our psychophysical definition of normal drinking to the point of mild intoxication and ensuing 'morning after' hangover.[25]

Five drinks: an *aperitif*; two glasses of wine; a liquor; and a brandy. This was Cain's *minimum*. My friends, this is *not* moderate drinking. By today's definition this is binge drinking – five or more drinks at a setting – and it is hazardous drinking for anyone. Alan Willoughby in his book, *The Alcohol Troubled Person,* also noted this passage and was appalled by Cain's excesses. Said Willoughby: "I can only react by saying that if that's 'normal' drinking, and one definitely gets the impression that he intends it as a possible standard daily dose, then I come from a different part of the world than he does."[26]

It is hard for people who habitually overdrink (or those of us who used to) to realize just how little average Americans drink, and how infrequently they imbibe. Researchers have found that up to seventy-five percent of all adults are either abstainers or are infrequent to light drinkers.[27] One way to measure Cain's over-exuberance is to observe that his recommendations may be read as allowing over forty-nine standard drinks per week. In the U.S. only five percent of adults drink that much or more.[28] In fact, if you drink more than *one drink per week*, you are drinking more than most adult Americans.[29] Although Cain's approach was not devoid of perceptive insights and interesting ideas, it is not too difficult to envision what probably caused his venture to end tragically as a fiasco.

Alcoholic Games: TA Challenges AA

The 1960s were a time of social change and experimentation. Probably not coincidentally, it was also a time of evolving eclecticism in the field of psychology. One popular psychological model in particular gave quite a bit of attention to alcohol and drug addiction. It created a stir by claiming that alcoholism was "a game," not a disease, and that alcoholics could be cured to become problem-free social drinkers.

"In game analysis there is no such thing as alcoholism or 'an alcoholic,' but there is a role called alcoholic in a certain type of game" wrote Dr. Eric Berne, M.D. in his 1964 best-selling book, *Games People Play*.[30] Berne's classic introduced TA – transactional analysis, a voguish system of self-help psychotherapy that achieved great popularity in the 1960s and 1970s.

Among other particulars, the TA method replaced technical Freudian terms with psychological "games" that had clever, non-technical monikers such as "Debtor," "Kick Me," "See What You

Made Me Do" and, of course, "Alcoholic." Berne also identified a game of "Addict," which was said to be "similar to 'Alcoholic,' but more sinister."[31]

By Berne's definition: "A game is a series of complimentary ulterior transactions progressing to a well-defined, predictable outcome."[32] In less technical terms, it is a bit of unhealthy social behavior involving a central character and a number of other "players" whose roles can be defined as contributing to the misbehavior of the central figure. In the game of "Alcoholic," for example, the roles of "Persecutor," "Rescuer," "Patsy," "Connection," and, of course, "Alcoholic," are identified.[33]

"The psychological cure for an alcoholic…" Berne felt, "lies in getting him to stop playing the game altogether, rather than simply change from one role to another."[34] He believed that "Alcoholics Anonymous … continues playing the actual game but concentrates on inducing the Alcoholic to take the role of Rescuer."[35]

Since alcoholism was believed to be a game not a disease, the goal of TA therapy was a return to social drinking, not abstinence. "The criteria of a true 'game cure' is that the former alcoholic should be able to drink socially without putting himself in jeopardy," Berne declared. "The usual 'total abstinence' cure will not satisfy the game analyst."[36] Berne waffled on his not-a-disease position quite a bit though: "If a biochemical or physiological abnormality is the prime mover of excessive drinking — and that is still open to some question — then its study belongs in the field of internal medicine," he wrote.[37] And he didn't neglect the credits to AA that were virtually mandatory at the time: "Alcoholics Anonymous is still for most people the best initiation into the therapy of over-indulgence."[38]

Berne died in 1970 but his work with the Alcoholic game was continued and expanded by his colleague and protégé, Claude Steiner, PhD. He, like Berne, emphasized that social interactions — "transactions" — are inherent in the game of Alcoholic. "[T]he transactional analyst," Steiner wrote, "would predict that an alcoholic stranded on a desert island with a large supply of alcohol will stop drinking because drinking is only part of a transactional situation; and without persons to transact with, the need for alcohol will disappear."[39]

Steiner added to Berne's thesis by formulating three distinct subtypes of Alcoholic Games. He named these: "Drunk and Proud"; "Lush"; and "Wino." For the "Drunk and Proud" player, drinking is only incidental to other misconduct such as gambling, adultery, or other transgressions aimed at abusing or humiliating the person who plays the role of Persecutor or Patsy, usually the spouse. "Lush," in transactional analysis theory, is played in response to emotional or sexual deprivations. "Wino," according to Steiner, is a game played by derelicts who obtain "strokes" by lifelong guzzling to the point of physical degeneration and illness.[40]

Steiner summarized his ideas in a December 1969 article in the *Quarterly Journal of Studies on Alcohol*. And in 1971 he developed them into a book, *Games Alcoholics Play*, an obvious sequel to *Games People Play* (and another best-seller). In 1979, Steiner released *Healing Alcoholism*, which was something of a revised version of *Games Alcoholics Play*, a book Steiner said he had become increasingly dissatisfied with.

In *Healing Alcoholism*, Steiner provided a certain amount of self-disclosure, reporting that he himself never had a problem with alcohol, of which he said he used "a very moderate amount."[41]

In this new book, Steiner moderated TA's stance on controlled drinking, but he added some harsh words for certain public institutions and the addiction treatment industry of that era. For example, in one passage Steiner wrote:

> People who have drinking problems and who come in contact with the courts or other public institutions, but who are not willing to relate to AA, will find themselves treated like heretics and will have a great deal of difficulty getting help from people who can affect their lives. Alcoholism workers who do not accept AA's total program will find they cannot find work. Their own ideas or suggestions will not be welcome in clinics or other institutions.[42]

On controlled drinking, Steiner's revision offered considerable backtracking based on his added clinical experience. "I am fully convinced," he wrote, "that people who have been habitual drinkers for many years have a strong tendency to return to this pattern. The past habits are like old ruts on the road; they remain part of you, and once you fall into them, they are very hard to get out of."[43]

In spite of this, or perhaps because of it, Steiner found that his patients – those who decided to try social drinking – inevitably landed in one of three groups:

Those in the largest group found that they were unable to drink any alcohol at all without the almost certain consequence of their drinking going out of control and becoming destructive.

Those in a second group found that, while they did not necessarily lose control, they were still uncomfortably attracted to alcohol. They found their alcohol use insidiously increasing and their thoughts becoming more and more involved with alcohol. Their drinking gradually evolved into "controlled alcoholic drinking," as opposed to true social drinking. Yet all was not lost. The members of this group, Steiner asserted, determined that drinking was not for them and usually stopped altogether, "without incident or harmful aftereffects."

People in the third group, by far the smallest, found that alcohol was no longer a problem or an unhealthy preoccupation. They were honestly able to take an occasional social drink without any observable ill effects.[44]

And, contrary to Dr. Cain, Steiner's idea of what constitutes social drinking is pretty realistic. In fact, Steiner almost seemed to be responding to Cain when he wrote:

> Having a couple of cocktails before dinner, some wine with the meal, and a snifter of after-dinner liqueur, having six or seven drinks at a party or a six-pack of beer during a hot afternoon is not social drinking. Social drinking is a glass of wine during dinner or a drink before dinner or a couple of beers

at a long party or a thimbleful of liqueur after a hearty meal.⁴⁵

In 1979 Steiner estimated that between 10 and 20 percent of those he worked with became this sort of moderate drinker.⁴⁶ Steiner recently revised *Healing Alcoholism* and in this unpublished version he lowered the estimate once again. He now figures that less than 10 percent of those with drinking problems will go on to become truly moderate consumers of alcohol.⁴⁷

Drinkwatchers and Similar Programs: Moderation Unlimited

Drinkwatchers, Responsible Drinkers, Responsible Users Group, Methods of Moderation and Abstinence: the 1970s and shortly thereafter saw the birth of a surprising number of organizations for moderate drinking and moderate or responsible use of drugs.

One such program was Responsible Drinkers (RD), a west coast group that broke away from the larger and better known Drinkwatchers. RD tried to recognize and deal with all of the facets of beverage alcohol: food, relaxant, mood elevator, social equalizer, drug, and poison. It believed that alcohol problems stemmed from too little respect being given to the powers of alcohol, the drug.⁴⁸

Another group or program was the Responsible Users Groups (RUG), a 1970s program for people who felt they were experiencing minimal problems, or no problems at all, with their use of alcohol or other drugs.⁴⁹ A third such effort, which came along in the 1980s, was called MOMA (Methods of Moderation and Abstinence). MOMA rose briefly and not too spectacularly from the ashes of the American Atheist's Addiction Recovery Groups (AAARG!), a recovery organization that was nominally supported by the American Atheists, Inc. Through an irregularly published newsletter, AAARG! and MOMA provided a forum for nonreligious persons who were seeking an alternative to AA or AA-styled Twelve Step programs.[50]

By far the most publicized and best documented of these programs was The Association of Drinkwatchers, International, Inc. or just plain Drinkwatchers (DW), which was formed in late 1974 as a non-profit, educational, self-help group. "Drinkwatchers' aim is to put alcohol in proper focus on the periphery of ... life rather than in central focus whether that be abstinence or moderate drinking," explained Drinkwatchers' founder, Ariel Winters.[51] It offered a choice of either abstinence or controlled drinking, but controlled drinking was what most attracted its members and the attention of the media.

The Drinkwatchers program had dozens of ideas, such as a suggestion advising three months of absolute sobriety at the start. It also had ten "Goals" – precepts that seem to answer, more or less, to AA's Twelve Steps. These goals were:

1. To put alcohol in its proper perspective in our lives, whether that be abstinence or moderate drinking.
2. To manage our own lives, rather than have it managed for us.
3. To learn that to abuse anything is self-defeating.
4. To assume responsibility for our lives, actions, and behavior.
5. To learn to overcome adversity, live creatively and accept the challenge of everyday life.
6. To understand that what we think of ourselves defines who we are.
7. To learn through a period of group identification how to stand on our own two feet.
8. To know that self-assurance and freedom from dependency are possible for us.
9. To live in cooperation with our fellowmen and with nature.
10. To share our knowledge, hopes, and perceptions with any persons seriously interested in sharing these common goals.[52]

During its brief existence, Drinkwatchers attracted quite a bit of publicity, mostly from periodicals such as *Newsday*, *Modern People*, and "Criswell Predicts," a newspaper column that purported to foretell the future. ("Criswell predicts that DW will be the big new thing."[53]) According to Winters, the publicity from these articles generated a considerable amount of mail, well over 30,000 letters. "The letters are great, sad, wonderful, revealing, inspirational, colorful, informative, funny, and wise," Winters thought.[54] Indeed, some of the comments DW received are of sufficient interest to warrant inclusion here:

C "I've felt the need for a 'reformed church' for a long time…"
C "I'm sick and tired of being branded an 'alcoholic.'"
C "Bravo! Never did I accept the idea of having a disease."
C "Hopefully, DW will be the answer to my husband's drinking problem, or at least a step in the right direction."
C "[I] was almost thrown out of an AA meeting for mentioning it!"
C "I have been drinking for over 40 years and have been in and out of AA for about 20, but to no avail. I've had little success there; maybe DW will work for me."
C "I'd rather be a Drinkwatcher than watch other people drink."[55]

A couple of inferences can be drawn from the above statements, which are fairly representative of the quotations that Winters included in her 1977 book, *Drinkwatchers*. For one thing, it is evident that the Drinkwatchers' program of moderation generated far more interest than the DW abstinence program, which was hardly mentioned at all. For another thing, it is clear that a good share of the attention came from people who were moving *away* from AA as opposed to moving aggressively *towards* Drinkwatchers.

One of the greatest weaknesses of the Drinkwatchers program was its tendency to rely upon generalities and slogans, as opposed to more specific, readily measurable rules and guidelines. Drinkwatchers had a variety of clever mottos such as, "Don't abuse, lightly use"; "With too much booze, you lose!"; "No more bullshit, please!"; "Enough *is* enough"; "Hold the line at feeling fine"; and "Just a few will do."[56]

Catchy apothegms, no doubt. But nowhere did Drinkwatchers specifically define its limits. Just what separates "light use" from "abuse?" Precisely how much "booze" is "too much?" Specifically, how much is "enough?" Where is "the line" that one must hold? Exactly what is meant by "feeling fine?" How many drinks are "just a few?" And just exactly what *is* "bullshit" to a Drinkwatcher, anyway?

Drinkwatchers may have been ill-defined. It may have been "ahead of its time"; or it may have been too much a creature of its own unique time in the hard-drinking 1970s. Ariel Winters' books provide photographs of the author, a strikingly beautiful woman. But the contents of those books reveal a person who is "into" everything – nutrition and all kinds of pop psychotherapy, for example – but concentrated upon nothing. Winters first book, *Drinkwatchers,* has 30 chapters that cover things like grief, depression, emotions, assertiveness, sex, dreams, diet, loneliness, rebellion, hosting a cocktail party, cooking with spirits, hangover cures (!!)… and so on.

Despite all the hype, you may never have heard of Ariel Winters because she is one of those that seemed to just disappear. Several years ago I tried to find out what I could about what happened to Winters and Drinkwatchers by writing to William R. Miller, PhD. I contacted him because he had provided a preface for one of Winter's books. This, in part, was his reply:

> I'm afraid I have very little information for you. I do know there was a *serious* problem with quality control of meetings. Virtually anyone could write in a[nd] get materials and permission to start a DW group. There were stories of 'flaming alcoholics in denial' starting up their own DW groups, with unfortunate results. I have no direct knowledge of such events… I only met once with Ms. Winters.

There were many rumors that I cannot confirm. I stopped hearing from her, mail was returned, and I heard somewhere that she had died...[57]

Moderation Management: The Promise and the Peril

Audrey Kishline didn't feel that she belonged in AA. Unlike other members, "I never felt... like I was coming 'home' when I walked into an AA meeting," she said.[58] And she wanted to know why. Why did AA's program seem to be the only way? "Why," she asked, "aren't there any support groups available for problem drinkers who have made the decision to moderate their drinking behavior?"[59]

Kishline apparently didn't know the history of moderation programs and if she did, perhaps it wouldn't have mattered. Working with some of the leading addiction professionals who advocate controlled drinking, she started her own peer-led support group for problem drinkers: Moderation Management or MM.

At first the MM program received lots and lots of media attention. Kishline got her full fifteen minutes of fame and more. She appeared on "Oprah," and other national TV shows. MM was the subject of numerous news and magazine articles. As an example of MM's ability to grab the spotlight, in June 1995 a major television news network actually carried reports on Moderation Management instead of covering AA's sixtieth anniversary convention.[60]

Kishline also wrote a book setting out the Moderation Management program, *Moderate Drinking: The New Option for Problem Drinkers*. "In the process of writing, I had the opportunity to speak with many experts in the addictions field," she reported.[61] Many of them thought that MM was a good idea that was too far ahead of its time, while a few said that MM *was* an idea whose time had come. She also talked to nonprofessionals. "When I asked laypeople for their response, almost all of them said it sounded like common sense, and most thought that it had already been done."[62] Score one for the laypeople, who apparently remembered

Drinkwatchers, possibly Arthur Cain, and perhaps the TA controversy better than the professionals.

In her book, Kishline told her personal story up to the founding of MM and described the Moderation Management program in detail. The essentials of the program can also be found on www.moderation.org, MM's official website.

The fundamentals of the MM program are: the MM Meeting Ground Rules; MM's Nine Steps; MM's concept of a Moderate Drinker; and the MM Limits. These have changed a little over the years but they are still largely as Kishline created them, with the help of some prominent addiction professionals.

MM Meeting Ground Rules

MM's Ground Rules are precepts by which the organization manages itself and sets standards for proper decorum. The Ground Rules are six in number, which is a change from Kishline's original version that had ten guidelines. In their current form, the Ground Rules are:

- An MM meeting is a safe, protected and confidential space. If you are concerned about your drinking, you are welcome here.
- We are here to help each other. The appropriate attitude is one of mutual respect and tolerance.
- People should not come to MM meetings intoxicated and we suggest abstaining from drinking altogether on meeting days.
- We discourage our members from socializing together in drinking situations, and alcohol is never allowed at meetings or official MM-related activities.
- We share our experiences and our knowledge; we do not stand in judgment of others and we try to avoid giving personal advice.
- We understand that individuals may choose paths other than ours; they are welcome if they are concerned about their drinking.

MM's Nine Steps Toward Moderation and Positive Lifestyle Changes

MM's nine steps are the centerpiece of the program. They are not only designed to reduce drinking, but are also intended to bring about other positive lifestyle changes. These have changed very little over the years. The only notable difference being the inclusion of on-line groups in addition to MM meetings. The nine MM Steps are:

1. Attend meetings or on-line groups and learn about the program of Moderation Management.
2. Abstain from alcoholic beverages for 30 days and complete steps three through six during this time.
3. Examine how drinking has affected your life.
4. Write down your life priorities.
5. Take a look at how much, how often, and under what circumstances you had been drinking.
6. Learn the MM guidelines and limits for moderate drinking.
7. Set moderate drinking limits and start weekly "small steps" toward balance and moderation in other areas of your life.
8. Review your progress and update your goals.
9. Continue to make positive lifestyle changes and attend meetings whenever you need ongoing support or would like to help newcomers.

MM's Concept of a Moderate Drinker:

According to MM's website: "When you have made the healthy decision to drink less, and you stay within moderate limits, you should not experience any health, personal, family, social, job-related, financial, or legal problems due to alcohol." According to MM, a Moderate Drinker also fits the following positive description:

- considers an occasional drink to be a small, though enjoyable, part of life
- has hobbies, interests, and other ways to relax and enjoy life that do not involve alcohol

- usually has friends who are moderate drinkers or nondrinkers
- generally has something to eat before, during, or soon after drinking
- usually does not drink for longer than an hour or two on any particular occasion
- usually does not drink faster than one drink per half-hour
- usually does not exceed the .055% BAC moderate drinking limit
- feels comfortable with his or her use of alcohol (never drinks secretly and does not spend a lot of time thinking about drinking or planning to drink)

The MM Limits:

According to MM, its portrait of a Moderate Drinker is meant to be flexible, but the limits are meant to be firm. It is also pointed out that these are *limits,* not targets or goals and that many successful moderate drinkers consume much less. In fact, by ordinary drinking standards the MM drinking limits are very liberal. In the U.S. only 11 percent of the men and 5 percent of the women drink that much.[63] The Limits are:

- Strictly obey local laws regarding drinking and driving.
- Do not drink in situations that would endanger yourself or others.
- Do not drink every day. MM suggests that you abstain from drinking alcohol at least 3 or 4 days per week.
- Women who drink more than 3 drinks on any day, and more than 9 drinks per week, may be drinking at harmful levels.
- Men who drink more than 4 drinks on any day, and more than 14 drinks per week, may be drinking at harmful levels.

The Accident

On March 25, 2000, at about 6 p.m., a head-on collision occurred on the eastbound side of Interstate 90 near Seattle. The occupants of the eastbound automobile, 38-year-old Richard "Danny" Davis and his 12-year-old daughter, LaShell Davis, were killed almost instantly. The driver of the westbound vehicle was seriously injured but survived to face two charges of vehicular homicide.

The driver was Audrey Kishline, founder of Moderation Management. She was going the wrong way on an interstate highway. She had beside her an open bottle of vodka. Her blood alcohol level was 0.26 percent, more than three times the legal limit, and toxicology tests showed that she also had high levels of antianxiety medications and antidepressants.[64]

Were it not for Kishline's ties to Moderation Management, this would almost certainly have been just another tragic accident involving alcohol. But because the drunk driver was the public face of a moderation program, both Kishline and MM received a lot of negative media coverage. However, as its supporters pointed out, the MM connection to the crash was complicated by the fact that about two months prior, Kishline had announced to an MM email list that she was giving up on moderation. She said she was attending AA and would also be attending Women for Sobriety and SMART Recovery.[65]

Supporters of the moderate drinking approach have taken this fact to argue that only then – after Kishline quit MM and rejoined AA – "did her drinking veer out of control."[66] The full story is not like that. In a 2007 book she co-authored with Sheryl Maloy, the crash victims' mother and ex-wife, Kishline described her real situation in MM, where she had been having problems for years:

> I had become a closet drinker, hiding my disease from everyone, including myself... All the while, I was going to my MM group, pretending I was the perfect picture of all that Moderation Management stood for... By 1996 [four years before quitting MM], I was drinking seven days a week. I was regularly drinking more than the allowed nine drinks a week or the maximum of three drinks a day for three days during one week.[67]

As a result of all this drinking, sometime in January 2000, an inebriated Kishline called 911. She feared she had seriously poisoned herself with alcohol. The responders took her to an alcohol detox center where she spent three days drying out. Only then, embarrassed and worried that the event might make the news and ruin MM, did Kishline tell the members of her program that she needed to resign. Sixty-five days later she drove drunk and killed two people. The facts are that Kishline was unable to change her ways with the help of AA and she was equally unsuccessful with Moderation Management. As one commentator put it, "she failed sobriety altogether."[68]

On June 29, 2000, Kishline plead guilty to two counts of vehicular homicide. On August 11, 2000, she was sentenced to four and one-half years in prison.[69]

MM Afterwards

In Kishline's absence, MM survived, carried on, and even continued to grow.[70] However, considering all the publicity, good and bad, it has not experienced anything like extraordinary growth.

One significant change at MM seems to be that mention of Audrey Kishline has almost disappeared. MM no longer sells her book, which had reached sales of 50,000. *Moderate Drinking* by Audrey Kishline has apparently been replaced by *Responsible Drinking: A Moderation Management Approach for Problem Drinkers* by Frederick Rotgers, Marc Kern and Rudy Hoeltzel. Of these, only Hoeltzel used MM to resolve a personal drinking problem. Rotgers and Kern are prominent professionals in the addictions field. Kern asserts that he overcame his own alcohol and drug habits before becoming a professional therapist roughly thirty years ago.

A post-Kishline study of MM showed that its members were generally successful and well educated: 81 percent were employed and 72 percent had at least a college education; almost half were female; about one-quarter were under age 35. Perhaps of greatest significance, it found that MM members had experienced significantly fewer alcohol-related problems than had members of other self-help or mutual-aid organizations. Thus it seemed that MM was succeeding in attracting the high-functioning, non-dependent drinker it was designed to serve.[72]

A more recent study conducted by Ana Kosok, who was MM's program director from 2000 to 2005, is posted on MM's website. It tends to support the previous findings with a couple of significant differences. The Kosok study found that the percentage of women in MM may be approximately 66 percent. It also found that MM may be attracting people with a higher level of alcohol dependence than previously thought. Furthermore, it reported that: "MM remains small in absolute numbers"[73] – and that most of its growth was due to members participating online. This study concluded with the following:

> MM continues to attract largely White, middle-class well-educated people who for the most part are mildly to moderately alcohol-dependent, though the degree of dependence may be increasing. Trends suggest that MM continues to be particularly attractive to female problem-drinkers and those who have a preference for participating online. It is an important option for individuals who have not previously sought help and for those seeking guidance as to whether to choose moderation or abstinence. Indications are that a controlled drinking option would be a choice for many if it were more widely available.[74]

HAMS: Reducing the Harm

Kenneth Anderson had what he called a "medium sized" drinking problem – until he joined AA. Then it became a *big* drinking problem. As he tells the story, during his short time in AA following a Twelve Step treatment program, he nearly drank himself to death. "I later learned that ... there are many other people like me who react badly to AA's spiritual program and whose drinking and/or mental health deteriorate severely after they are exposed to AA," he wrote.[75]

Anderson found his solution in the harm reduction approach to addictions. Using its principles, he tells us that he "went from being a homeless guy shaking with alcohol withdrawal in the county detox to leading an online harm reduction discussion group and entering the New School University in New York City to take a master's degree in psychology and substance abuse counseling."[76] HAMS is the harm reduction recovery program that he founded.

HAMS stands for Harm reduction, Abstinence, and Moderation Support. The harm reduction philosophy aims to reduce the negative consequences of drinking and/or drug use. It differs from Moderation Management, which HAMS calls a harm *elimination* program because, theoretically, keeping within the MM limits will eliminate all alcohol-related harm.

HAMS concentrates on problems with alcohol, marijuana, nicotine and caffeine, which it calls "soft" drugs. Primarily, HAMS deals with alcohol; it does not directly deal with "hard" drugs such as heroin, cocaine, methamphetamine, and so forth. The HAMS website contains a referral list of other organizations that address these hard drug problems.

HAMS is a peer support group for anyone who wants to improve his or her drinking habits. A fairly new organization, it has a book by its founder and director, Kenneth Anderson: *How to Change Your Drinking: a Harm Reduction Guide to Alcohol*. It also has a well-developed website (http://hamsnetwork.org). Those who belong to or subscribe to the HAMS organization call themselves "Hamsters."

The HAMS program has seventeen "elements" which are roughly analogous to AA's steps. The elements are optional and no one is required to do all of them or to do them in any particular order. The HAMS seventeen elements, as found in Anderson's book *How to Change Your Drinking,*[77] (with some brief comments or explanations by this author) are:

ELEMENT ONE: *Do a Cost Benefit Analysis (CBA) of your drinking.*
A Cost Benefit Analysis weighs the pros and cons of drinking behavior and the pros and cons of changing that behavior. The HAMS website and book have forms and examples for doing a CBA.

ELEMENT TWO: *Choose a drinking goal – safer drinking, reduced drinking, or quitting.*
Goals can be combined. For example, a pledge never to drive after drinking (safer drinking) can be combined with a goal of reduced drinking. Notice that HAMS also includes the goal of quitting.

ELEMENT THREE: *Learn about risk ranking and rank your risks.*
According to HAMS, "there are two types of risks associated with drinking alcohol – risks associated with the quantity consumed and risks associated with situations and behaviors while drinking."[78] HAMS also recognizes that there is a hierarchy of risks. It is safest to engage only in no-risk drinking or abstinence, but it is most critical to eliminate the drinking and behaviors that have high or extremely high levels of risk. These risks can include death, prison, delirium, cirrhosis, AIDS and other drug use (extremely high risks), along with job loss, divorce, drunk driving arrests, sweats, shakes, and so forth (high risk drinking).

ELEMENT FOUR: *Learn about the HAMS tools and strategies for changing your drinking.*
These tools include easily learned psychological methods and techniques, habit changes such as eating before you drink, control techniques such as charting your drinks and behaviors, and the possible use of medications and dietary supplements.

ELEMENT FIVE: *Make a plan to achieve your drinking goal.*

HAMS recommends that you make this plan in writing. The HAMS book and website provide worksheets and examples.

ELEMENT SIX: *Use alcohol-free time to reset your drinking habits.*

Alcohol-free days can help reset drinking habits to a lower tolerance. HAMS recommends having alcohol free days but it also warns daily drinkers about the risks of withdrawal.[79] It recommends that those who have stayed drunk for several days in a row, gotten drunk every night for a month or more, drank throughout the day for a month or more, and people with a history of alcohol withdrawal symptoms, taper off or seek medical attention.[80] If in doubt about your condition, I strongly recommend seeking medical attention because alcohol withdrawal can be fatal.

ELEMENT SEVEN: *Learn to cope without booze.*

HAMS offers helpful worksheets and other ways of coping with life's problems without resorting to alcohol.

ELEMENT EIGHT: *Address outside issues that affect drinking.*

Outside issues may include such things as mental health, housing, financial difficulties, and so forth. HAMS believes that such problems should be addressed concurrently with alcohol issues. "Although HAMS cannot solve these issues for you since they are beyond our scope," says the HAMS workbook, "you are welcome to discuss outside issues at HAMS any time you wish."[81]

ELEMENT NINE: *Learn to have fun without booze.*

List all the fun things you can think of that do not involve drinking.

ELEMENT TEN: *Learn to believe in yourself.*

HAMS encourages building up your self-confidence.

ELEMENT ELEVEN: *Use a chart to plan and track your drinks and drinking behaviors day by day.*

The HAMS "tool kit" includes a drinking chart and a risk tracking chart. According to HAMS, tracking "is a highly effective tool for behavioral change."[82]

ELEMENT TWELVE: *Evaluate your progress – honestly report struggles – revise plans or goals as needed.*

If what you are doing isn't working, you can change your goal and/or methods at any time.

ELEMENT THIRTEEN: *Practice damage control as needed.*

If you slip or slip up, don't beat yourself up.

ELEMENT FOURTEEN: *Get back on the horse.*

HAMS strongly advocates the old adage: "if at first you don't succeed, try, try again." It is a fact that most efforts to change do not succeed the first time. Success comes with repeated trying.

ELEMENT FIFTEEN: *Graduate from HAMS, stick around, or come back.*

HAMS doesn't tell people that they must remain members for life. You have a choice to "graduate" and move on with your life, to keep working with HAMS to help others after your personal problems appear to be solved, or to come back at any time for a tune-up or to work on a new goal.

ELEMENT SIXTEEN: *Praise yourself for every success!!*

According to HAMS, "you deserve to praise yourself for every positive change."[83]

ELEMENT SEVENTEEN: *Move at your own pace – you don't have to do it all at once.*

In the HAMS program, "everything is optional... Move at a pace that is comfortable for you and keep things doable."[84]

Taking These Roads

If you are thinking of taking any of these roads, there are two important things you need know. The first is that the more serious your alcohol or drug problem, the less chance you have of controlling it.[85] If you're not sure how serious your problem is, you could and should have it professionally evaluated. The second thing to know is that moderate drinking isn't the only alternative to Twelve Step Anonymous programs.

I didn't know either one when I decided to experiment with a return to "social" drinking in the 1980s. My experience was probably typical enough, started good – lasted about a year, and ended bad. But I was laboring under the impression that true moderate drinking should come naturally, so bothersome details like counting drinks weren't part of my plan. I might have done better if I'd have had more knowledge and applied it correctly, but today I'm happier as a virtual teetotaler. That's just me.

If you're thinking about practicing moderation, it makes a big difference whether you're currently drinking or currently sober. To some, that may almost seem as if the sober person is being discriminated against, but the fact is that if you're a drinker and you absolutely don't want to quit, you have nothing to lose by trying to cut down. In fact, anyone who drinks over the recommended limits should try to drink less. But if you're sober and getting your life together, you may be risking a lot. If you're currently sober but just not liking the Twelve Step programs, or whatever else it is that you're doing now, try some other programs or support systems first before you try moderation. Maybe try two or three, OK? That's my advice. There's more to life than drinking alcohol.

If you want help, there are professional therapists who will work with you on a goal of moderation. Two of these programs are Drink/Link, which was started in 1988 by Donna Cornett (http://www.drinklinkmoderation.com/) and the Alcohol Management Program, which was formerly called DrinkWise (http://hr.umich.edu/mhealthy/programs/alcohol/management/).
Both are for-profit organizations. There are also a number of books

from which you could learn the principles of control. One of the best, or at least the most tested, is *Controlling Your Drinking: Tools to Make Moderation Work for You*, by William R. Miller and Ricardo F. Munoz. This work is balanced, clearly laying out the program and its risks in a helpful, nonjudgmental way.

Clapp's ***Square Pegs, The Society of Seven Sinners*** and ***The Association of Drinkwatchers*** are no more, of course, (although an organization called UK Drinkwatchers exists in the United Kingdom).

The ***Transactional Analysis*** approach is still around and still available, although it is not the cultural phenomenon it once was. For those who want to work this as a self-help program, Dr. Steiner has a website (www.claudesteiner.com) where you can download *Healing Alcoholism* for free. There is also a website for the International Transactional Analysis Association (www.itaa-net.org) and the TA Association in the United States (www.usataa.org).

Moderation Management is available on the web (www.moderation.org) and, in certain locations, as live face-to-face meetings. MM's basic text is *Responsible Drinking: A Moderation Management Approach for Problem Drinkers* by Frederick Rotgers, Marc Kern and Rudy Hoeltzel. The mail address for MM is 22 West 27 Street, 5th floor, New York, NY 10001. The email address is MM@moderation.org

Live ***HAMS*** meetings seem to be limited at the present time. There is a meeting in New York City and there may be more in different places as time goes on. The *HAMS* website (http://hamsnetwork.org) has email lists and live chats. The *HAMS* workbook, *How to Change Your Drinking: a Harm Reduction Guide to Alcohol,* by Kenneth Anderson, can be ordered from the website and elsewhere online. The *HAMS* mailing address is: The *HAMS* Harm Reduction Network, Inc., P. O. Box 498, Prince Street Station, New York, NY 10012. The email address is: hams@hamshrn.org. The telephone number is 347-678-5671.

There is another program, described in Chapter V, that allows for moderation goals. It is ***My Way Out (MWO)***, a peer-lead,

Internet-based, self-help program that allows goals of abstinence *and* moderation. There are no face-to-face meetings for this program, only a very active Internet site and discussion lists (http://www.mywayout.org/). The program consists of four parts: 1) anti-addiction prescription medications; 2) hypnosis CDs; 3) vitamin, amino acid and herbal supplements; and 4) light exercise. Chapter IX also describes a program that allows harm reduction as a goal. It is the **Glide Memorial Church** program.

There are two ways of viewing imperfect moderation and harm reduction. One is that if harm is only *reduced*, there is still some harm or damage being done. The other view is that it is better to do something (anything!) than to do nothing and live with a harmful status quo.

Whatever choices you make, may good luck, good fortune and success follow you!

Chapter Endnotes

1. B., Dick (1995) *Design for Living: The Oxford Group's Contribution to Early AA*, San Rafael, CA: Paradise Research Publications, page 102.
2. Clapp, Charles Jr. (1946) writing as "Charly C." (sic) "It Works," *AA Grapevine,* Vol. 2, No. 9, February (downloaded from AAGrapevine.org).
3. Clapp (1946)
4. Miller, William R. (1983) "Controlled Drinking, a History and a Critical Review," *Journal of Studies on Alcohol,* Vol. 44, No. 1, January, pages 68-83.
5. Miller, William R. and Ricardo F. Munoz (2005) *Controlling Your Drinking*: *Tools to Make Moderation Work for You*, New York: The Guilford Press, page 12.
6. Miller and Munoz (2005) page 11-12.
7. Miller and Munoz (2005) page 12.
8. Clapp, Charles, Jr. (1942) *Drunks Are Square Pegs,* New York: Island Press, page 3.

9. Clapp (1942) pages 30-31.
10. Clapp (1946)
11. Clapp (1946)
12. Clapp (1946)
13. Clapp, Charles, Jr. (1949) *Drinking's Not the Problem,* New York: Thomas Y. Crowell Company, page 145.
14. B., Dick (1997) *Turning Point: A History of Early AA's Spiritual Roots and Successes,* San Rafael, CA: Paradise Research Publications, page 150.
15. Cain, Arthur H. (1963) "Alcoholics Anonymous: Cult or Cure?" *Harper's Magazine,* 226:48-54, February.
16. Cain, Arthur H. (September 1964) "Alcoholics Can be Cured – Despite AA" *Saturday Evening Post,* 237:6+, September 19.
17. Cain, Arthur H. (1964) *The Cured Alcoholic: New Concepts in Alcoholism Treatment and Research,* New York: John Day Company, page 179.
18. Cain, Arthur H. (1967) *Paul King's Rebellion,* New York: John Day Company, page 152.
19. For Arthur Cain's biographical information see: Commire, Anne (1972) *Something About the Author,* Vol. 3, Detroit: Gale Research Book Tower, pages 33-34.
20. Cain (1967) pages 162-163.
21. Cain (1967) page 181.
22. Madsen, William (1974) *The American Alcoholic: The Nature-Nurture Controversy in Alcoholic Research and Therapy,* Springfield, IL: Charles C. Thomas Publisher, page 74.
23. Cain (1964) page 189.
24. Cain (1964) page 229.
25. Cain (1964) page 228.
26. Willoughby, Alan (1979) *The Alcoholic Troubled Person: Known and Unknown,* Chicago: Nelson-Hall, page 60.
27. Beauchamp, Dan E. (1980) *Beyond Alcoholism: Alcohol and Public Health Policy*, Philadelphia: Temple University Press, page 89.

28. Miller, William R. and Ricardo F. Munoz (1982) *How to Control Your Drinking* (revised edition), Albuquerque, NM: University of New Mexico Press, page 5
29. Miller and Munoz (2005) page 189.
30. Berne, Eric (1964) *Games People Play: The Psychology of Human Relationships,* New York: Grove Press, Inc., page 73.
31. Berne (1964) page 76.
32. Berne (1964) page 48.
33. Berne (1964) page 74.
34. Berne (1964) page 77.
35. Berne (1964) page 76.
36. Berne (1964) page 77.
37. Berne (1964) page 73.
38. Berne (1964) page 78.
39. Steiner, Claude M.(1969). "The Alcoholic Game," *Quarterly Journal of Studies on Alcohol,* Vol. 30, No. 4, December, pages 920-941.
40. Steiner, Claude M.(1971) *Games Alcoholics Play,* New York: Ballantine Books, pages 83-103.
41. Steiner, Claud M. (1979) *Healing Alcoholism,* New York: Grove Press, Inc., 1979. page 14.
42. Steiner (1979) page 34-35.
43. Steiner (1979) page 36.
44. Steiner (1979) page 35.
45. Steiner (1979) page 33.
46. Steiner (1979) page 35.
47. Steiner, Claud M. (2008) *Healing Alcoholism* (unpublished revision), manuscript privately provided to the author, November. (Available at: http://www.claudesteiner.com/healing.htm)
48. Winters, Ariel (1978) *Alternatives for the Problem Drinker: AA Is Not the Only Way*, New York: Drake Publishers, page 147.
49. Winters (1978) page 146-147

50. Fox, Vincent (1993) *Addiction, Change & Choice: The New View of Alcoholism*, Tucson, AZ: See Sharp Press, pages 86, 105.
51. Winters (1978) page 143.
52. Winters, Ariel (1977) *Drinkwatchers*, Haverstraw, NY: Gullistan Press, page 29.
53. Winters (1977) page 25.
54. Winters (1977) page 26.
55. Winters (1977) page 26-27.
56. Winters (1977) page 28.
57. Miller, William R., personal communication with the author, December 21, 1995.
58. Kishline, Audrey (1994) *Moderate Drinking: The New Option for Problem Drinkers,* Tucson, AZ: See Sharp Press, 1994. page 6.
59. Kishline (1994) page 1.
60. The major network news coverage that I happened to see was the ABC Nightly News.
61. Kishline (1994) page 2.
62. Kishline (1994) page 2.
63. Miller and Munoz (2005) page 32.
64. Kishline, Audrey and Sheryl Maloy (2007) *Face to Face,* Des Moines: Meredith Books, page 51.
65. Kishline and Maloy (2007) page145-146.
66. Peele, Stanton (2000) "After the Crash," *Reason Online,* November. Retrieved 11/27/2013 from: www.reason.com/0011/fe.sp.after.html
67. Kishline and Maloy (2007) page 126.
68. Heckman, Candace (2000) "Arrest trips up 'moderate drinking' crusader's cause," *Seattle Post-Intelligencer*, August 11.
69. Humphreys, Keith (2004) *Circles of Recovery: Self-Help Organizations for Addictions,* Cambridge: Cambridge University Press, page 72.
70. Humphreys (2004) page 72.
71. Humphreys (2004) page 73.

72. Humphreys, Keith. and E. Klaw (2001) "Can targeting non-dependent problem drinkers and providing Internet-based services expand access to assistance for alcohol problems? A study of the Moderation Management self-help/mutual aid organization." *Journal of Studies on Alcohol,* 62, 528-532..
73. Kosok, Ana (2006) "The Moderation Management Programme in 2004: What type of drinker seeks controlled drinking?" *International Journal of Drug Policy,* 17, page 300.
74. Kosok (2006) page 302.
75. Anderson, Kenneth (2010) *How to Change Your Drinking: a Harm Reduction Guide to Alcohol,* New York: The HAMS Harm Reduction Network, page 12.
76. Anderson (2010) page 12.
77. Anderson (2010) page 14.
78. Anderson (2010) page 15.
79. Anderson (2010) page 16.
80. Anderson (2010) pages 56 - 60.
81. Anderson (2010) page 16.
82. Anderson (2010) page 17.
83. Anderson (2010) page 18.
84. Anderson (2010) page 18.
85. Miller and Munoz (2005) page xi.

CHAPTER VIII:
FAITH-BASED RECOVERY:
"BE NOT AMONG WINEBIBBERS"[1]

Fremont Older was managing editor of the *San Francisco Bulletin* and a long-time enemy of W. S. "Sam" Leake, a man who had once been the editor of a rival newspaper named the *San Francisco Call*. Older described his former rival thusly:

As I recall Leake's early life, the habit of drinking came upon him while he was at work on his newspaper, and in a few years alcohol had gained mastery over him to such an extent that he was no longer able at any time to hold full possession of his very unusual qualities, and after he left the paper he went rapidly downward to a point where he was regarded as a hopeless drunkard.[2]

Another observer found Leake's condition to be even worse: "he looked like an old man, stooped, his legs shriveled to poles, his eyes half blind."[3] Then one day Older happened upon Jim Wilkins, an old friend of Leake's. "Jim," he asked, "what has become of Sam Leake? Is he dead?"

"Dead! I should say not." Wilkins exclaimed. "He is very much alive. At this very moment he is in the library reading and looking the picture of health, rosy-cheeked, clear-eyed and erect. Every inch a man."

Older was amazed. He couldn't believe it possible that a man who was in the condition Leake was in the last time he saw him could have recovered so much. "How did it come about?" he asked.

"Christian Science,"* said Wilkins.

"Christian Science!" Older exclaimed. "Is it possible that Leake has been saved through Christian Science?"

"It is not only possible," Wilkins said, "it is true."[4]

---

* Christian Science is not related in any way to Scientology, the religion founded by L. Ron Hubbard and practiced by some Hollywood celebrities such as Tom Cruise.

Sam Leake was but one of thousands upon thousands of alcoholics and drug addicts who have been restored to wholeness by religion. "Make no mistake," Leake said. "The battle was not won by the superb will power (sic) of Sam Leake. I didn't leave drunkenness; drunkenness left me."[5]

Leake revealed little of how his Christian Science practitioner had healed him, but it is known that she told him never to decline a drink when he wanted one. "Leave him alone," she told some friends when they urged her to alter Sam's treatment. "I do not care if he swims home in whiskey every night."[6] She believed that Sam would be healed ... and he was. One morning he awoke with absolutely no desire for alcohol, and he never drank again for the rest of his life.

> Once Sam's healing was accomplished, he set about helping others as his Christian Science practitioner had helped him. For a while he was known as "a one-man Alcoholics Anonymous," but in the long run, little came of it. "What methods he used, whether he formalized them or worked only by his sympathy and intuition, one does not know," said Dwight Anderson, a future Director of Public Relations for the Medical Society of New York. "He did not bother with schemes and statistics; he kept no record of what proportion of his patients remained sober after how many years."[7]

According to Anderson, in less than two decades inquiries about Leake "were fruitless, his name was only a memory in newspaper circles."[8] However, Sam Leake's personal recovery was a huge success. He never touched alcohol again and surely the same could be said for many of the people he had helped.

This chapter will discuss various faith-based recovery programs, most of which have been longer-lived than Sam Leake's. In this context, "faith-based" applies to most western and Mideastern religions, not exclusively to Christianity.*

Jerry McAuley and Gospel Rescue Missions: But for the Grace of God...

Jerry McAuley was a brawler, a thief, a drunkard, a con-man and an inmate at New York State's Sing-Sing prison. He was sent there after being convicted of highway robbery, a crime he swore he did not do. But he had committed enough other crimes in his young life to more than justify his fifteen-year sentence. Nevertheless, he burned with resentment. Although he tried to be a model prisoner, his rage and anger got the best of him.

"I got ugly and thought it was no use," McAuley explained, "and then they punished me. Do you know what that is? It's the leather collar that holds and galls you. You are strapped up by the arms with your toes just touching the floor, and it's the shower bath that leaves you in a dead faint till another dash brings you out. I've stood it all and cursed God while I did."[9]

> Until the morning he heard a familiar voice. In his own words:
>
> It was one Sunday morning. I'd been in prison five years. I dragged myself to the chapel and sat down; then I heard a voice I knew and looked up. There by the chaplain was a man I'd been on a spree with, many and many a time – Orville Gardner. He stepped down off of the platform. "My men," he said, "I've no right anywhere but among you, for I've been one of you in sin," and then he prayed till there wasn't a dry eye there but mine. I was ashamed to be seen

---

* Certain New Thought churches, along with Buddhism and Paganism, will be discussed in Chapter X, New Age Recovery.

crying, but I looked at him and wondered what had come to him to make him so different.[10]

Orville Gardner – a man whose reputation was so terrible that he was known far and wide as "Awful" Gardner – had gotten religion. As Gardner told the prisoners his story, he quoted the Bible and that got McAuley to reading the Good Book – which led him to prayer until, eventually, the Lord revealed Himself. As McAuley described his experience:

> All at once it seemed as if something supernatural was in my room. I was afraid to open my eyes. I was in an agony, and the sweat rolled off my face in great drops. Oh, how I longed for God's mercy! Just then, in the very height of my distress, it seemed as if a hand was laid upon my head, and these words came to me: "My son, thy sins which are many are forgiven." I do not know if I heard a voice, yet the words were distinctly spoken. Oh, the precious Christ! How plainly I saw him lifted on the cross for my sins! What a thrill went through me. I jumped from my knees; I paced up and down my cell. A heavenly light seemed to fill it; a softness and a perfume like the fragrance of sweet flowers. I did not know if I was living or not. I clapped my hands and shouted, "Praise God! Praise God![11]

"And the Lord began to use me in the prison, among my fellow-convicts," McAuley wrote. "A great work was commenced there, and spread from cell to cell. The prisoners began to read their Bibles, to call upon God, and to praise the name of Jesus."[12]

McAuley spent the next two years in prison, contentedly working to save others and certain that the Lord would answer any reasonable prayer. On March 8, 1864, an answer came. After McAuley had served about half his time, the state of New York pardoned him and restored his citizenship.

"[I]t does not seem to me right to turn men out of prison, and make no provision for their future well-doing," McAuley mused. "If I had found a single Christian friend it would have saved me years of misery."[13] As it was, the only friend he could find took him to a lager-bier saloon. Lager-bier, or lager beer as it's written in English, wasn't around when McAuley went to prison and he didn't know what it was. He was told it was a healthy drink, so he drank it – and his old appetite returned. McAuley stayed drunk until well after the Civil War. He went back to a life of crime and almost drowned trying to rob boats out on the river. "God has saved you for the last time," a Voice said to him. "If you ever go out on the river again, God will let you drop into hell and be lost."[14]

At last, a city missionary befriended him and later on he met and married a woman named Maria. She was a former drunk, an ex-prostitute and, according to Jerry's biographer, "his greatest source of strength, aside from God."[15]

In due time McAuley had another spiritual experience, a "sort of a trance or vision," he called it:

> I was singing at my work and my mind became absorbed, and it seemed as if I was working for the Lord down in the Fourth Ward [the meanest section of New York]. I had a house, and people were coming in. There was a bath, and as they came in I washed and cleansed them on the outside and the Lord cleansed them inside. They came at first by small numbers, then by hundreds, and afterwards by thousands.
>
> Before I came out of this vision, I was in tears. Then something said to me, "would you do that for the Lord if he should call you? Would you do it for Jesus' sake?" And I answered, "Yes Lord, open the way and I will go."[16]

"Then," McAuley said, "the Lord opened the way for me to begin the work in a small way at 316 Water Street."[17] The McAuley Water Street Mission in the blighted Fourth Ward of New York City was born. Originally called "A Helping Hand for Men," it was the first gospel rescue mission in the United States and one of the first such enterprises in the world.

Today there are rescue missions in virtually every city of the US and in many foreign countries. The rescue mission treatment method is a simple one. Men (and sometimes women) are lured in with the promise of free food and a place to sleep. Before they are fed, however, they must attend a gospel prayer service where still suffering alcoholics and drug addicts are urged to come forward to give their lives to Christ. The next morning, those who responded to the call are interviewed by mission workers who are themselves recovering alcoholics. If a candidate seems to have a reasonable chance of recovery, the mission becomes his temporary home. He is assigned a bed and a locker, and in some cases he may receive medical aid. The mission helps him to stay straight, find a job and reconcile with his family (if he has one). Afterwards he may affiliate with Christian recovery groups such as Alcoholics Victorious, Alcoholics for Christ or Overcomer's Outreach. As a result of Jerry McAuley's ministry, literally millions of lives have been transformed.[18]

The Salvation Army: "Go See Sally"

"Sally" is what skid row vagrants call the Salvation Army (SA). When those folks are at the end of their meager resources, they ofttimes "go see Sally" for a free meal and a place to sleep. The SA's approach to recovery is similar to the mission programs, but more varied and complex. Comparing the two systems, the inducements of hot food and a cot are about the same and the evening services vary only in certain details. But according to pastoral counselor Howard Clinebell, the Salvation Army's program is different in that "the resources of social work, psychiatry, medicine, and AA have been integrated with their basic evangelicalism."[19]

The Salvation Army was founded in England in 1852 by William Booth. The army motif was present almost from the beginning when the organization was called "The Christian Mission" and Booth held the position of general superintendent. His followers called him "General Booth" and at some point his "volunteer army" became The Salvation Army – and it has been so ever since.

Booth's army has grown into a world-wide organization with outposts in 109 different countries. In the United States, the SA has a presence in every city and many smaller communities. In addition to its rescue work, the Army has a formal alcohol/drug rehabilitation program with both inpatient and outpatient options. Although programs may vary from location to location, a minimum six month commitment is usually required for the long-term residential program.

Today, the Salvation Army works closely with AA and uses its Twelve Steps exactly as they were written by Bill Wilson in 1939. But perhaps this wasn't always so. In the 1940s the SA had steps that were "similar to the 'Twelve Steps' of AA," but only nine in number. These are found in Howard Clinebell's *Understanding and Counseling the Alcoholic,* along with the caveat that "there is a real question as to how widespread the use of these steps are in actual practice."[20] The SA's nine steps are (or were):

1. The alcoholic must realize that he is unable to control his addiction and that his life is completely disorganized.
2. He must acknowledge that only God, his Creator, can recreate him as a decent man.
3. He must let God through Jesus Christ rule his life and resolve to live according to His will.
4. He must realize that alcohol addiction is only a symptom of basic defects in his thinking and living, and that the proper use of every talent he possesses is impaired by his enslavement.

5. He should make public confession to God and man of past wrong-doing and be willing to ask God for guidance in the future.
6. He should make restitution to all whom he has willfully and knowingly wronged.
7. He should realize that he is human and subject to error, and that no advance is made by covering up a mistake; he should admit failure and profit by experience.
8. Since, through prayer and forgiveness, he has found God, he must continue prayerful contact with God and seek constantly to know His will.
9. Because the Salvation Army believes that the personal touch and example are the most vital forces in applying the principles of Christianity, he should be made to work continuously not only for his own salvation but to help effect the salvation of others like himself.[21]

According to Professor Edward McKinley, in modern times the Salvation Army is "the largest and most successful rehabilitation program for transient alcoholic men in the United States."[22]

America's Keswick Colony of Mercy

Born in 1857 to "good Christian parents," William Raws (an Englishman) married at the tender age of 21. "Up to that time I did not know the taste of liquor," he said. Unfortunately, though, his wife did, "although a woman of splendid qualities in other respects;" and this proved to be the rock upon which we made shipwreck of our lives. We owned considerable property, had money in the bank, a well-furnished home, etc., when I first gave way to the curse of strong drink. Oh the misery, the heartache, the wretched experiences and the ruin of the next ten years! I shudder when I think of it…[23]

In an attempt to escape from the evils of drunkenness, Raws left England to come to America; and when nothing good came of that, he "cried unto God" – and God answered him! He heard my cry and saved me. Jesus Christ "was manifested, that he might destroy the work of the devil." For days and nights thereafter I could neither eat nor sleep. I was on the verge of delirium tremens. I had had them before. But peace came at last and victory through our Lord and Savior Jesus Christ.[24]

In a short time, Raws felt called to take up mission work. He opened a mission at the site of the saloon where he used to get drunk and named it "The Whosoever Gospel Mission and Rescue Home." Next he bought 880 acres near Whiting, New Jersey where he founded America's Keswick Colony of Mercy, an enterprise that survives to this day.

On September 18, 1910, William Raws left this life. He was succeeded as head of the Colony by his son, Addison Raws, who was succeeded by his own son, the Rev. William A. Raws.[25]

America's Keswick was named after the village of Keswick in the UK, which is the site of an annual evangelical Christian convention. America's Keswick is not a Twelve Step treatment but a Christ-centered regime of work therapy, Bible study, church services, scripture memorization and pastoral counseling. It requires a 120 day commitment. After leaving the colony, the men are encouraged to find support through recovery programs such as Alcoholics Victorious or other Christian groups. There is also a nonresidential ministry called "Women of Character" for the wives and fiancées of the men.

A First Century Christian Fellowship, The Oxford Group, Moral ReArmament and Initiatives of Change: One Program with Many Names

In the early 1910s, Pennsylvania State College had a reputation as "the most godless university in the country."[26] (And needless to say, not the driest.) The man who supplied the college with its booze was a bootlegger with the unusual name of Bill Pickle. That's right, Pickle. His real name was William Gilliland but he, his wife, and their twelve children were all known as "the Pickles" who lived on "Pickle Hill" (also known as "Heinz Heights").

Into this unpromising environment stepped Franklin N. D. Buchman, a young Lutheran minister at the start of his extraordinary career. He had been hired as the campus's YMCA secretary, with the challenge of moving Penn State "Godwards." Foreshadowing his strategy of concentrating on "key people," Buchman worked first at making friends with Blair Buck, a graduate student who was that era's version of a B.M.O.C. (Big Man On Campus). Buchman's intention was to have Blair help with the conversion of Bill Pickle. Garth Lean, in his *Frank Buchanan: A Life,* told the story:

> Bill Pickle was the illegitimate son of a colonel, and had served in the Civil War as a drummer boy. He sported a "furious walrus moustache", "looked like a roaring pirate" and had been heard to declare that he would like to stick a knife in Buchman's ribs. Buchman was rather nervous about him, and was alarmed when one day Buck pointed him out as they walked the town together, because he knew he must make a move towards him or lose Buck's respect. "I've got a big nose," Buchman related later, "so when I walked up to Bill, I put my hand on his biceps so that if he did haul off, he wouldn't haul so hard["]. The thought flashed through my mind, "Give him your deepest message." "Bill," I said, "we've been praying for you."[27]

Buchman was surprised when Bill Pickle, the man who "looked like a roaring pirate," turned mellow. Instead of "hauling off" on Buchman, tears came to his eyes and he started a conversation: "See that church over there?" Pickle said, "I was there when the cornerstone was laid. There's a penny of mine under it."[28] And the two became friends.

A few months later, Buchman and Blair Buck talked (and bribed) Bill Pickle into going with them to a meeting in Toronto.

Believe it or not, while there Pickle decided to become a Christian. He completely stopped drinking and bootlegging – and the change was permanent.

Without a handy bootlegger to supply its liquor, the school's alcohol consumption declined and sobriety began to spread. One of the converts was "Pop" Golden, Penn State's grizzled football coach. "[F]or whatever reason," Garth Lean reported, "the football team won 26 games and lost only two in the four years after his change."[29]

The Bill Pickle episode was the first of Buchman's successes at rescuing drunks and it would certainly not be his last. Explained Linda Mercadante, author of *Victims and Sinners: Spiritual Roots of Addiction and Recovery:* "Although the Oxford Group looked at a panoply [variety] of problem behaviors, compulsive drinking was an issue they tackled frequently."[30]

Early on, Buchman gave up a conventional minister's career in order to found A First Century Christian Fellowship, which soon became the Oxford Group (OG). The OG became Moral Re-Armament (MRA) in the 1930s and endured as such until 2001, when the name was changed again to Initiatives of Change (IofC). Under all these names, but especially as the Oxford Group, the movement maintained a nonexclusive interest in rescuing men and women who had been lost to alcoholism.

As we saw in Chapter II, the Oxford Group was the forerunner of AA, and the OG program contains many elements that are also found in Alcoholics Anonymous. However, the Oxford Group had other practices that have been dropped, ignored, watered down or forgotten by the Twelve Step Movement. According to James Houck, a *very long time sober* OG member who lived to be 100 years old, "Frank [Buchman] incorporated three key elements into the Oxford Group program. They were the Four Standards [or 'Four Absolutes'] of Honesty, Purity, Unselfishness and Love; the concept of two-way prayer; and the use of restitution to change lives."[31] Some observers, including Wally Paton, author of *How to Listen to God,* believe that the Oxford Group used a four-step program of surrender, sharing, restitution and guidance. Referencing *What is the*

Oxford Group?– a book written anonymously by "A Layman With a Notebook," Paton described the four "steps" as:

> STEP 1. **Surrender** our life, past, present and future, into God's care and direction.
>
> STEP 2. **Sharing** with God and another person the characteristics of self, which have separated us from our creator.
>
> STEP 3. Make **Restitution** to all whom we have wronged, directly or indirectly.
>
> STEP 4. Listen to, and accept and rely on God's **Guidance** and carry it out in everything we think, say or do, great or small.[32]

Guidance is unquestionably one of the most important items in the OG's toolbox. The Oxford Groupers sought guidance from God during what they called "quiet time" or "two way prayer." About this, James Houck said:

> The idea is to set aside time every morning to receive guidance from God. Most people know how to pray, but very few know how to listen. Just as we pray to God through our minds, God talks to us through our minds. The key to the whole process is to get quiet, write down what you hear and share what you've written with another person.[33]

The "Five C's of Life Changing": *Confidence, Confession, Conviction, Conversion* and *Continuance* were another important tool used by the OG. Garth Lean, Buchman's main biographer, explained the origin of the "Five C's":

> While on [a] ship… en route for China, a Miss Constance Smith asked Buchman one evening how

he helped individuals. Next day, he answered her with a rough formula which he called 'the five Cs' - *Confidence, Confession, Conviction, Conversion,* [and] *Continuance*... Nothing could be done until the other person had *confidence* in you, and knew that you would keep confidences. *Confession* – honesty about the real state of the person's life – would lead to a *conviction* of the seriousness of sin and the desire to be freed from its control. For *conversion* to take place there must be a free decision of the will – often cold-blooded, seldom emotional. But [by] far the longest and most neglected part was *continuance.* You were responsible for helping the newly orientated person to become increasingly the person God meant him or her to be.[34] [emphases added]

Frank Buchman's contribution to religion was immense, but his contribution to self-help psychology may have equaled it. Howard Clinebell described Buchman as one of the foremost pioneers of the modern self-help or mutual-assistance philosophy.[35] Minister and author T. Willard Hunter reported that: "Buchman, as much as anyone, broke people out of the assumption that problem persons had to go to a professional. He demonstrated that they might get more help from other persons with the same problem."[36] And Paul Tournier, a pioneer of person-centered psychotherapy, said this: "The whole development of group therapy in medicine cannot all be traced back to Frank, but he historically personified that new beginning..."[37]

In plain words, nearly all of the mutual-help and self-help programs found in this book –as well as many other such groups and programs worldwide– owe a debt of gratitude to the founder of the Oxford Group. And Buchmanism, as it is sometimes called, continues to influence people through the latest reincarnation of its program, *Initiatives of Change*, which is headquartered in Caux, Switzerland.

The Venerable Matt Talbot: Patron of Alcoholics and Addicts

By the time Matt Talbot reached his twenty-eighth birthday, he had lived half his life as a hopeless drunk. Friends who knew him when he was young said that back then "he wanted only one thing – the drink."[38] And according to Morgan Costello, one of Talbot's many biographers: "For ten years his life was 'one long soak.'"[39]

Talbot was born May 2, 1856 in Dublin, Ireland. He was the second child of a large family who lived in poverty because of their father's alcoholism. As a child, Matt had only a couple of years of sporadic schooling before going to work at the age of twelve. His job was messenger boy for a wine merchant and beer bottling firm and, unfortunately, he took the opportunity to sample the wares as often as he could.

Although Matt was a chronic alcoholic, he quit drinking abruptly one Saturday in 1884 when his friends disappointed him during a hard weekend. He had not worked the previous week so he had no paycheck that day, but he was certain that his friends would help him get through it. He waited for hours outside of O'Meara's pub, but not a single friend offered to buy him a drink. Talbot, who was generous to a fault when he had money, said that this experience cut him "to the heart."

He gave it up, returned home sober, and told his mother he was going to take a pledge to quit drinking. "Go in God's name," his mother said, "but don't take it unless you are going to keep it."[40] He kept it. The first time he signed a pledge for three months, then for longer periods, and finally he took the pledge for life. All told, he kept the pledge for 41 years, until the day of his death in 1925.

He didn't find it easy. Everywhere he went he ran into drinking establishments and old drinking companions. The only place he felt safe was in a church; and one day he wasn't safe even there. On that day Matt went to receive Holy Communion and found himself stuck to the floor! He couldn't move and a voice in his head kept saying: "It's no use, you'll never give up drink. You'll always be a drunkard." He tried another church and then another with the same results. Finally he fell to his knees and called for help. "Jesus mercy, Mary help," he cried; over and over, "Jesus mercy, Mary help!" And They heard him. He arose, took communion and was never bothered again by such strange happenings.[41]

Talbot's sober life came to be grounded in numerous religious exercises such as prayer, meditation, spiritual reading, fasting, mortification, restitution and alms giving. It is said that he modeled his life after sixth and seventh century Irish monks, whose lives have been summed up as: "pray daily, fast daily, study daily, work daily." One of the priests who counseled Matt called him "the holiest man in Dublin whose prayers are always answered."[42]

Much has been made of the similarities between Talbot's method for quitting drink and the Twelve Steps of AA. Indeed, there are some clear parallels such as prayer, meditation, and making amends. However, a lawyer by the name of Philip Maynard studied Matt Talbot's life and found there a program that is intended to be used, not with, but *instead of* AA's recovery model.

Maynard himself is a recovered alcoholic who happens to disagree with the Twelve Steps. Specifically, his sticking point was Step One,* admitting he was "powerless over alcohol." As Maynard described his plight:

> I tried Alcoholics Anonymous several times. Although I was amazed and often moved by the stories members told of their past drinking and how AA was able to help them stop, I could never bring myself to accept the idea that I was powerless over alcohol, at least not in any permanent sense.

---

* AA's Step One reads: *"We admitted we were* powerless *over alcohol – that our lives had become unmanageable."* [emphasis added]

> I was willing to accept my powerlessness while I continued to drink, but I was determined that if I was going to give it up, my powerlessness would end with it... AA's motto of "One day at a time" may have worked wonders with others, but if I was going to quit, I would quit for good.[43]

Furthermore, Maynard alleges that:

> For all its remarkable successes, Alcoholics Anonymous has only scratched the surface of the problem of alcoholism. At best, less than one of every fifteen alcoholics attend its meetings. And if you include "problem drinkers," less than one in twenty five... For some of those left untouched by AA... the Way to Sobriety inspired by the example of Matt Talbot may be the only approach that works.[44]

Upon Talbot's death, it was discovered that he had taken to wearing heavy cords and chains wrapped about his legs and body. This was part of a spiritual discipline called "Slavery to Mary," whose purpose is to become closer to Christ through devotion to His mother Mary. Slavery to Mary calls for a "little chain" to be worn as "a *symbol* of having 'voluntarily surrendered oneself to the glorious slavery of Jesus Christ.'" Says Philip Maynard: "In his usual fashion of not going easy at anything... Matt chose to interpret this literally and in a penitential way."[45]

Concerning the asceticism involved in this practice, Philip Maynard says: "In assessing [Talbot's] extraordinary penances and how today they might fit in with the Matt Talbot Way to Sobriety, we find that they really do not fit at all." Maynard points out that such practices have been out of favor and even forbidden by the Catholic Church for some time.[46]

Philip Maynard's alternative program follows the example set by Matt Talbot, but leaves out the austerities and mortifications. It's a seven-step recovery program that he calls "The Matt Talbot Way"

– and every one of the Seven Steps is intended to be used and practiced every day. The essence of the Matt Talbot Way is to increase your love of Jesus Christ to the point where you voluntarily and happily make an offering to Him of whatever pleasures you were experiencing from your addiction.

The first step of the Matt Talbot Way is the *Daily Offering,* which is a morning prayer expressing your love of Christ. Once your love is sufficient to overcome your addiction problem, you can make a daily offering to Christ by your decision to forego the pleasures of alcohol, drugs, or other addictions. For this offering, Maynard suggests a prescribed prayer beginning with "Heavenly Father, being mindful of the heroic example of your servant Matt Talbot, I offer you during this day myself… and in particular, the worldly pleasures and delights of alcohol [and/or drugs, etc.] which I forego, as an expression of love for your son, Jesus Christ…"[47]

The next step is *Christ Centered Prayer.* For this prayer, Maynard recommends the "Jesus Prayer" (also known as the "Prayer of the Publican" and/or the "Sinner's Prayer"): "Lord Jesus Christ, Son of God, have mercy on me, a sinner." Maynard instructs that you should say it slowly and from the heart, one hundred or more times each day.

The third step of the Matt Talbot Way is *Dedication of Prayers of the Day.* Maynard offers a prescribed prayer for this step also. It begins "O Holy Spirit, may I receive Jesus Christ into my heart through you…" etc. Says Maynard: "You don't ask God to keep you from drinking or even for the virtue of temperance; rather, you pray solely that your love for him may increase – particularly for the person of Jesus Christ."[48]

The next step is *Spiritual Reading.* Maynard says that "Ten or fifteen minutes a day should be spent in spiritual reading with an emphasis on the Bible, particularly the New Testament."[49]

The fifth step is saying *Short Prayers During the Day.* Maynard says that an example of this may be saying grace before dinner. He also recommends the Jesus Prayer, and for Catholics he recommends prayers such as the Rosary and other specifically Catholic devotions.

Next in order is the *Evening Prayer.* Although Maynard offers an example of an "excellent evening prayer," he states that each person has complete freedom to select a prayer or prayers of his or her choice. "This is a good time," he says, "to rededicate all of the day's prayers to your primary objective of growing in love for Jesus Christ."[50]

The final step of the Matt Talbot Way is Step Seven: *Christian Living.* "You are not expected to be perfect," Maynard says, "but you must at least dispose yourself to trying to lead a Christian life."[51] In addition to conquering drug and alcohol addictions, Philip Maynard suggests that the Matt Talbot Way can be used for other troubles such as quitting cigarettes and losing weight.

Another exciting use of the saintly example set by Matt Talbot is found in the *Matt Talbot Retreat Movement.* The Movement was founded in 1943 by a small number of recovering alcoholics. Its purpose is to assist alcoholics with their spiritual aspirations by placing special emphasis on AA's Fourth, Fifth and Eleventh Steps. These are the steps calling for moral inventory, confession of wrongdoing, and practicing prayer and meditation. All these steps were taken by Matt Talbot, especially Step Eleven: "Sought through prayer and meditation to improve our conscious contact with God AS WE UNDERSTOOD HIM, praying only for knowledge of His will for us and the power to carry that out." Contrary to the advice given by Philip Maynard, the Retreat Movement encourages its members to ask Matt Talbot to intercede or pray on their behalf. The effectiveness of Talbot's intercessions has been shown by the many favors that have been reported by Matt Talbot devotees from around the world.

The Calix Society: "Replacing the Cup that Stupefies with the Cup that Sanctifies"

In 1947 five recovering alcoholics in Minneapolis were meeting regularly for mutual support and prayer. With the help of a priest, that informal prayer meeting grew into the Calix Society, an

"Eleventh Step" program for Catholics involved in Alcoholics Anonymous. Calix does not regard itself as an alternative to AA. It describes itself as an extension of the Twelve Step program whose purpose is to help Catholics practice AA's Eleventh Step, the step of prayer and meditation.

Calix is Latin for chalice or cup. The motto of the organization is "Sobriety through AA—Sanctity through Calix."[52] According to THE CALIX CREDO, the Society has three main goals:

> Our first concern is to interest Catholics with an alcohol problem in the VIRTUE of total abstinence. Our second stated purpose is to promote the spiritual development of our membership... [and] our third objective...[is] to strive for the sanctification of the whole personality of each member.[53]

The CREDO also states that: "We welcome other alcoholics, not members of our Faith, or any others, non-alcoholics, who are concerned with the illness of alcoholism and wish to join with us in prayer for our stated purpose."[54] Most Calix groups hold monthly meetings featuring mass, a prayer breakfast and a speaker.

Alcoholics Victorious: We Are Free in Christ

Jerry Dunn found Jesus Christ in 1948. He was serving time in a Texas prison when he started reading a Gideon Bible. *"The thief cometh not, but for to steal, to kill and to destroy,"* he read. *"I am come that they might have life, and that they might have it more abundantly."*[55] "That broke me," Dunn confessed. "[I]f that's what You've got for me, that's what I want," he told God.[56] And there and then Jerry Dunn made his commitment to Christ. It was a decision that would change Jerry's life and alter the destiny of Alcoholics Victorious (AV).

AV was founded in 1948, the same year that Jerry Dunn accepted Jesus as his Savior, but Dunn was not the founder. It was founded by William Seath, director of the Chicago Christian Industrial League.[57] Seath was an admirer of Alcoholics Anonymous but felt that the power of the program could be greatly increased by naming Jesus Christ as the Higher Power.

Originally, the AV program was intended to serve just the 80 to 85 men in Seath's Chicago mission. But as others heard of the program, they too wanted to start AV chapters. Alcoholics Victorious continued to grow until about 1955, but after that it declined to almost nothing. Then in 1965, Jerry Dunn wrote *God Is for the Alcoholic,* an all-time best selling Christian recovery book and a book that endorsed Alcoholics Victorious. As a result of Dunn's recommendation, the AV program began to prosper again and it remains so today.

Not only did Jerry Dunn save Alcoholics Victorious, Alcoholics Victorious continued to save Jerry Dunn. He remained active in AV for the rest of his life, leading one observer to say that "Jerry Dunn's life *is Alcoholics Victorious.*"[58] [emphasis added]

For most of its existence, Alcoholics Victorious has used the Twelve Steps of AA correlated with Biblical passages, but in the 1970s or thereabouts, AV apparently used a seven step program. AV's "Seven Steps to Victory for the Alcoholic" are found in *How to Live with an Alcoholic and Win* by Jim and Cyndy Hunt. These seven steps are:

1. I know that I cannot overcome alcohol dependency by myself. I believe that the healing power of Jesus Christ is available to help me. (Correlates with Romans 3:23)
2. I believe that through my acceptance of Jesus Christ as my Savior and Lord, I will become a new person. (Correlates with II Corinthians 5:17)
3. I pray this prayer of commitment:
   Dear Lord Jesus: I know that I am a lost sinner and need forgiveness. I believe that you died for my sins. I want to turn from my sins. I invite you to come into my heart and life. I want to trust you as my Savior and follow you as Lord.

Deliver me, Lord Jesus, from this addiction and heal my mind. Thank you Jesus. Amen. (Psalms 51; I John 1:9)
4. I recognize my need for daily prayer and Bible study as the only guide for victorious Christian living. (I Thessalonians 5:17; II Timothy 2:15)
5. I will seek the Will of God and the Power of the Holy Spirit through daily prayer and scripture readings. (Acts 1:18; II Peter 1:3)
6. I will seek the fellowship of other Christian believers and worship God through the Church of my choice; I will begin to praise and thank God in ALL circumstances of my life. (Hebrews 10:25; I Thessalonians 5:18)
7. As a disciple of Christ, I will proclaim the Gospel to all men and through His strength, help others to victory. (Mark 16:15; Isaiah 40:31)[59]

Another very important part of the AV program is the Alcoholics Victorious Creed. Its five statements are all rooted in 2 Corinthians 5:17: *"Therefore if any man be in Christ, he is a new creature: old things are passed away; behold, all things are become new."* The five statements of the AV creed are:

1. I realize I cannot overcome the drink habit by myself. I believe that the power of Jesus Christ is available to help me. I believe that through my acceptance of Him as my Savior, I am a new man [or woman].
2. Because the presence of God is manifested through continued prayer, I will set aside two periods every day, morning and evening, for communion with my Heavenly Father. I realize my need for daily Bible reading and use it as a guide for my daily living.
3. I recognize my need for Christian fellowship and will, therefore, have fellowship with Christians through the church of my choice. I know that in order to be victorious, I must keep active in the service of Christ and his church and I will help others to victory.

4. I do not partake of any beverage containing alcohol. I know it is the first drink that does the harm. Therefore, "I do not drink."
5. I can be victorious because I know that God's strength is sufficient to supply all my needs.[60]

In addition to the boost it got from Jerry Dunn's 1965 book, AV got another shot in the arm in 1974 when Jim and Cyndy Hunt founded a Minneapolis chapter and began to actively promote the AV program. Today, there are Alcoholics Victorious meetings in more than one third of the states in the US.[61]

Alcoholics for Christ

According to the *Alcoholics for Christ* (A/C) website: "AC is an inter-denominational, non-profit, Christian fellowship that ministers to three groups: Alcoholics or Substance abusers, Family members – those who relate regularly with an alcoholic or substance abuser, and Adult Children – individuals who were raised in alcoholic, substance abuse (sic) or dysfunctional families."[62]

A/C got its start in 1976 when a born-again recovering alcoholic organized a slightly different sort of retreat for AA men. The difference was that all of the retreat's leaders were born-again Christians. It was regarded as a miracle when, by the end of the retreat, nearly all of the attendees had made a commitment to Jesus Christ. Then in February of the next year, "another men's retreat was organized and it too had the same miraculous results."[63]

Alcoholics for Christ uses the Twelve Steps with some significant modifications that make them explicitly Christian. For example, the A/C's second step reads: "Came to believe that through Jesus Christ we could be restored to right relationship with God the Father, and subsequent sanity and stability in our lives."*[64]

---

* AA's second step: *"Came to believe that a Power greater than ourselves could restore us to sanity."*

"Overcomers "Recovery Groups

There are at least three faith-based recovery programs that use the word "Overcomers" as part of their name. They are: Overcomers Outreach, the Overcomers Recovery Support Program, and Overcomers In Christ. Although the names are similar, these programs are independent of one another.

According to William L. White, *Overcomers Outreach* (O.O.) was founded in 1977.[65] The founders were Bob and Pauline Bartusch. The program's slogan is: "Bridging the gap between 12 Step groups and churches of all denominations."[66]

The O.O. Preamble, which is said to be "the very heart of each Overcomers Group," declares that O.O. members "strongly believe that our 'Higher Power' is Jesus Christ, our Savior and Lord." The Preamble also lists O.O.'s five-part mission:

Our five-fold purpose, based directly upon the Word of God is set forth as follows:

(1) To provide fellowship in recovery; (2) To be and live reconciled to God and His family; (3) To gain a better understanding of alcohol and mood-altering chemicals; (4) To be built up and strengthened in our faith in Christ; (5) To render dedicated service to others who are suffering as we once were.[67]

To organize this, O.O. uses the acronym F.R.E.E.D., which stands for: Fellowship; Reconciliation to God and His family; Education about chemicals and addiction; Edification through faith in Christ; and Dedicated service to others.[68] The Preamble goes on to say that: "We practice the suggested recovery program of Alcoholics Anonymous, Al-Anon, and other 12-Step groups because we believe these to be the practical application of these life-changing principles which are so clearly set forth in the Scriptures."[69]

The *Overcomers Recovery Support Program*, the second of the three "Overcomer" programs, was founded in 1985 by Charles and Sharon Burton. It is a Twelve Step program that addresses the problems of alcoholism, drug addiction, gambling, sexual addiction, pornography, eating disorders and the cycle of criminal behaviors. In 2000, the Burtons wrote and published *A Daily Choice:*

Overcoming Life-Controlling Problems, which is a workbook outlining a 90-day plan to enhance self-respect and teach members how to make better decisions for an addiction free life. In addition to completing the workbook, when and wherever possible members are encouraged to attend weekly Overcomers Recovery Support Program meetings.

"The Twelve Steps of the Overcomers Program" are worded somewhat differently from the Twelve Steps of AA, but they are much the same in essence. For example, the Overcomers Recovery Support Group's first step reads: "I admit that I am powerless over the problem controlling my life"[70] (as opposed to *"powerless over alcohol"*).

The third and final "Overcomers" recovery program – *Overcomers In Christ* or *OIC* – celebrated its twenty-fifth anniversary in 2012. The founders were Bill and Mary Fear and the surviving founder, Mary Fear, still heads the organization. According to the *OIC* website, "Overcomers In Christ is a nondenominational, faith-based ministry that empowers people to walk daily in victory."[71] Instead of the ubiquitous Twelve Steps, the *OIC* program uses *Twelve Goals*.

The Twelve Goals of the Overcomers In Christ program are:

1. We face the truth knowing that **Truth** forms our lifeline to recovery.
2. We choose a positive **Attitude** because attitudes lead to action.
3. We practice Christ-honoring habits one day at a time to build our **Health**.
4. We find freedom to determine our destiny by making wise **Decisions**.
5. We put our **Faith** in Jesus Christ who is the source of inner peace.
6. We forgive others as we experience and appreciate God's **Forgiveness**.
7. We **Surrender** our will to discover God's plan for our lives.

8. We make time for daily **Devotions** so God can transform our lives.
9. We maintain **Fellowship** with the Lord and those friends who support our recovery.
10. We keep a personal **Inventory** and allow the Lord to remove our defects.
11. We transfer our dependency to God to claim the **Victory** that is ours in Christ.
12. We gratefully **Outreach** by sharing the message of victory in Christ.[72]

JACS: Jewish Alcoholics, Chemically dependent persons and Significant others

"Oy oy oy, shikker is a goy." A drunk is a non-Jew; therefore, if someone is a drunkard, he or she must be a Gentile. Everybody knows that, right? Jews just don't have alcohol or drug problems.

Not so. Jewish alcoholics, Jewish addicts, and Jewish communities have been poorly served by the myths of genetic or cultural immunity. Jews have been told that they would not be alcoholics if they were better Jews – and some Jewish addicts have been asked if they're sure they are Jewish. (One insensitive rabbi is reported to have put it this way: "Are you sure you know who your mother [or your father] is"?!)[73]

Contrary to myth, however, alcoholism and drug addiction are a reality for Jews. As pioneer alcoholism and addiction specialist Sheila Bloom put it:

> There have been Jewish alcoholics (and addicts) right along. Addictions in the Jewish community have been there all the while. Whether there are more of them or less of them is less important than the recognition that it is there, and getting prevention and treatment to the community.[74]

On the other hand, addicted Jews have also had difficulties with Twelve Step programs. These include going to meetings in Christian church basements, reciting the Lord's Prayer, and getting down on one's knees for the Seventh Step prayer[*] and other such occasions – as some old-time sponsors are apt to suggest. While credible arguments reveal that none of these practices are forbidden by Jewish law, they still make many Jews uncomfortable.

However, from its founding in 1979, Jewish Alcoholics, Chemically dependent persons and Significant others (JACS) was never meant to be a substitute for Twelve Step meetings. It's a supplemental program that allows Jewish alcoholics, addicts, and their families to meet together as Jews who are also members of AA, NA, Al-anon and other such groups. As Rabbi Malcolm Stern wrote:

> JACS is no substitute for AA and the other agencies. It came into being to offer a Jewish component to treatment: to provide recovering Jewish addicts opportunities to gather under Jewish auspices, to offer insights from Jewish tradition, and to provide intellectual and spiritual support.[75]

Virtually from the beginning, JACS has had a three-fold mission:

1. To encourage and assist Jewish alcoholics, chemically dependent persons and their families, friends and associates to explore recovery in a nurturing Jewish environment;
2. To promote knowledge and understanding of the disease of alcoholism and chemical dependency as it involves the Jewish community; and

---

[*] Seventh Step: *"Humbly asked Him to remove our shortcomings."* Original wording: *"Humbly,* on our knees, *asked Him to remove our shortcomings – holding nothing back."* [emphasis added]

3. To act as a resource center and information clearinghouse on the effects of alcoholism and drug dependency on Jewish family life.[76]

Retreats are another important JACS function. There are semi-annual week-end retreats and more that 400 periodic, all-day retreats.[77] Furthermore, JACS founders Audrey Waxman and David Buchholz say this: "Through JACS, there are more than 500 rabbis across the country who have received an education about addiction and recovery."[78] Quite an accomplishment. Additionally, JACS sponsors about four alcohol-free Jewish holidays each year. These celebrations include "Sober Purim Parties" and "Recovery Seders."* To sum up, an anonymous posting at www.williamwhitepapers.com informs us that:

> For more than three decades, JACS has directly assisted thousands of alcoholic and chemically addicted Jews and [their] families and reached tens of thousands more through publications, community presentations and the media. JACS has also provided leadership to the Jewish recovery movement and fostered the development of dozens of independent JACS groups nationally and internationally.[79]

Celebrate Recovery®

John Baker was a successful businessman – a wunderkind, actually, a person who achieves great success while still relatively young. He boasted that he had "reached all my life's career and financial objectives and goals by the time I was thirty!"[80]

---

* *Purim* is a Jewish holiday based on the Book of Esther. It is celebrated in part by drinking until one cannot tell the difference between "cursed be Haman" (the villain) and blessed be Mordecai" (a hero). Most Jews do not take this literally. A *Seder* is a meal that is held in the home during Passover. The meal includes wine and special foods.

But he was also an alcoholic – "a functioning alcoholic," according to him. But functional or dysfunctional, he awoke one morning *knowing* that he could never take another drink. He joined AA and put his whole self into it. He actually went to *more* than ninety meetings in ninety days.

When John Baker was a boy of thirteen, he asked Jesus Christ to come into his heart, but obviously he had done some backsliding in the years since then. In the meanwhile his estranged wife Cheryl had joined the Saddleback Valley Community Church, a mega-church in Southern California. One Sunday his kids asked him to take them to church at Saddleback and he said yes. He hadn't been to church for five years. "I heard the music and Pastor Rick Warren's message and I knew I was home," he said.[81]

> However, there were problems. At church, his men's group didn't want to discuss his addiction issues. When he raised the topic they responded with: "How about those Dodgers?" or something like that. And when he went to AA meetings he was mocked if he told them that Jesus Christ is his Higher Power. He couldn't find a safe place to share. So he wrote to Rick Warren, the senior pastor at Saddleback. He sent Warren a "short and concise" thirteen page, single spaced letter explaining his vision for a Christ-centered and Bible-based recovery program. "Great John, you do it," was Pastor Rick's reply.

That was over twenty years ago and John Baker is now an associate minister at Saddleback. Since then over 17,000 people have completed the Celebrate Recovery (CR) program, and the mega-church has been able to start the program at over 10,000 other churches where over half a million individuals have completed it.[82] CR also has a ministry for prisoners serving both long- and short-term sentences.

Celebrate Recovery uses a "big tent" philosophy. It addresses a wide variety of "habits, hurts and hang-ups." According to CR:

"Examples include dependency on alcohol or drugs, pornography, low self-esteem, need to control, anger, co-dependency, depression, fear of rejection, fear of abandonment, perfectionism, broken relationships, and abuse."[83]

Like numerous other Christian recovery programs, CR uses the Twelve Steps paired with appropriate verses from the Bible. It also uses Eight Principles, which are based on the Beatitudes (the verses from Christ's "Sermon on the Mount" that usually begin with "Blessed [or Happy] are the meek…" etc.). CR's Eight Principles, along with their corresponding Beatitudes, are:

1. **R**ealize I'm not God. I admit that I am powerless to control my tendency to do the wrong thing and that my life is unmanageable.
   Happy are those who know they are spiritually poor." *(Matthew 5:3)*
2. **E**arnestly believe that God exists, that I matter to him, and that He has the power to help me recover.
   "Happy are those who mourn, for they shall be comforted." (Matthew 5:4)
3. **C**onsciously choose to commit all my life and will to Christ's care and control.
   "Happy are the meek." (Matthew 5:5)
4. **O**penly examine and confess my faults to myself, to God, and to someone I trust.
   "Happy are the pure in heart." (Matthew 5:8)
5. **V**oluntarily submit to every change God wants to make in my life and humbly ask Him to remove my character defects.
   "Happy are those whose greatest desire is to do what God requires." (Matthew 5:6)
6. **E**valuate all my relationships. Offer forgiveness to those who have hurt me and make amends for harm I've done to others, except when to do so would harm them or others.
   "Happy are the merciful." (Matthew 5:7)
   "Happy are the peacemakers." (Matthew 5:9)

7. **R**eserve a daily time with God for self-examination, Bible reading, and prayer in order to know God and His will for my life and to gain the power to follow His will."
8. **Y**ield myself to God to be used to bring this Good News to others, both by my example and by my words.
"Happy are those who are persecuted because they do what God requires." (Matthew 5:10)[84]

Notice that the first letter of each Principle spell the word "RECOVERY." CR uses a lot of these *acrostics*. For example, the letters of the word HOPE stand for: **H**igher Power, **O**penness to change, **P**ower to change, and **E**xpect to change.[85]

Another virtually unique feature of Celebrate Recovery is its refusal to allow coeducational meetings. CR has a list of "things we are" and a list of "things we are NOT." Among the "things we are": "A safe place to share." And among the "things we are NOT": "A place to look for dating relationships."[86]

LDS Recovery: The Mormon Way

How does the Church of Jesus Christ of Latter Day Saints (LDS or Mormon) view addiction? Is it possible that they view it with a degree of insight and understanding? The first page of their *Guide to Addiction Recovery and Healing* hints at it.

> Many of us began our addictions out of curiosity. Some of us became involved because of a justifiable need for a prescription drug or as an act of deliberate rebellion... Whatever our motive for starting and our circumstances, we soon discovered that the addiction relieved more than just physical pain. It provided stimulation or numbed painful feelings or moods. It helped us avoid the problems we faced – or so we thought. For a while, we felt free of fear, worry, loneliness, discouragement, regret, or boredom. But

because life is full of the conditions that prompt these kinds of feelings, we resorted to our addictions more and more often. Still, most of us failed to recognize or admit that we had lost the ability to resist and abstain on our own.[87]

In creating its Addiction Recovery Program or ARP in 1985, LDS Family Services took the Twelve Steps of AA and "Mormonized" them. A good example of this is their version of Step Five: "Admit to yourself, to your Heavenly Father in the name of Jesus Christ, to proper priesthood authority, and to another person the exact nature of your wrongs."*[88]

Although the ARP's steps are based on Mormon doctrine and the Book of Mormon as well as the Bible, meetings are open to anyone. Merlin O. Baker, a Mormon missionary who wrote a book titled *Understanding Alcohol and Drug Addiction,* says this: "Addicts do not come to an LDS 12-step meeting because it is a Church meeting... They come because it is a 'good' 12-step meeting, and they are familiar with the format." Furthermore, he adds: "Many come because it is their last hope. They may have gone through four or more rehabilitation programs, but yet they are still addicted to alcohol or drugs." Another primary purpose of the LDS Addiction Recovery Program is to help addicts who have been disfellowshipped or excommunicated from the Mormon church.[89]

Millati Islami

Millati Islami (MI) actually means "path of peace." MI was founded in 1989 at Baltimore, Maryland. It remained a local effort until 1992 when a Muslim AA group in Washington, DC adopted the Baltimore group's Steps and Traditions. From there it grew into

---

* AA's version of Step Five: *"Admitted to God, to ourselves, and to another human being the exact nature of our wrongs."*

a national recovery program with as many as 42 groups meeting in sixteen states.⁹⁰ According to the MI website:

> "We have sought to integrate the treatment requirements of both Al-Islam and the Twelve Step approach to recovery into a simultaneous program… Just as Narcotics Anonymous was founded out of its need to be non-specific with regard to substance, so Millati Islami was born out of our need to be religiously specific with regard to spiritual principles."⁹¹

Millati Islami's Steps and Traditions keep the familiar "twelve by twelve" essence of AA but they also depart from AA's usual orthodoxy in some significant ways. Millati Islami members do not do things "one day at a time." Instead they recover from *Salaat* to *Salaat* (from prayer to prayer).⁹² Other interesting variations are that MI members do not take the Fifth Step with another person, and the MI Traditions make no mention of anonymity.

The Millati Islami steps that make the most meaningful departures from the usual Twelve Steps are steps 1, 5, 11, and 12. Compared with the Twelve Steps of AA (with significant differences marked by *italics*) these are:

ALCOHOLICS ANONYMOUS	MILLATI ISLAMI
1) We admitted we were *powerless over alcohol* – that our lives had become unmanageable.	1) We admitted that we were *neglectful of our higher selves* and that our lives have become unmanageable.
5) Admitted to God, to ourselves, *and to another human being* the exact nature of our wrongs.	5) We admitted to Allah and to ourselves the exact nature of our wrongs.
11) Sought through prayer and *meditation* to improve our conscious contact with God AS WE UNDERSTOOD HIM, *praying only for knowledge of His will*	11) We sought through *Salaat* (prayer service) and *Iqraa* (reading and studying) to improve our understanding of *Taqwa* (G-d consciousness;

for us and the power to carry that out.	proper love and respect for Allah) and *Ihsan* (though we cannot see Allah, He does see us).
12) Having had *a spiritual awakening* as the result of these steps, we tried to carry this message to alcoholics, and to practice these principles in all our affairs.	12) Having increased our level of *Iman* (faith) and *Taqwa* [G-d consciousness], as a result of applying these steps, we carried this message to humanity and began practicing these principles in all our affairs.[93]

Concerning the Twelve Traditions, MI's Tradition Twelve makes a significant departure from AA's Twelfth Tradition. Again comparing MI with AA, Millati Islami's Tradition Twelve is:

ALCOHOLICS ANONYMOUS	MILLATI ISLAMI
12) *Anonymity* is the spiritual foundation of all our Traditions, ever reminding us to place principles before personality.	12) *Iman* (faith) [not anonymity] is the spiritual foundation of all our traditions, reminding us to place principles before personalities.[94]

Bahá'í Faith

Founded in the mid Nineteenth Century, The Bahá'í Faith is the newest and one of the fastest growing monotheistic religions in the world. It was founded in Persia (now Iran) by a man who took the title of Bahá'u'lláh (the Glory of God). The Bahá'í Faith's leadership was passed down through Bahá'u'lláh's son and grandson until the mid-Twentieth Century, when it evolved into an administrative order of elected and appointed leaders. Since 1963, the ultimate authority for the Bahá'í Faith has been the Universal House of Justice, an elected body that is seated in the city of Haifa, Israel.

While Bahá'ís are welcomed in most parts of the world, they continue to be persecuted in Iran, Egypt and some other Islamic countries.

Today, there are more than five million Bahá'ís living in 253 countries, making it one of the most widespread religions in the world (second only to Christianity).[95] Bahá'ís have no quarrel with any of the other major religions. Like Christians, they believe that Jesus Christ is the son of God. And Bahá'ís, like Moslems, believe that God has sent numerous prophets, including Buddha, Jesus, and Muhammad. In the Bahá'í religion, Bahá'u'lláh is believed to be the latest messenger of God. Bahá'ís see gender equality, racial equality, and world peace as not only attainable, but inevitable.

Bahá'ís are forbidden to drink alcohol or to take drugs unless prescribed by a physician. In 1986 the Universal House of Justice ruled that there is no reason for Bahá'ís not to be members of Alcoholics Anonymous and that the "sharing of experiences which [AA] members undertake does not conflict with the Bahá'í prohibition on the confession of sins."[96] Probably no one knows how many alcoholics, drug addicts and their families have found refuge in the Bahá'í religion, but in the 1980s, at least, there were enough to form a support group called the Bahá'ís in Recovery Fellowship. Although this fellowship has apparently gone dormant in recent years, the Bahá'í Faith still offers a large sober fellowship of progressively minded people.

Taking These Roads

My goodness, *faith-based* roads to recovery are many! They range from programs that originated long before the modern Twelve Step Movement (rescue missions, recovery colonies, and the Salvation Army), to programs of more recent origin that offer an alternative to the Twelve Steps (Christian Science, The Matt Talbot Way), to a lot of faith-based programs that make good use of the Steps. Those who want to integrate their step work with a bonafide religion have many programs to choose from. And there are probably a lot more than the ones described in this chapter. Many churches have their own recovery ministries which are only known locally – and I understand that there are even a few *Twelve Step Churches* which preach the Twelve Step program 100 percent of the time.*

The website for ***Christian Science*** (CS) is: http://christian science.com/. If you are interested in the *Christian Science* way of recovery, perhaps you should know that not all CS practitioners are as easygoing as Sam Leake's wonderful healer. I know little of Christian Science except that it is not associated in any way with Tom Cruise's favored religion, Scientology, but I do have a December 28, 1992 edition of the *Christian Science Sentinel*. That issue is subtitled "God's control *overcomes* addiction," and the stories and letters therein seem to indicate that some Christian Science practitioners expect their patients to pray *with* them and to study Mary Baker Eddy's *Science and Health with Key to the Scriptures,* along with the Bible.[97]

Jerry McAuley's Gospel Rescue Mission continues to serve New York's needy, as it has since 1872. It is now called the *New York City Rescue Mission* and is located at 90 Lafayette Street, New York, NY 10013. Rescue Missions now exist in foreign countries and in many cities and large towns across the USA. Many of these belong to the ***Association of Gospel Rescue Missions (AGRM)*** whose searchable website is: http://www.agrm.org/.

The Salvation Army's official USA website is: http://salvationarmyusa.org/. This site allows you to search for *Salvation Army* centers near you.

> The official website for ***America's Keswick Colony of Mercy*** is: http://www.americaskeswick.org/. The physical address is: America's Keswick, 601 Route 530, Whiting, NJ 08759. The phone number for the

---

* There are also some churches that are highly critical of the Steps. See for example: *12 Steps to Destruction* by Martin and Deidre Bobgan, *Alcoholics Anonymous Unmasked* by Cathy Burns, and *The Useful Lie* by William Playfair.

Colony of Mercy is: 732-350-1187 ex. 46. Email: addictionrecovery@americaskeswick.org.

America's Keswick is far from being the only recovery colony in the US. Its website has a page (http://www.americaskeswick.org/688964.ihtml) with a long list of similar programs. The page includes this disclaimer:

> America's Keswick is glad to provide the following referral list of addiction centers and shelters. The list combines programs for both men and women... This list is by no means exhaustive. Although we are making the list available to you, you must bear the responsibility to contact the shelters and check on requirements, philosophies, and religious affiliations. We are not recommending any particular program. Since each person's background and needs are different, each individual must evaluate the information and make a selection based on their own need.[98]

As was previously discussed, the ***Oxford Group*** is now known as ***Initiatives of Change***.

It is no longer conspicuously involved with helping people recover from addictions, but Fr. Bill Wigmore, a recovering alcoholic who attended an international IofC conference titled "Tools for Change," reported this:

> Going to this conference was like going back in time. Many of these people didn't know the 12 Steps but they knew and practiced the very same principles that had formed them....[T]hey held meetings and told stories of spiritual awakenings.... People learned the tool of Quiet Time, being silent and listening to God or to their conscience or to what some called their

Inner Voice. They wrote down the thoughts that came and shared them with a friend. Often what they shared helped the listener as much or more than it helped them....Next year the teams will again return with more stories of change. Maybe next year there'll be more than one alcoholic among them.[99]

If you are a Twelve Step group member looking for something more, or a person whose recovery program has somehow gone stale, *Initiatives of Change* may be an interesting option for you.

The Matt Talbot Way is laid out in Philip Maynard's book: *To Slake a Thirst: The Matt Talbot Way to Sobriety* (2000, published by Alba House in New York). I don't know of any groups that are working this program, but if you are using *The Matt Talbot Way*, by itself or in conjunction with some other program, I would be interested in hearing from you. The **Matt Talbot Retreat Movement** is strong among Catholics. The official website for the Movement is: http://matttalbotretreats.org/. The physical address is: Matt Talbot Retreat Movement, Inc., 32 Watkins Drive, Sandy Hook, CT 06482. Email: secy@matttalbotretreats.org.

The main website for the **Calix Society** is: http://www.calixsociety.org/. Their mailing address is: P.O. Box 9085, St. Paul, MN 55109. The phone number is 651-773-3117; toll free for the USA and Canada: 800-398-0524.

The official **Alcoholics Victorious** headquarters website is found at: http://alcoholicsvictorious.org/. It has tabs for finding an AV group and for starting an AV group.

Alcoholics Victorious is loosely associated with **Christians In Recovery** (http://christians-inrecovery.org/). You can contact *CIR* at: Christians in Recovery, 48 Pleasant Street, Dorchester, MA 02125. There is also an **Addictions Victorious** program (http://www.addvicinc.org /index.html) and an **Addicts Victorious** program (http://www.addictsvictorious.com/).

Alcoholics for Christ is headquartered at 10096 Highland Rd., Suite 216, Hartland, MI 48353. Its official website is:

http://www.alcoholicsforchrist.com/. The phone number is 248399-9955; email: office@alcoholicsforchrist.com.

Overcomers Outreach has a website at: http://overcomersoutreach.org/. Its physical address is: 12828 Acheson Dr., Whittier, CA 90601. Phone: 562-698-9000; toll free: 800-3103001. The website will allow you to send emails to Trusted Servants Jeff M. and Betty K. *Overcomers Outreach* also has websites and email addresses for O.O. programs in Canada, the UK, Sweden, Germany and Australia.

http://recoverysupport.org/ is the Internet address for the **Overcomers Recovery Support Program.** Their mailing address is P.O. Box 29623, Shreveport, LA 71149; telephone: 318-6874777. ORSP's workbook, *A Daily Choice: Overcoming Life-controlling Problems,* can be purchased from their website or elsewhere on the Internet.

Overcomers In Christ has a website at: http://overcomersinchrist.org/. Mail is delivered to them at: P.O. Box 34460, Omaha, Nebraska 68134; telephone: 866-573-0966. Emails can be sent to OIC via their website.

The website for **Jewish Alcoholics, Chemically dependent persons and Significant others** is: http://www.jbfcs.org/programs-services/jewish-community-services-2/jacs/. Their telephone number is: 212-632-4600. The website also has phone numbers and email addresses for the Program Coordinator and the Program Director.

http://www.celebraterecovery.com/ is *Celebrate Recovery's* website. There are also websites and Facebook pages for some of the 10,000 or so churches using the *Celebrate Recovery* program.

One advantage of the **LDS Recovery Program** may be that the Mormon church offers a large fellowship of total abstainers. The *LDS Program* has a website at: http:// addictionrecovery.lds.org/ This website allows you to search for meetings in your local area. Most *LDS* recovery meetings are focused on general addiction problems, with pornography and sexual addiction being second.

Millati Islami World Service has a website at: http://www.millatiislami.org/. The postal address is: P.O. Box 2100, Douglasville, GA 30133; email: INFO@MILLATIISLAMI.ORG.

It may be worth noting that while the ***Bahá'í Faith*** has certain features that are very progressive, it has other features that are quite conventional. In addition to abstaining from alcohol and illicit drugs, Bahá'ís do not smoke or gamble and sexuality is limited to conventionally married couples. For those who are enticed, or at least not deterred by such things, the *Bahá'í Faith* has an international website (in English, Spanish, Arabic and other languages) at: http://www.bahai.org/; and a website for Bahá'ís of the United States: http://www.bahai.us/.

Other *faith based* recovery programs such as *Free'N'One* and *One Church-One Addict* are covered in Chapter IX on Afrocentric Recovery. And a few *faith-based* recovery programs such as *Lion Tamers, Mountain Movers, High Ground* and *Victorious Lady* are not included in this chapter although they have been mentioned in scholarly papers on the subject. The reason is simply because they do not have websites or other means to access information about them. They may be defunct, or your local minister or priest may have information about them.

Yes, there are indeed many *faith-based* roads to recovery. Whether you choose to use these religious programs alone, in conjunction with one or more secular or 'spiritual' programs, or not at all, is up to you. And whatever choices you make may:

The Lord bless you and keep you; the Lord make His face to shine upon you and be gracious unto you;
the Lord turn His face toward you and give you peace.
~Numbers 6:24-26 (NIV)

Chapter Endnotes

1. Proverbs 23:20 (King James Version)
2. Older, Fremont (circa 1920) "My Personal Recollections." In Leake, W. S. (1920) *The Healing of "Sam" Leake,* Los Angeles: The Rob-Mar Press, page 86.
3. Anderson, Dwight with Page Cooper (1950) *The Other Side of the Bottle,* New York: A. A. Wyn, Inc., page 160.
4. Adapted from Older (circa 1920) page 86. (Some lines were edited or paraphrased.)
5. Anderson with Cooper (1950) page 161.
6. Leake (1920) page 45.
7. Anderson with Cooper (1950) pages 159, 161-162.
8. Ibid., page 162.
9. McAuley, Jerry and Duane V. Maxey, ed. (2000) "Life Story of Jerry McAuley," Atlanta: Repairer Publishing Company. Retrieved 12/11/2013 from: http://wesley.nnu.edu/wesleyctr/books/1801-1900/HDM1855.pdf
10. McAuley and Maxey (2000).
11. McAuley, Jeremiah (1876) *Transformed; or, the History of a River Thief, Briefly Told,* Published by himself, pages 28-29.
12. Ibid., page 31.
13. Ibid., page 36.
14. Ibid., page 45.
15. Bonner, Arthur (1990) *Jerry McAuley and His Mission,* revised edition, Neptune, NJ: Loizeaux Brothers, page 37.
16. McAuley (1876) pages 62 - 63.
17. Ibid., pages 63-64.
18. "The Life and Ministry of Jerry McAuley" (n.d.) Retrieved 12/19/2013 from: http://www.agrm.org/agrm/Jerry_McAuley.asp
19. Clinebell, Howard J., Jr. (1968) *Understanding and Counseling the Alcoholic Through Religion and Psychology,* Nashville: Abingdon Press, page 99.
20. Ibid.

21. Clinebell (1968) page 98.
22. McKinley, Edward (1986) *Somebody's Brother: A History of the Salvation Army Men's Social Service Department, 1891-1985*, Lewiston, NY: The Edwin Mellon Press, page 2.
23. Raws, William (n.d.) "The Miraculous Story of William Raws, Founder of America's Keswick." Brochure retrieved 12/16/2013 from: http://www.americaskeswick.org/files/
24. Ibid.
25. White, William L. (1998) *Slaying the Dragon: The History of Addiction Treatment and Recovery in America,* Bloomington, IL: Chestnut Health Systems/Lighthouse Institute, page 76.
26. Lean, Garth (1985) *Frank Buchman: A Life,* Printed in Great Brittan by St. Edmundsbury Press, page 33.
27. Ibid., page 37.
28. Buchman, Frank (1948) "The Story of Bill Pickle... *A story told by Dr. Frank Buchman at the World Assembly for Moral Re-Armament, Riverside, California, June 1948,"* Retrieved 12/20/2013 from: http://stepstudy.org/2008/05/21/the-story-of-bill-pickle-by-frank-buchman/
29. Lean (1985) page 37.
30. Mercadante, Linda A. (1996) *Victims and Sinners: Spiritual Roots of Addiction and Recovery,* Louisville: Westminster John Knox Press, page 57.
31. Paton, Wally (2000) *How to Listen to God: Overcoming Addiction Through Practice of Two-Way Prayer,* Tucson, AZ: Faith With Works Publishing Company, page 14.
32. Ibid., page 154.
33. Ibid., page 15.
34. Lean (1985) page 79.
35. Lean (1985) page 153.
36. Hunter, T. Willard with Mel B. (Aug 1988?) "AA's Roots in the Oxford Group." Retrieved 12/31/2013 from: http://silkworth.net/melb/oxfordgroup.html
37. Lean (1985) page 153.
38. Purcell, Mary (1972) *The Making of Matt Talbot,* Dublin, Ireland: Messenger Publications, pages 4 and 7.

39. Costelloe, Morgan (1987) *Matt Talbot: Hope for Addicts,* Dublin, Ireland: Veritas Publications, page 15.
40. Ibid., page 16.
41. "Matt Talbot - The Road to Recovery" (n.d.). Retrieved 1/24/2014 from: http://www.matttalbot.ie/recovery.htm.
42. Costelloe (1987) page 4, 8.
43. Maynard, Philip (2000) *To Slake a Thirst: The Matt Talbot Way to Sobriety,* Staten Island, NY: St. Pauls/Alba House, pages xv - xvi.
44. Ibid., page xix.
45. Ibid., page 107.
46. Ibid., page 134, 131.
47. Ibid., pages 157-158.
48. Ibid., page 41.
49. Ibid., pages 44,160.
50. Ibid., page 45.
51. Ibid., page 46.
52. White (1998) page 223.
53. The Calix Society (n.d.) "A Word for the Problem Drinker! And Program of Prayer,"Minneapolis: The Calix Society (booklet).
54. Ibid.
55. John 10:10 (King James Version)
56. Dunn, Jerry G. with Bernard Palmer (1980) *What Will You Have to Drink? The New Christian Password,* Alberta: Horizon Books, pages 75-76.
57. White (1998) page 222.
58. Anonymous. In Dunn (1997, 2003, 2012) page 35.
59. Hunt, Jim and Cyndy Hunt with Robert Allen Hill (1978) *How to Live with an Alcoholic and Win,* Minneapolis: Ark Books, page 87.
60. Ibid., page 14.
61. "Alcoholics Victorious - Database of Meetings" (n.d.). Retrieved 1/7/2014 from: http://alcoholicsvictorious.org/database.html

62. "About Alcoholics for Christ - Statement of Faith" (1997-2001). Retrieved 1/20/2014 from: http://www.alcoholicsforchrist.com/au.htm
63. "About Alcoholics for Christ - History" (1977-2001). Retrieved 1/16/2014 from: http://www.alcoholicsforchrist.com/aua.htm
64. "Alcoholics for Christ - 12 Step, Christ Centered, Program for Alcoholics and Substance Abusers" (1977-2008) .Retrieved1/24/2014 from: http://www.alcoholicsforchrist.com/sa.htm
65. White, William L. (2013) "Addiction Recovery Mutual Aid Groups: A Chronology of Founding Dates. Retrieved1/17/2014from: http://www.williamwhitepapers.com/pr/2013 Addiction Recovery Mutual Aid Chronology.pdf
66. "Overcomers Outreach – Home" (n.d.) Retrieved 1/24/2014 from: http://overcomersoutreach.org/
67. Bartosch, Bob and Pauline Bartosch (1994, 2000, 2004, 2009) *Overcomers Outreach: A Bridge to Recovery,* Enumclaw, WA: Pleasant Word, page 295-296.
68. Bartosch, Bob and Pauline Bartosch (1985, 1986, 1989) *Overcomers Outreach: FREED!,* LaHarbra, CA: Overcomers Outreach, Inc. Page 1-2.
69. Bartosch and Bartosch (1994, 2000, 2994, 2009) page 296.
70. Burton, Charles and Sharon Burton (2000) *A Daily Choice: Overcoming Life-Controlling Problems,* Shreveport, LA: Overcomers, Inc., page VI.
71. "Overcomers In Christ 25th Anniversary Fundraiser Banquet" (2012). Retrieved 1/15/2014 from: http://www.overcomersinchrist.net/index.php
72. "The Overcomer's Goals" (1999) *Think Overcoming Your Problems is Impossible? Think Again! All Things Are Possible Through Christ Jesus!* (brochure). Retrieved 3/7/2014 from: http://overcomersinchrist.org/wp-content/uploads/woocommerce_uploads/2013/01/brochure.pdf.

73. White, William L. (2013) "JACS and Alcohol Problems Within the Jewish Community: An Interview with Lisa Auerbach." Retrieved 1/31/2014 from: http://www.williamwhitepapers.com/pr/Lisa Auerbach JACS.pdf
74. Bloom, Sheila, quoted in: Waxman, Audrey H. (2007) "A Brief Historical Perspective on Jews, Women and Addiction." Retrieved 2/4/2014 from: http://www.williamwhitepapers.com /pr/Historical Perspective on Jews Women and Addiction.pdf
75. Rothberg, Samuel (2011) "JACS: A Jewish Response to Alcoholism." Retrieved 2/4/2014 from: http://www.jacsweb.org/article-12.html
76. JACS Mission Statement (2011). Retrieved 2/4/2014 from: http://www.jacsweb.org/about.html
77. "JACS Fact Sheet" (n.d.). Retrieved 2/4/2014 from: http://www.williamwhitepapers.com/pr/JACS Fact Sheet.pdf
78. Waxman, Audrey and David Buchholz (May 2004) "A Detailed History of JACS 19792004, pages 12 and 13. Retrieved 2/6/2014 from: http://www.williamwhitepapers.com/pr/History of JACS 1979-2004.pdf
79. "About JACS" (n.d.) Retrieved 2/4/2014 from: http://www.williamwhitepapers.com/pr/About JACS 2013.pdf
80. Baker, John (1998, 2005) *Celebrate Recovery®Leader's Guide: A Recovery Program Based on Eight Principles From the Beatitudes,* Grand Rapids: Zondervan, page 15.
81. Baker, John (n.d.) "Pastor John's Testimony." Retrieved 2/5/2014 from: http://www.celebraterecovery.com/site-map/pastor-john-s-testimony.
82. Baker (n.d.) "Pastor John's Testimony." *And* Baker (1998, 2005) page 21.
83. "Is Celebrate Recovery for me?" (n.d.). Retrieved 2/5/2014 from: http://www.celebraterecovery.com/site-map/faq (The original listed "depression" twice. I have corrected that.)

84. Baker (1998, 2005) page 9.
85. Baker (1998, 2005) page 74.
86. Baker (1998, 2005) page 231.
87. LDS Family Services (2005) *Addiction Recovery Program: A Guide to Addiction Recovery and Healing,* Salt Lake City: The Church of Jesus Christ of Latter-day Saints, page 1.
88. Ibid., page 29.
89. Baker, Merlin O. (2004) *Understanding Alcohol and Drug Addiction: An LDS Perspective,* Cedar Fort, Inc., pages 63, 65, 66.
90. Millati Islami World Service (n.d.) "What is Millati Islami and how did it start?" Retrieved 2/14/2014 from: http://www.millatiislami.org/Welcome/islamic-12-step-program (Data dated Mar 2, 1996)
91. Millati Islami World Services (n.d.) "What is Millati Islamic?" Retrieved 2/14/2014 from: http://www.millatiislami.org/
92. Millati Islami World Service (n.d.) "Meeting Format." Retrieved 2/14/2014 from: ://www.millatiislami.org/meeting-format
93. "Twelve Steps to Recovery" (n.d.) *Millati Islami World Service.* Retrieved 3/11/2014 from: http://www.millatiislami.org/Welcome/12-steps
94. Millati Islami World Service (n.d.) "Twelve Traditions of Millati Islami." Retrieved 2/14/2014 from: http://www.millatiislami.org/Welcome/12-traditions
95. McCabe, Des (2012) *The Five Minute Guide to the Bahá'í Faith* (Kindle edition) Retrieved from Amazon.com
96. Bahá'ís in Recovery Fellowship (1988) "The Twelve Steps: Bahá'í Writings and recovery from substance abuse." Retrieved 4/27/2014 from: http://bahai-library.com/compilation _twelve_step_program
97. See e.g., Hansen, Eva (Dec 28, 1992) untitled letter, *Christian Science Sentinel,* Vol. 94, No. 52, pages 38-40.
98. "Referral List" (2011). Retrieved 2/18/2014 from: http://www.americaskeswick.org/688964.ihtml

99. Wigmore, Bill (Oct 2008) "Whatever Became of the Oxford Group?" Retrieved 12/28/2013 from: http://www.recoverytoday.net/October_2008/wigmore.html

CHAPTER IX:
Afrocentric Recovery:
From Frederick Douglass to Malcolm X and Beyond

In 1845, a young fugitive American slave wrote:

> I have no accurate knowledge of my age, never having seen any authentic record containing it. By far the larger part of the slaves know as little of their ages as horses know of theirs, and it is the wish of most masters within my knowledge to keep their slaves thus ignorant... A want of information concerning my own [age] was a source of unhappiness to me even during childhood. The white children could tell their ages. I could not tell why I ought to be deprived of the same privilege.[1]

Thus were the sad and humble beginnings of one of America's greatest men, Frederick Douglass. Douglass was born as Frederick Augustus Washington Bailey in Talbot County, Maryland in what most historians agree was the year 1818. His mother was a slave and his father, who was rumored to be his master, never acknowledged paternity. In 1838 he escaped to the free state of Massachusetts, whereupon he changed his last name to Douglass to avoid recapture.

As a free man, Douglass became the most famous Black abolitionist *in the world*. An abolitionist is someone who works to abolish slavery and Douglass devoted much of his life to that cause. He also favored other causes such as women's rights, economic opportunity and temperance, a movement to reduce or eliminate the use of alcoholic beverages.

It was common for nineteenth century reformers to advocate several such causes, which were sometimes grouped together under titles such as "the Sisterhood of Reforms."[2] Among Black reformers, the temperance and abolitionist causes were often found together.[3]

When he was in the United States, Douglass spoke mostly of slavery, but on a tour of the British Isles in 1845–1847 he opened up about his temperance beliefs and his own experience with demon alcohol. "I used to love drink – that's a fact," Douglass told an audience in Glasgow, Scotland on February 18, 1846. "I found in me all the characteristics leading to drunkenness – and it would be an interesting experience if I should tell you how I was cured of intemperance [drunkenness], but I will not go into that matter now."[4] Douglass never did reveal how he was cured, but he did offer other hints about his personal drinking problem – enough to lead some modern researchers to conclude that *"Frederick Douglass may be the most prominent of early African Americans in recovery."*[5] [Emphasis added.] What is known for certain is that after a few years of excessive drinking and several years of abstaining, Douglass took a total abstinence pledge from Father Theobald Mathew, the Irish apostle of temperance.[6] And he kept that pledge for the rest of his life.

Douglass favored temperance not only because intemperance, drunkenness and drug addiction are bad, but also because those evils reflect poorly on the reputation of Black communities. "We have a large class of free people of color in America," Douglass told an audience at Cork, Ireland. He added:

> [T]hat class has, through the influence of intemperance, done much to retard the progress of the anti-slavery movement – that is, they have furnished arguments to the oppressors for oppressing us; they have pointed to the drunkards among the free colored population, and asked us the question tauntingly — "what better would you be if you were in their situation?"[7]

Of course, Frederick Douglass was not the only African American to support temperance. In the early 1870s William

Washington Browne, a well-known Black man, applied for membership in the Independent Order of Good Templars (IOGT), a leading temperance fraternity of the time. Browne was denied membership because of his race but the IOGT offered a compromise, which was the creation of a new organization for Blacks called the Grand United Order of True Reformers. Browne accepted the offer and began organizing "fountains" (local chapters) throughout the South. The reason for calling them "fountains" was because: "A fountain is always running; it sends forth its waters pure and clear at all times."[8]

In addition to being a successful temperance fraternity, the True Reformers became the largest and most successful Black business enterprise in America.[9] In 1889, the True Reformers opened a bank, which became the first Black-owned, Black-operated financial institution to be chartered in the United States; and as the fraternity continued to prosper, it acquired other properties, including fourteen meeting halls, three farms, an office building, and a fifty-room hotel.[10]

But the True Reformers never forgot that temperance was the foundation of their order. Only those who "pledged themselves to a life of total abstinence"[11] were initiated into membership and the order's rituals were rich with reminders that intemperance "wears the garb of an enemy."[12] Initiation into the Second, or Hope Degree called for an even greater obligation – an obligation that is very similar to the duties of modern day recovery group members. In this rite, the Worthy Grand Master charged the initiates:

> [I]t shall be your duty, as well as ours, to go to that desolate wife, and those famishing children and tell them you have come to comfort them... Go also to the poor inebriate, and whisper in his ear that for him there is yet hope; that though his prospects are cheerless and gloomy, he may yet live to Mess [take care of, feed or dine with] his wife and children, and cause joy and gladness to spring up in their hearts.[13]

So the True Reformers were rescuing drunks more than 60 years before AA and other mainstream recovery groups began to "carry the message!"

William Whipper, another remarkable Black abolitionist and temperance crusader, was born on February 22, 1804 in the free state of Pennsylvania. He inherited a small lumber yard from his father, which he and his business partner built into a successful wholesale enterprise that made them both quite wealthy. According to one report, Whipper "epitomized the unique prosperity that northern Blacks were able to attain in the mid-19th century."[14]

Much of Whipper's wealth was used in aiding the escape of fugitive slaves. For several decades he operated a "station" on the Underground Railroad.* Concerning Whipper's work on the "Railroad," Leroy Hopkins wrote the following:

> Once in Columbia [Pennsylvania] the fugitives were sent by Whipper in one of two directions: either west by boat to Pittsburgh or east by train to Philadelphia. In this way, by his own account, between 1847 - 1859 Whipper "passed hundreds to the land of freedom, while others, induced by high wages, and feeling that they were safe in Columbia, worked in the lumber and coalyards of that place."[15]

William Whipper favored temperance in part because of his belief "that alcohol consumption was a contributing factor for Africans [in Africa] selling their own people into slavery."[16] For much of his life Whipper also believed that prejudice against Blacks came "not from the color of their skin, but from their condition."[17] Therefore he linked temperance for free Blacks with abolition for their enslaved brethren. As the African American Registry put it: "Although some did not see moral reform by Black leaders

---

* The Underground Railroad was not a real railroad. It was a secret network of people and safe houses known as "stations" that helped runaway slaves escape to free states or Canada.

connected to the abolitionist cause and the plight of the southern black population, Whipper saw a direct connection between them."[18]

In a speech titled "The Slavery of Intemperance," Whipper explained: "I firmly believe that if three hundred thousand free colored people possessed such a [temperate] character, the moral force and influence it would send forth would disperse slavery from our land."[19] In other words, Whipper agreed with Frederick Douglass who earlier in this chapter was heard to say that intemperate free Blacks had "done much to retard the progress of the anti-slavery movement."[20]

An even clearer statement was made at the African Temperance Society meeting in New York City in 1842: "whenever it can be said that the free blacks are sober and industrious and intelligent people capable of self-government, the only argument in favor of slavery falls to the ground."[21]

But Whipper added: "I wish not to be understood to insinuate that we are more intemperate than the whites, for I do not believe it."[22] In that, he was absolutely correct. Prior to about 1900, Blacks enthusiastically embraced the temperance cause. A modern introduction to Whipper's speech stated: "By 1840 most black communities had some form of temperance society and many had temperance boardinghouses, stores, restaurants, and newspapers."[23] And according to Denise Herd, author of "We Cannot Stagger to Freedom," "blacks had spearheaded a major black temperance campaign that rivaled the general American temperance movement in scope and intensity."[24]

Frederick Douglass, in the same speech at Cork, Ireland where he criticized his fellow freemen for their intemperance, also said:

> I am pleased to be able to say, that the change in their situation, with regard to intemperance, has been great in the last seven years. Take Philadelphia, for example: there are 1500 colored people there, and there are now not less than 80 Temperance Societies among that class.[25]

And Ira V. Brown, Professor Emeritus of American History at Pennsylvania State University, added this remarkable assessment:

> Douglass reported the progress which African Americans had made in Lynn, Massachusetts, the place of his residence. Five years earlier he could not walk in the streets without insult on account of his complexion. He could not ride on a railroad or in an omnibus. He could not send his children to school. He could not attend a lyceum, all because this badge of color was upon him. Now [c. 1847] the state of things was changed. No class of people was now more respected, more kindly treated, or cordially met than men of color.[26]

Around the turn of the century, however, the politics changed. Temperance advocates, anxious to enroll White southerners in their cause, gradually abandoned Black civil rights and the movement became downright racist. Again, according to Denise Herd:

> The racist policies of the post-Reconstruction anti-liquor movement greatly diminished black interest and support for the twentieth-century anti-liquor movements. This period was associated with an overall intensification of alcohol use among blacks and a subsequent rise in alcohol-related problems.[27]

While it was absolutely deplorable that the anti-alcohol movement gave in to racism, it was tragic that Blacks abandoned temperance. Experts tell us that the West African tradition from which most American Blacks are descended "placed a high value on moderate drinking and expressed strong disapproval of socially disruptive behavior."[28] By enthusiastically embracing the temperance cause, Blacks were living up to that noble tradition.

Today, African Americans are again discovering that the strengthening of cultural roots is a way of overcoming the evils of addiction. As one exasperated Black radical put it, ordinary programs "were never intended to cure Black addicts. They can't even cure the White addicts they were designed for."[29] This chapter will explore several culturally nuanced and Black church supported recovery programs for African American alcoholics and drug addicts.

Malcolm X and the Nation of Islam: "Recovery by Any Means Necessary"

Roughly one hundred years after the heyday of the Black temperance movement,[*] another African American reformer, Malcolm X, also framed recovery as a political act. Using words reminiscent of his nineteenth century forebears, Malcolm X told a Cleveland audience that "we have to get together and remove the ... alcoholism, drug addiction, and other evils that are destroying the moral fiber of our community."[30] Furthermore, in his autobiography, Malcolm X wrote "black junkies are trying to narcotize themselves against being a black man in the white man's America, but ... the black man taking dope is only helping the white man to 'prove' that the black man is nothing."[31]

Compare these statements with what Philip Foner and Robert Branham wrote about the Black temperance movement: "Black community leaders in the temperance movement argued that the use of alcohol, while understandable as an act of despair over thwarted aspirations and limited opportunities, was a destructive force akin to slavery."[32] Surely the nineteenth century temperance reformers and abolitionists would be in agreement with Malcolm X.

William White and others have noted that the story of Malcolm X can be told by describing his serial identities. First there was the infant named Malcolm Little, one of eleven poor children who were raised on a diet of day-old bread, cornmeal mush and dandelion greens. Then there was the child called "Milky" and "Snowflake,"

---

[*] Known as the "colored temperance movement" in the nineteenth century.

who believed he was favored by his father for his light skin color and disfavored by his mother for the same reason, a child who was virtually orphaned at a young age by the murder of his father and the mental illness of his mother.

Also there was "Detroit Red," the pimp, dope dealer, hustler and smalltime criminal who was "always high." Then there was "Satan," the convict who showed such remarkable animosity toward religion that he impressed even the hardened criminals who were his prisonmates. Next came Malcolm X, the popular and controversial minister for the Nation of Islam (NOI); and finally there was El Hajj Malik el Shabazz, the moderate Sunni Muslim who was assassinated in 1965 after breaking with the NOI.[33]

Like Frederick Douglass, Malcolm X's recovery story was overshadowed by the other achievements and controversies of his life. What we know is that "Detroit Red," the hustler, pimp and two-bit criminal, was always high on marijuana, cocaine, opium and amphetamines; and he continued taking drugs after being sent to prison for burglary in 1946. "I viewed narcotics as most people regard food," Malcolm said.[34] After his conversion to the Nation of Islam, however, he completely stopped using drugs, alcohol and tobacco – and he challenged other recovered addicts to "return to the 'junkie jungle' to salvage those who were still suffering."[35]

Malcolm X bragged that "a lot has been written ... about the Nation of Islam's phenomenal record of dope-addiction cures of longtime junkies."[36] He added that the NOI's success was due to a six-point process:

FIRST, the addict is brought to admit to himself that he (or she) is an addict.

> *"Like the alcoholic, the junkie can never start to cure himself until he recognizes and accepts his true condition. The Muslim sticks like a leech, drumming his old junkie buddy, 'You're hooked man!' It might take months before the addict comes to grips with this. The curative program is never really underway until this happens."*

SECOND, the addict is taught *why* he (or she) uses narcotics.
> *"Still working on his man, right in the old jungle locale ... the Muslim often collects audiences of a dozen junkies. They listen only because they know the clean-cut proud Muslim had earlier been like them. Every addict takes junk to escape something, the Muslim explains."*

THIRD, the addict is shown that there is *a way* to stop addiction.
> *"The Muslim can tell when his quarry is ready to be shown that the way for him to quit the dope is through joining the Nation of Islam."*

FORTH, the addict's shattered self-image is built up until the addict realizes that he (or she) has, *within*, the self-power to end the addiction.
> *"The addict is brought ... among proud, clean Muslims who show each other mutual affection and respect instead of the familiar hostility of the ghetto streets. For the first time in years, the addict hears himself called, genuinely, 'Brother,' 'Sir,' and 'Mr.' No one cares about his past... Everyone...is confident that he will kick the habit."*

FIFTH, the addict voluntarily undergoes a cold turkey break with drugs.
> *"When the addict's withdrawal sets in, and he is screaming, cursing and begging, 'Just one shot man!' the Muslims are right there talking junkie jargon to him. 'Baby, knock that monkey off your back! Kick that habit! Kick Whitey off your back.'"*

SIXTH, fully cured, the ex-addict completes the cycle by "fishing" for other addicts and supervising their salvaging.
> *"He will never forget these brothers who stood by him during this time. He will never forget that it was the Nation of Islam's program which rescued him from that special hell of dope. And that black brother (or sister, whom Muslim sisters attend) rarely ever will he return to the use of narcotics. Instead, the ex-*

addict when he is proud, clean, renewed, can scarcely wait to hit the same junkie jungle he was in, to 'fish' out some buddy and salvage him!"[37]

According to Mark Sanders, a counselor and faculty member of the Addictions Studies Program at Governors State University: "The Nation of Islam is perhaps the most successful program in reaching African American male substance abusers in the criminal justice system."[38] In 1995, that same Mark Sanders interviewed ten formerly addicted African American men who were active in the Nation of Islam. All had been involved with two or more traditional treatment programs prior to joining the NOI and Sanders asked all of them what the Nation of Islam did that traditional substance abuse programs did not. His selection of their responses was first published in an article titled "The Response of African American Communities to Addiction ..." in the third quarter 2002 edition of *Alcoholism Treatment Quarterly*. Below is a summary of his selected responses:

1. *A Sense of Hope* - One man felt that Malcolm X had a greater problem than he did. After reading Malcolm's story, he had hope that he could turn his life around.
2. *Physical Changes* - After joining the Nation of Islam, a man started wearing a suit and tie every day. When he looked better on the outside, he started to feel better on the inside.
3. *Role Models* - The number of Black ex-convicts in the NOI who were now living productive lives provided others with "something to shoot for."
4. *Ethnic Pride and Dignity* - The Nation's teachings about the primacy of the Black man created a feeling of pride about being Black.
5. *Encouraged to Read* - The Nation encourages reading, something often neglected in the ghetto. One man reported that: "Reading changed my life."

6. *Proper Diet* - The Nation's dietary code eliminates pork and much of the other "soul food" that Blacks were forced to eat during slavery. One man found this to be very liberating.
7. *Help with Employment and Classes on How to Live* - The Nation helps with finding employment. One man said that the classes "taught me how to eat to live, how to treat women, and the responsibilities of man."
8. *No Labels* - One man reported that he had been seeing counselors and other helpers since he was eleven years old. He always felt labeled by them, but when NOI members came into his jail, he said he felt loved.[39]

Glide Memorial Church: "Telling the Truth and Living in the Spirit"

When Cecil Williams was ten years old, a train came for him.

It came to kill him. "The voices warned of the train's intention," William's wrote in *I'm Alive,* his first autobiography, "but they really didn't have to. I knew what the train was after, and for four months that wore like years, I felt and believed I would die in the darkness."[40]

He was having a nervous breakdown.

Usually, Williams attributes his breakdown to the stress of growing up in a highly segregated Texas community. Other times, however, he allows that it might have been influenced by the birth of a baby brother, an event that dethroned him from the position of youngest in the family. Whatever it was, he recovered completely, though he still hears the voices from time to time, he says, even in the eighth decade of his life.[41]

Perhaps it is because his family and his neighbors stuck with him during this dark and some would say shameful episode that he has always championed society's outcasts: sex workers, convicts, drug addicts and – even prior to the homosexual revolution – gays, lesbians and transgendered individuals of every persuasion.

Even as a boy, Williams was nicknamed "the Rev" and anointed to be the family member who is called to the ministry. After completing his seminary training and suffering through a couple of assignments that did not fit his personality, Williams was assigned to take over the ministry of Glide Memorial United Methodist Church in San Francisco. Glide had a proud history, a generous endowment and a spacious building, but the congregation had shrunk to just 35 members when Williams arrived in 1963.[42]

Glide is located in the notorious, high-crime Tenderloin district of San Francisco. The previous minister had tried to deal with this by keeping the neighborhood's residents out of the church, but Cecil decided to open its doors and let them in. The result was a dramatic increase in parishioners. The congregation exploded and the church prospered.

> In the late 1980s, according to Cecil, the Tenderloin district "began to smell [of] death."

About this, he wrote:

> I began to see women, many young mothers, strung out on Crack (sic) cocaine, straggling through Boeddeker Park. They'd pull along their little children who were so dispirited they didn't even want to play in the concrete play yard. The mothers were holding the hands of their children as they all meandered down a path of despair. Crack cocaine was causing that stench of death.[43]

And Glide Memorial Church decided to do something about it. The recovery process Glide invented is culturally based and involves four basic acts: recognition (not powerlessness), self-definition (not society's definition), rebirth (facing the pain and telling the truth), and community (moving further into relationships with people of all colors).[44]

"Since 1989," Cecil wrote, "hundreds of Crack addicts have come to Glide to plant faith in themselves, sow belief in the Spirit, cultivate resistance to death and addiction, and celebrate recovery of life."[45]

Most of the addicts who come to Glide are African American, and very early on it was discovered that traditional (Twelve Step) recovery programs do not work well for them. In *No Hiding Place,* the book Cecil wrote about Glide's recovery process, he said this:

> The Twelve Steps focus on individual recovery as if independently getting clean and sober were the ultimate goal. But African Americans are a communal people – we fought for our freedom together. A recovery program that focuses mainly on the individual doesn't jibe to a people whose identity rests in belonging to an extended family and being a member of the black community.[46]

> Other shortcomings of the Twelve Step programs for Blacks were also noted: 1) when Afro-American addicts attend Twelve Step meetings, they are often the only Crack addicts or the only people of color in the room; 2) many of the Tenderloin's addicts have never been in the mainstream; to get clean and sober they need to learn how to empower their lives, not how to surrender to powerlessness; and 3) the principle of anonymity does nothing for the underclass – they have already felt invisible and unheard for most of their lives.

"It wasn't long ... [until] the press began to show up at Glide..." Cecil wrote. "Much of the initial coverage was negative."

> Some of the [news] articles presented some widely held assumptions as if they were facts. Crack addicts don't recover... Forget them, they'll go away. What is the church doing messing with recovery? Doesn't

Glide know the only role the church has to play in recovery is to rent out its basements for AA meetings…?[47]

Soon, however, it became evident that the people going through Glide's recovery process *were* recovering. The first few "generations," as Cecil calls them, developed a capsulized program that replaced AA's Twelve Steps. Instead of Steps, they coined *Ten Terms of Resistance,* which are:

1. I will **gain control over my life.**
2. I will **stop lying.**
3. I will **be honest with myself.**
4. I will **accept who I am.**
5. I will **feel my real feelings.**
6. I will **feel my pain.**
7. I will **forgive myself and forgive others.**
8. I will **rebirth a new life.**
9. I will **live my spirituality.**
10. I will **support and love my brothers and sisters.**[48]

"These ten terms are not steps…" Cecil warned. "They are not a new set of commandments. They are the lifeline that keeps us afloat as we risk recovery and have faith that day by day we will live into our freedom."[49] The *Ten Terms of Resistance* are read at every Glide recovery meeting, much as Alcoholics Anonymous and Narcotics Anonymous members sometimes read the Twelve Steps.

People seeking recovery at Glide are allowed to openly express their feelings of anger and rage. According to Mark Sanders: "This is significant" because many of the African American men he interviewed "feared being kicked out if they really expressed their anger and rage while in treatment."[50] Recovering Glide members are also taught that their individual recovery is important to the African American community. At one time – and perhaps even now – 80 percent of Glide's congregation was in recovery.

Glide's recovery program has been operating successfully for several decades and somewhere along the way a man who owes his recovery to Glide had this to say: "I mean if someone has reached out a hand and pulled you up from the bottom, you'll never forget it. That is what Glide has done for me."[51]

Free N One: Free from Drugs and Alcohol, and One in Christ

"The church can no longer sit idle when drugs and alcohol addiction is the No. 1 killer and destroyer of families in our community today!"[52] says Elder Ron Simmons, who founded Free N One in 1987 along with Ronald Wright and Rene Whitehead, all recovering alcoholics or addicts.

Free N One is a church supported, nonprofit, drug- and alcohol-free program. Its goals include: "To establish, provide and maintain inner-city drug and alcohol free meetings centered in the Church." "To educate the Church about the disease of addiction." "To provide help for the family and significant others through drug/alcohol support groups..." And: "To bring the Church together as one; to fight this affliction that is destroying our people, our cities, and our nation."[53]

The Free N One program is similar to AA and other Twelve Step models, but it is supercharged with an emphasis on Jesus Christ and the Bible. Instead of the traditional Twelve Steps, Free N One uses Twelve Spiritual Steps to Recovery. Each of the Spiritual Steps is correlated with one or more Bible passage, which users are apparently expected to look up on their own. The Twelve Spiritual Steps to Recovery are:

1. We admitted that we could not control our addiction and our lives became unmanageable (Romans 7:15-25)
2. Learned to believe that God can and will restore us to a right relationship with Him through Jesus Christ. (Matthew 11:28-30, Romans 3:22-23, Romans 5:9-10)

3. Made a quality decision to let God have complete control over our will and lives through His Word. (Joshua 24:15, Psalms 119:4, Proverbs 3:5-6, Matthew 6:24, 33)
4. Made a thorough and fearless moral examination of ourselves on paper. (2 Corinthians 13:5)
5. Confessed to God in the name of Jesus and admitted to ourselves and unashamedly admit the exact nature of our wrongs to another human being. (Proverbs 28:13, James 5:16, 1 John 1:9)
6. Became entirely ready to have God take away all these blocks to our freedom in Christ. (Galatians 5:1, Hebrews 12:1,2, Psalms 86:10-13, Psalms 119:57-59)
7. Humbly asked God in the name of Jesus and thanked Him for His mercy and for giving us the strength to overcome our faults. (John 16:24, 1 Peter 5: 6-10, James 4:10, Psalms 51:10, Psalms 19:12-14)
8. Wrote down all those persons we had harmed and became willing to make restitution to them all. (Matthew 5:23-24, Luke 19:8-10)
9. Made direct restitution to such persons whenever possible except when to do so would injure them or others. (James 5:16, Luke 6:31, 36-37)
10. Examined ourselves daily to see if we are being doers of the Word and not just hearers only. If wrong promptly confess it. (James 1:22, James 5:16, 1 John 1:8-10, Ephesians 4:26)
11. Continue to pray, study and meditate on the Word, and maintain consistent fellowship with believers, to improve our relationship with God. (Joshua 1:8, Psalms 1:1-3, 1 Thessalonians 5:17, 2 Timothy 2:15, Hebrews 10:25)
12. Having had a born again experience and having been freed from our addiction we shared our testimony with those who are still in bondage and continued to be doers of the Word in all our affairs. (Matthew 28:19-20, Romans 1:16, Galatians 5:1 and 13, 1 Timothy 6:18, John 3:3)[54]

Although Free N One is a religious program, it also has a traditional approach for those who prefer it.

One Church - One Addict

In the late 1980s, Father George Clements, a Black Catholic priest, befriended a middle school child by the name of Tommy. Tommy was a bright boy, valedictorian of his junior high class and an outstanding football player. He had earned a scholarship to one of the best high schools in the city. "Do you think I could be a doctor?" Tommy asked the priest. Father Clements told him he was certain that he could.

Later that night, Father Clements received a phone call from a hospital emergency room. A delirious boy with no identification had been calling his name. When the priest arrived at the hospital, the boy was dead. It was Tommy, dead of a drug overdose.

"How could I not have known?" the stunned priest asked himself. The tragic incident led Father Clements to found One Church - One Addict, an ecumenical, church-based recovery program.[55]

"Addiction itself is a spiritual disease and needs a spiritual cure," Father Clements opined, "and where better to find it than in our Christian churches, Buddhist and Bahá'í temples, Muslim mosques and Jewish synagogues, which are supposed to be the repositories of love?"[56]

One Church - One Addict is ecumenical, meaning that all faiths are encouraged to do something about alcoholism and drug addiction in their own communities. Addicts and alcoholics are encouraged to seek one-on-one counseling from volunteers trained by One Church - One Addict. They usually enter the program after undergoing detox or rehab and usually stay for about nine months, although there is no time limit on participation. According to a June 27, 2012 article, "More than 1,000 churches in thirty-five states now belong to the program."[57]

African American Survivors Organization

"African Americans experience racism; yet this is rarely mentioned in 12-step group meetings," says Benneth Lee, founder of the African American Survivors Organization.[58] The Survivors program was created to give African American men a place to discuss issues that are not commonly raised in traditional recovery group meetings. According to Mark Sanders:

> The format of an African American Survivors meeting begins with a reading entitled, "Who is a Survivor?" and "What is an African American Survivors Group Meeting?" This is followed by reading the Seven Principles of Nguzo Saba, which are followed during a Kwanza celebration, and teach group members some of the principles of African culture. They are unity, self-determination, collective works and responsibility, cooperative economics, purpose, creativity – You have a responsibility to do as much as you can to leave your community more beautiful than how you found it – and faith. The eleven personal development principles, based on the work of Wade Nobel, are then read.[59]

After the readings, group members share whatever is in their hearts or on their minds. The meetings both support and challenge members to use the principles of African and Afro-American culture to solve problems in their own lives.[60]

Taking These Roads

Mark Sanders, a Black counselor who has been quoted throughout this chapter, offered his fellow addiction counselors some sage advice: "Since it is difficult to have complete knowledge of another culture, it is possible for a counselor to inadvertently insult clients by 'saying the wrong thing.' Helper sincerity is the one thing that allows clients to forgive helpers who violate a cultural boundary."[61] I say that if this applies to counselors, it applies equally to writers. Since I am not an expert on African American or any other culture, I sincerely apologize in advance for any missteps I may have made.

You may be aware that the ***Nation of Islam*** is a controversial organization. Among the controversies is the assassination of Malcolm X, which has never been resolved. The original *Nation of Islam* was implicated because three of its members (or former members) were convicted of the crime. However, there are still rumors, including speculation that the CIA or the FBI may have been involved. And then there is the so-called Yacub (or Yakub) myth. According to this teaching, which is central to the Nation's theology, approximately 6,000 years ago an evil scientist named Yacub created White people as a "race of devils."[62] (It may be the case, however, that some of the younger NOI members do not take such teachings literally.) A third source of controversy has been Minister Louis Farrakhan's pronouncements against Jews, Whites, Christians and homosexuals. These may or may not be things that concern you.

In 1975, upon the death of Elijah Muhammad who had led the Nation for forty years, his son Wallace Deen Muhammad (later changed to Warith Deen Muhammed) was appointed leader. According to Jeffery O. G. Ogbar, author of *Black Power: Radical Politics and African American Identity,* "Wallace assumed the daunting task of dismantling the racist theology of the Nation.... The name was changed to the World Community of Islam in the West... and it ceased to be a black nationalist organization."[63] Today, the World Community of Islam in the West is known as the American Society of Muslims.

A small faction of followers kept to the teachings of Elijah Muhammad. Louis Farrakhan gained control of this faction and, again according to Ogbar, "pursued the difficult task of rebuilding the organization run by Muhammad for forty years."[64] Today,

Farrakhan's *Nation of Islam* is popularly accepted as the continuation of Elijah Muhammad's organization *and it remains very active in reforming criminals and drug addicts.*[65]

If you feel that the *Nation of Islam* may be the recovery road for you, Good! Check it out.

"Recovery by any means necessary." The Nation's headquarters is in Chicago (7351 South Stony Island Ave., 60649; phone: 773-324-6000). It also has mosques in many other large cities. Its official website is: http://www.noi.org/

Cecil Williams has retired from the ministry, but **Glide Memorial Church** continues to provide recovery support for many addicts and alcoholics. *Glide* offers a 90-day outpatient recovery program, a Certified Recovery Program (by appointment) and drop-in Recovery Circles. The drop-in circles are from Tuesday through Thursday, 11:00 am to 12:30 pm and they are for all addicts seeking help. Glide also offers harm reduction services. According to *Glide's* website: "Meeting our patients where they are at, and allowing them to define their goals and priorities in the process, is what we do. We are partners working together to accomplish what they define as success."[66]

Unfortunately, *Glide's* range of service is limited to the San Francisco Bay Area. Acknowledging this, Cecil Williams wrote: "Now there is only one Glide, it can't be duplicated. Yet the Glide attitude is one that can be chosen and adapted to any church, community, or city. Anyone, especially you, can take the risk of telling the truth and living in the Spirit."[67] *Glide* is located at 330 Ellis Street (Main Building), San Francisco, CA 94102. The phone number is 415-674-6000. Email: info@glide.org. *Glide's* website is at: https://www.glide.org/.

Free N One is headquartered at 5838 South Overhill Dr., Suite #3, Los Angeles, CA 90043 (telephone: 323-295-0009; fax: 323-295-0022; email: freenone@msn.com). There is a *Free N One* website at: http://www.free-n-one.org/. *Free-N-One* is primarily active in Los Angeles and Chicago. For a directory of meetings go to: http://freenone.org/content/other related-continuum-of-care/directory-of-meetings/.

I have been unable to locate contact information for *One Church - One Addict* and the *African Americans Survivors Organization.* It may be possible to find out more about *OCOA* through your local Christian minister, Buddhist or Catholic Priest, Jewish Rabbi, Muslim Imam or Bahá'í Faith chairperson. Although Father Clements has retired, I've been assured that *OCOA* continues its good work. In addition to *One Church One Addict*, Father Clements founded *One Church - One Child,* an organization that encourages churches to find adoptive parents for orphaned Black children, and *One Church - One Inmate,* which encourages churches to "adopt" ex-inmates and help them to stay straight and reintegrate into society. The *African American Survivors Organization* was founded by Benneth Lee and is based in Chicago. Though it does not appear to be a national program, it is an interesting concept and ambitious individuals may want to start similar programs in their communities.

A resource not previously mentioned is the *Winner's Circle Program (WCP)*. It is active in Illinois and was started by Treatment Alternatives for Safe Communities (TASC), a non-profit organization that provides behavioral health and recovery management services for individuals in the criminal justice and other social service systems. *WCP* is loosely patterned after AA but it does not abide by AA's formal or informal traditions. Members introduce themselves by saying: "My name is _____ and I'm a winner." Crosstalk is permitted. The meetings are peer-led and, according to Thomas Lyons and Arthur Lurigio, authors of "The Role of Recovery Capital in the Community Reentry of Prisoners with Substance Use Disorders": "The [WCP] program provides information about employment, reduces the stigma of addiction, and connects former prisoners with the local recovery community."[68] Further contact information was not available.

Another localized resource is the *African American Family Services* program (*AAFS*), which is a grassroots organization providing culturally specific services for chemically dependent people of color.[69] The program is active in Minneapolis and Saint Paul, Minnesota. The website for *AAFS* is http://www.aafs.net. The phone number is: 612-871-7878.

Altogether, there are multiple choices available for African Americans seeking recovery. In addition to those mentioned here, there may be others sponsored by your local church, synagogue, mosque or temple. Says Mark Sanders: "Each denomination of church in the African American community has its own faith-based recovery ministry."[70] Furthermore, there are about 100 integrated programs – religious, secular, spiritual, special interest and professional – that are described in other chapters of this book. You may (or may not) be especially interested in the Muslim program, *Millanti Islami,* described in Chapter VIII on Faith-Based Recovery.

And please do not assume that *Twelve Step* programs are of no use to Blacks. African Americans do recover in *Twelve Step* programs, although they appear to be under-represented in such groups.[71] A common complaint is that there are few, if any, people of color in attendance at *Twelve Step* meetings, but this may be resolving itself with the passage of time. Concerning this situation, William L. White, author of *Slaying the Dragon,* had this to say:

> It is my observation that the ability of A.A. [and NA, etc.] in any one locality to attract large numbers of ... people of color depends on reaching [a] critical mass of such involvement. Retention rates may be low until that critical mass is reached; after that, growth can be quite rapid.[72]

So there is a cornucopia of recovery possibilities for African Americans. For Blacks, the roads to recovery truly are many. Whatever road or roads you take, my very best wishes go with you!

Chapter Endnotes

1. Douglass, Frederick (1845a) *Narrative of the Life of Frederick Douglass,* New York: Dover Publication, Inc., 1995, page 1.

2. Walters, Ronald G. (n.d.) "Abolition and Antebellum Reform." Retrieved 10/25/2013 from http://www.gilderlehrman.org/history-by-era/slavery-and-anti-slavery/essays/abolition-andantebellum-reform.
3. Quarles, Benjamin (1969) *Black Abolitionists,* New York: Oxford University Press, page 93.
4. Douglass, Frederick (1846) "Intemperance Viewed in Connection with Slavery: An Address Delivered in Glascow (sic) Scotland, on February 18, 1846." Glasgow *Saturday Post*, February 21, 1846. In Blassingame, John (*et al,* eds). *The Frederick Douglass Papers: Series One – Speeches, Debates, and Interviews.* New Haven: Yale University Press, 1979. Vol. I, p. 165.
5. White, William and Mark Sanders (2002) "Addiction and Recovery Among African Americans Before 1900," *Counselor* 3(6): 64-66.
6. "Theobald Mathew (temperance reformer)" (Oct 9, 2013) *Wikipedia, the free encyclopedia.* Retrieved 10/28/2013 from: http://en.wikipedia.org/wiki/Theobald_Mathew_(temperance_reformer)
7. Douglass, Frederick (1845b) "Intemperance and Slavery: An Address Delivered in Cork, Ireland, on October 20, 1845," *Truth Seeker,* 1: 142-44 (1845-46). Reprinted in Blassingame, John (*et al,* eds.). *The Frederick Douglass Papers: Series One – Speeches, Debates, and Interviews.* New Haven: Yale University Press, 1979. Vol. I, p. 55.
8. Burrell, W. P. and D. E. Johnson, Sr. (1909) *Twenty Five Years History of the Grand Fountain of the United Order of True Reformers, 1881-1905,* Richmond, VA, page 23. Quote retrieved 11/14/2013 from "United Order of True Reformers": http://www.stichtingargus.nl/vrijmetselarij/r/uotr_en.html
9. Hollie, Donna Tyler (Dec 4, 2012) "Grand Fountain of the United Order of True Reformers," *Encyclopedia Virginia.* Retrieved 10/3/2013 from:

http://www.encyclopediavirginia.org/Grand_Fountain_of_the_United_Order_of_True_Reformers
10. Ibid.
11. "Grand United Order of True Reformers Ritual of the First, or Faith Degree" (1875) Retrieved 10/19/2013 from: http://www.stichtingargus.nl/vrijmetselarij/r/guotr_r1.html
12. "Grand United Order of True Reformers Ritual of the Third Degree or Degree of Charity (1875). Retrieved 10/19/2013 from: http://www.stichtingargus.nl/vrijmetselarij/r/guotr_r3.html
13. "Grand United Order of True Reformers Ritual of the Second, or Hope Degree (1875) Retrieved 10/19/2013 from: http://www.stichtingargus.nl/vrijmetselarij/r/guotr_r2.html
14. *Alpha MINDS* (n.d.) "William Whipper." Retrieved 11/1/2013 from: http://www.minds.com/search/result/wikipediaWilliamWhipper
15. Hopkins, Leroy (1985) "Black Eldorado on the Susquehanna: The Emergence of Black Columbia, 1726 - 1861," *Journal of the Lancaster County Historical Society,* Vol. 89, No. 4, page 129. Quoted in Zimmerman, David (n.d.) "William Whipper in the Black Abolitionist Tradition." Retrieved 11/1/2013 from: http://archive.is/UNr31
16. *Alpha MINDS* (n.d.).
17. Ripley, C. Peter, ed. (1985) *The Black Abolitionist Papers,* Vol. 2, Chapel Hill: University of North Carolina, page 119. Quoted in Zimmerman (n.d.).
18. African American Registry (1996) "William Whipper, A Thoughtful Abolitionist," *Encyclopedia Britannica,* Fifteenth Edition. Retrieved 11/1/2013 from http://www.aaregistry.org/historic_events/view/william-whipper-thoughtful-abolitionist
19. 19. Whipper, William (Jun 21–28 and Jul 5, 1834) "The Slavery of Intemperance," *Liberator*. In Foner, Philip S. and Robert James Branham, eds. (1998) *Lift Every Voice: African*

American Oratory 1787– 1900, Tuscaloosa, Alabama: The University of Alabama Press, page 151.
20. Douglass (1846)
21. *The Northern Star and Freeman's Advocate* (Feb 17, 1842). Quoted in Cheagle, Roslyn V. (Aug 19, 1969) *The Colored Temperance Movement: 1830-1860,* M.A. Thesis, Washington, DC: Howard University, page 23.
22. Whipper (Jun 21–28 and Jul 5, 1834) page 151.
23. Foner, Philip S. and Robert James Branham, eds. (1998) *Lift Every Voice: African American Oratory 1787– 1900,* Tuscaloosa, Alabama: The University of Alabama Press, page 145.
24. Herd, Denise, "'We Cannot Stagger to Freedom: A History of Blacks and Alcohol in American Politics." In Brill, Leon and Charles Winick, eds. (1985) *Yearbook of Substance Use and Abuse, Volume III,* New York: Human Sciences Press, Inc., page 146.
25. Douglass (1845b)
26. Brown, Ira V. (Autumn 2000) "An Antislavery Journey: Garrison and Douglass in Pennsylvania, 1847," *Pennsylvania History,* Vol. 67, No. 4, page 537.
27. Ibid., page 142.
28. Ibid., page 144.
29. Tabor, Michael "Cetewayo" (1970) "Capitalism Plus Dope Equals Genocide." Retrieved 10/8/2013 from: http://www.marxists.org/history/usa/workers/black-panthers/1970/dope.htm
30. X, Malcolm (Apr 3, 1964) "The Ballot or the Bullet" speech, Cleveland Ohio. Retrieved 11/8/2013 from: http://www.edchange.org/multicultural/speeches/malcolm_x_ballot.html
31. 31. X, Malcolm and Alex Haley (1964, 1965) *The Autobiography of Malcolm X,* New York: Ballantine Books, page 260.
32. Foner and Branham (1998) page 145.

33. White, William L., Mark Sanders and Tanya Sanders (2006) "Addiction in the African American Community: The Recovery Legacies of Frederick Douglass and Malcolm X," *Counselor,* 7(5), 53-58.
34. X and Haley (1964, 1965) page 138.
35. White, Sanders and Sanders (2006).
36. X and Haley (1964, 1965) page 259.
37. Assembled from: X and Haley (1964, 1965) pages 260 - 262.
38. Sanders, Mark (2002) "The Response of African American Communities to Addiction: An Opportunity for Treatment Providers." In McGovern, Thomas F. and William L. White, eds. (2002) *Alcohol Problems in the United States: Twenty Years of Treatment Perspective,* New York: Haworth Press, Inc., pages 167 - 174.
39. Sanders (2002).
40. Williams, Cecil (1980) *I'm Alive,* San Francisco: Harper & Row Publishers, page 1.
41. Williams, Cecil and Janice Mirikitani (2013) *Beyond the Possible,* Harper One, page 10.
42. The United Methodist Reported (Feb 14, 2013) "Cecil and Janice – Unlikely Pair Writes of Leading Glide Memorial UMC." Retrieved 11/28/2013 from: http://unitedmethodistreporter.com/2013/02/14/cecil-and-janice-unlikely-pair-writes-of-leading-glide-memorial-umc/
43. Williams, Cecil, with Rebecca Laird (1992) *No Hiding Place: Empowerment and Recovery for Our Troubled Communities,* New York: Harper Collins Publishing, page 2.
44. Morell, C. (May 1996) "Radicalizing Recovery: Addiction, Spirituality, and Politics," *Social Work,* Vol 41, No. 3, pages 306-312.
45. Williams with Laird (1992) page 6.
46. Ibid., page 8.
47. Ibid., page 48.
48. Ibid., page 86.
49. Ibid.
50. Sanders (2002).

51. Williams with Laird (1992) page 188.
52. Jackson-Fossett, Cora (Jun 7, 2012) "Free N One Offers Faith-Based Recovery Training,"*Los Angeles Sentinel.*
53. Simmons, Ronald (2001) *Understanding Christian Drug and Alcohol Recovery,* Los Angeles: Free N One Books, page 146.
54. Simmons (2001) page 80. (Number 10: hearer corrected to hearers)
55. Ragghianti, Marie (1995?) "To Help Those Living on the Edge." Reprinted from *Parade* magazine in Congressional Record 104th Congress (Dec. 13, 1995) page S18566. Retrieved 11/15/2013 from: http://thomas.loc.gov/cgi-bin/query/z?r104:S13DE5-B298:
56. Quoted in: Taylor, Susan L. (1995) *Lessons in Living,* New York: Anchor Books Doubleday, page 154.
57. Allen, Mark (Jun 27, 2012) "Father George Clements Honored In Chicago For Health Advocacy and New Chairmanship of Hepatitis C Health Organization." Retrieved 12/17/2013 from: http://www.chicagonow.com/and-the-ordinary-people-said/2012/06/father-george-clements-honored-in-chicago-for-health-advocacy-and-new-chairmanship-of-hepatitis-c-health-organization/
58. Quoted in Sanders (2002).
59. Sanders (2002).
60. Sanders (2002). (Cites "Personal Communications" with Benneth Lee.)
61. Sanders, Mark (Feb 1, 2003) "Building Bridges Instead of Walls: Effective Cross-Cultural Counseling With Corrections Clients," *Corrections Today,* Vol. 65, Nbr. 1.
62. Ogbar, Jeffrey O. G. (2004) *Black Power: Radical Politics and African American Identity,* Baltimore: The Johns Hopkins University Press, page 13.
63. Ibid., page 202.
64. Ibid., page 203.
65. Ibid.

66. "RecoveryServices"(n.d.)*I am GLIDE* website. Retrieved 11/16/2013 from:http://66.211.107.100/page 380
67. Williams with Laird (1992) page 219.
68. Lyons, Thomas and Arthur J. Lurigio (2010) "The Role of Recovery Capital in the Community Reentry of Prisoners with Substance Use Disorders," *Journal of Offender Rehabilitation,* 49:445-455.
69. "Our History" (2010) *African American Family Services.* Retrieved 12/6/2013 from: http://www.aafs.net/history.html.
70. White, William L. (2013) "ROSC from an African American Community Perspective: An Interview with Mark Sanders," Retrieved 11/24/2013 from: http://www.williamwhitepapers.com/pr/2013 Mark Sanders Interview ROSC African American Perspective.pdf
71. "Special Composition Groups in AA" (n.d.) Retrieved 6/25/2013 from: http://www.barefootsworld.net/aaspecialgroups.html
72. White, William L. (1998) *Slaying the Dragon: A History of Addiction Treatment and Recovery in America,* Bloomington, IL: Chestnut Health Systems/Lighthouse Institute, pages 161-162.

CHAPTER X:
New Age Recovery:
Ancient Wisdom for Modern Times

Is God dead?

In the early and middle parts of the Twentieth Century a diminutive Black preacher who went by the name of Major Jealous Divine (and was better known as Father Divine) allowed and encouraged his many thousands of followers, both Black and White, to believe that he was God incarnate. Now, of course, Father Divine is gone. He passed away on September 10, 1965 after a long period of declining health. So – is God dead?

Of course not. God can't be dead and Father Divine wasn't God, except in the sense that we are all rays or sparks of God's infinite Self – which is actually what he taught, but in practice only Divine himself was believed to be God. Nevertheless, the story of this mysterious "short and squat" 5' 2" minister is one of the more interesting and perplexing tales in the annals of new religious movements.

We don't know exactly when Father Divine was born, probably in the late 1870s, but most of his biographers do agree that his original name was George Baker. There is no such agreement on *where* he was born. Some say it was Georgia or "somewhere in the Deep South;" another says Maryland.[1] As an adult, Divine settled in the Northeast, where he established his headquarters in New York and Harlem before moving to Philadelphia in the 1940s.[2]

Father Divine's religion is still alive today, though just barely so. His program is called the International Peace Mission Movement and it has spiritual, political and economic components. Spiritually, the Peace Mission Movement has been described by Daniel Schneider as "a unique combination of Emersonianism, the Social Gospel, the Protestant Ethic and New Thought."[3]

New Thought is a New Age phenomenon that is sometimes called the Mind-cure Movement. Although that appellation is somewhat misleading, Father Divine's followers did offer many testimonials of spiritual healings attributable to him, including at least two people who were allegedly raised from the dead.[4]

Politically, the movement campaigned for racial integration, the abolishment of lynching and equal rights for all. Economically, Father Divine was a very astute businessman who provided jobs and a decent standard of living for many of his followers, even during the very difficult depression years of the 1930s. And he astonished everyone with his ability to feed thousands with lavish "Holy Communion" banquets, which were held almost daily, free of charge or at a very nominal cost. "How can he afford it?" people asked. It seemed almost as if Father Divine was reenacting Christ's miracles of feeding the multitudes.[*]

These accomplishments are all the more remarkable when considering that Divine recruited many of his disciples from some of the roughest areas in America's big cities. In San Francisco his followers were housed in the notorious Barbary Coast district; and in Seattle his Peace Mission operated in an area that was actually called Skid Row (the namesake for all of the other Skid Rows in America). Furthermore, according to Robert Weisbrot, Divine's Peace Missions in the Northeast operated primarily along the poorest streets of Harlem and other ghetto neighborhoods.[5]

Stories of Father Divine's followers finding relief from alcoholism and other addictions are commonplace. According to Professor Keith V. Erickson: "Father Divine numbered among his followers hundreds who had come from lives of crime, prostitution, vagrancy, alcoholism, and rascality."[6] Furthermore, Divine's most recent biographer, Jill Watts, wrote this: "At a time when few treatments existed for alcoholism, the Peace Mission offered

---

[*] Also known as "the miracles of the loaves and fishes." Jesus performed these miracles of feeding thousands with a few loaves of bread and a few small fish on two occasions. See Matthew 14:13-21 and 15:32-39; Mark 6:31-44 and 8:1-9; Luke 9:10-17; and John 6:5-15.

support-group therapy that encouraged alcoholics to take control of their lives."[7]

Considering all his good works *and* his outrageous claims, was Father Divine a holy man, a flim-flam man, or maybe a little of both? Like some other charismatic religious leaders, Father Divine's career was marred by scandal. There were allegations of sexual improprieties and financial misappropriations. At one point he was mocked as "God in a Rolls Royce." Although Father Divine may have had legal troubles and may have lived extravagantly, Keith Erickson concluded that he did more good than anything else:

> Father Divine distinguished himself from Harlem's other prophets by serving his followers' physical and spiritual needs, whereas others stole from the disadvantaged and returned to them only platitudes and vacuous promises. Father Divine not only provided shelter and sustenance, he also reshaped the faithful's perception of themselves and their lives...[8]

While the International Peace Mission Movement was not exclusively an addiction recovery program, it is one example of addiction recovery using New Age ideas. Of course the New Age, sometimes called the Aquarian Age, is not really new. Generally it is based on ancient wisdom that is thousands of years old. This chapter will explore several Aquarian Age recovery programs –none as cultish as Father Divine's– that can be loosely grouped together under the rubric of "New Age." They range from programs that incorporate the Twelve Steps to programs that are somewhat critical of that method.

Abraham-Hicks and Their New Twelve Steps

Who is Abraham? Is Abraham male or female? One or many? The last question is easy. Abraham is many. Abraham has been described as "a group of non-physical entities." Esther Hicks (the

Hicks of Abraham-Hicks) calls them "infinite intelligence." Her husband, the late Jerry Hicks, said they are "the purest form of love I've ever experienced."[9]

The second question is difficult. Abraham may be male/female, neither male nor female, or the group may be half males and half females. One admirer says that "they are neither male nor female. It is pure positive energy."[10] Since they describe themselves as "usually a nebulous mist," they may simply have no use for gender identities.[11]

Abraham is "interpreted" by Esther Hicks while she is in something of a trance-like state. She doesn't use the word "channeling," though that is pretty much what it is. She says it is not "channeling" but "interpreting" because she doesn't receive the messages as spoken words. She has to *interpret* or *translate* them into English – which, by the way, results in some rather strange uses of certain words. Outside of Abraham-Hicks, have you ever heard of "rockets of desire?"* I didn't think so.

Whatever the group named Abraham is, I have been duly impressed by some of their words. For instance, speaking through Esther Hicks, they said: "What we've noticed about the [Twelve Step] program, and we've interacted with so many people who have been part of it, is that in the beginning, it is all downstream [going in a healthy direction] for them. But after a little while, when they begin gaining their balance, to say those same things are upstream [going in an unhealthy direction] for them."[12] This was certainly my experience when I was doing AA in the 1970s and 80s.

To deal with these changing currents, Abraham suggests a *second* set of steps. "So we think if we were standing in your physical shoes," they said, "we would introduce the 12 Step Program as the first 12 steps and [then] we would tell them there are 12 more."[13] What follows is a *brief summary* of Abraham-Hicks' Second Twelve Steps. The full version of these Second Twelve Steps is available on *Beyond the Twelve Steps: Breaking Free of Addiction*, a DVD and a CD by Abraham-Hicks Publications.

---

* "Rockets of desire" are simply intentions or desires to have or do something.

The ***First Step*** of the Second Twelve Steps is about *not* admitting you are powerless. Says Abraham: "While you've been saying in the first 12 Steps that there is a power greater than you, there has never been a power that is greater than you are." The ***Second Step*** is about telling yourself that you did the best you could do. According to Abraham: "You are the creator of your own experience and you are doing the best that you know how to do, every step along the way." The ***Third Step*** is: "I am where I am, and where I am is all right, because it has to be, because it's the only choice I have." This leads to the ***Fourth Step,*** which says: "I am a worthy being, who is an extension of Source Energy, and I came forth with powerful intention, and got crossways of it… And when I got crossways of it, I went nuts." This led to "pain beyond pain," which caused drugs and alcohol to become involved as poor "solutions" for that pain. Rather than beating yourself up about this, Abraham suggests saying: "while I would not return to something that is numbing [alcohol and/or drugs]… I've never known anyone who would deny anyone some sort of a solution or solving of some kind of pain."

The ***Fifth Step*** of the Second Twelve Steps says "I will make peace with those who did not understand how I felt." And the ***Sixth Step*** is: "I forgive all of them from this new point of view." The ***Seventh*** and ***Eighth Steps*** are: "Now that I am more sure of who I am… it is my promise to myself that even if I were to do something that formerly I thought was a mistake, that I'm determined that I will offer no self-condemnation, ever again" (*Step Seven*). "And" (*Step Eight*) "if I should… ever take a drink again, it is my promise to myself: I'm not going back through those first 12 steps. I know too much. I've come too far." (This too would have been good advice for me when I tried going back to AA in the 1980s.)

The ***Ninth Step*** of the Second Twelve Steps counsels "sincere appreciation for the first 12 Steps, because they were there for me when I most needed them;" and the Second ***Step Ten*** says: "I am appreciating everything that ever gave me grief, because from it was born clarity of desire." The Second ***Eleventh Step*** says "I encourage no one to go through what I went through in order to get where I am." And the ***Final (Twelfth) Step*** of the Second Twelve Steps says:

"I adore knowing that I am the creator of my own reality... And I think all 24 steps are part of me being able to now do that."[14]

Addiction Alchemy:™ The True Gold of Recovery

Alchemy is sometimes called "the yoga of the West," *and it isn't just about making gold.* Alchemy is also defined as "a power or process that changes or transforms something in a mysterious or impressive way."[15] Such is the intent of Addiction Alchemy (AddA*), which was founded by Renee Bledsoe, a minister who is also the founder of the Church of Spiritual Light in Ft. Myers, Florida. Even though she personally has never been hooked on any substance, Renee's brother is reported to have died of drug addiction and alcoholism. Hence her strong interest in addiction and recovery.[16] Furthermore, according to Bledsoe:

> "The eclecticism and elasticity of Addiction Alchemy could allow an entire population, who for whatever reason could not connect with the 12 Steps of Alcoholics Anonymous, to connect to the overarching power of archetypal energy healing."

This observation aside, however, the AddA website states that: "Addiction Alchemy... can be used in conjunction with the 12 Step programs, or it can be used as an alternative to the traditional 12 Steps."[17]

MEDICINE WHEEL

---

* My abbreviation.

With either method of utilization, the primary recovery tool used by Addiction Alchemy is the Medicine Wheel, which is similar to the Medicine Wheels described in Chapter I, the chapter on Native North American recoveries. In that chapter we learned that: "In its simplest form, the Medicine Wheel is a circle containing an equal-armed cross... The circle represents the universe or the 'circle of life,' which the cross divides into quadrants."[18] The points where the cross meets the circle represent the four cardinal directions and, like the Native American medicine wheels, have many other symbolic correspondences. Some of these include the four seasons: spring, summer, autumn and winter and the basis colors: yellow, red, black, white. These correspond to the directions: east, south, west and north, respectively.

AddA's basic program is a series of five "gatherings" – one for each of the four cardinal directions on the Medicine Wheel and one for the center. The gatherings are held about every two months so it takes around eight to ten months to complete a cycle. Apparently, most Addiction Alchemists choose to go around the Wheel more than once.

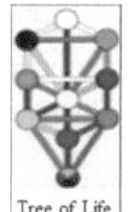
Tree of Life

According to Bledsoe, the AddA curriculum includes: "the Medicine Wheel, Tree of Life, Meditation, Archetypes, Nature and the Elements, Animals, Energy Healing and much more."[19] Next to the Medicine Wheel, the second most important symbol used by Addiction Alchemy appears to be the Kabalistic Tree of Life. Kabala (or Cabala) is usually associated with Jewish mysticism, but the Cabala and the Tree of Life are also part of the broader Western esoteric tradition. The Tree of Life is a symbol made up of ten circles or sephira and twenty-two lines or paths, one for each trump card in the Tarot deck and one for each letter of the Hebrew alphabet. The circles or sephira represent a number of things and ideas, but one basic correspondence is to the planets of astrology. Starting from the top sephira the correlations are: Neptune, Uranus, Saturn, Jupiter, Mars, Sun, Venus, Mercury, Moon and Earth or physical manifestation.

One interesting meditation used by Addiction Alchemy and based on the Tree of Life is "The Pattern on the Trestleboard." This is a series of eleven affirmations numbered from zero through ten, with the numbers one through ten representing the Tree of Life's ten sephira and zero representing the No-Thing that precedes manifestation. Heretofore, The Pattern on the Trestleboard has been known mostly to Western esotericists who have studied the work of Paul Foster Case, a Twentieth Century cabalist who wrote extensively on Tarot, spiritual alchemy and Rosicrucianism. Its eleven statements are:

1. All the Power that ever was or will be is here now.
1. I am a center of expression for the Primal Will-to-Good which eternally creates and sustains the universe.
2. Through me its unfailing Wisdom takes form in thought and word.
3. Filled with Understanding of its perfect law, I am guided, moment by moment, along the path of liberation.
4. From the exhaustless richness of its Limitless Substance, I draw all things needful, both spiritual and material.
5. I recognize the manifestation of the Undeviating Justice in all the circumstances of my life.
6. In all things, great and small, I see the Beauty of the Divine Expression.
7. Living from that Will, supported by its unfailing Wisdom and Understanding, mine is the Victorious Life.
8. I look forward with confidence to the perfect realization of the Eternal Splendor of the Limitless Light.
9. In thought and word and deed, I rest my life, from day to day, upon the sure Foundation of Eternal Being.
10. The Kingdom of Spirit is embodied in my flesh.[20]

Says Renee Bledsoe: "Read this every day from top to bottom. Then start at the bottom and read it from bottom to top. Do this every day. If you do nothing for yourself beyond this one thing, you will shift your energy in subtle and pervasive ways that you may not yet even be able to imagine."[21]

TM:® Transcendental Meditation

"Yes, I know TM. I practice it every time I go to the dentist," an experienced AA oldtimer said to me, a Twelve Step rookie, back in the 1970s.

"How's that?" I asked.

"I don't take any painkillers because I *transcend dental medication!* Har, har, har."

Passing over the fact that having dental work done without taking anything for pain is sometimes quite discomforting,[*] the above vignette may speak to the sorts of meditations that were practiced by Twelve Steppers of that era and in that small prairie city. Nowadays, I understand that some Twelve Step groups do encourage their members to learn formal meditation methods such as TM, but I would hazard a guess that most groups are of the same mind-set as my old home-group on the Dakota plains. To some, this may seem a little odd because TM is very well known, meditation is specifically called for in the steps and, according to social scientists such as Patrick G. Williams, over two dozen scientific studies have concluded that Transcendental Meditation enhances the stability and length of sobriety for all kinds of people.[22]

So, what is Transcendental Meditation? According to the TM website (www.tm.org) Transcendental Meditation "is a simple technique practiced 20 minutes twice each day while sitting comfortably with eyes closed." It goes on to say that: "The TM technique is easy to learn and enjoyable to practice, and is not a religion, philosophy or lifestyle. Over five million people have learned it – people of all ages, cultures, and religions."[23]

The TM technique is taught (for a fee) in a series of seven lessons or "steps." The first three steps, which can be taken free of charge, are an Introductory Lecture, a Preparatory Lecture and a Personal Interview. The last four steps are taken on four consecutive days. They are a Personal Introduction and three sessions of "Checking" to verify the correctness and your understanding of the

---

[*] Of course, if you believe that taking painkillers will lead to a slip in your sobriety foregoing the medication may be the right decision for you.

mechanics of the TM technique and the development of higher states of consciousness.[24]

TM was founded by Maharishi Mahesh Yogi in the late 1950s. It is a form of mantra meditation, which is the mental repetition of a word or sound for a period of time. In the case of Transcendental Meditation, the mantras are said to be meaningless sounds of one to three syllables. Each student receives a secret mantra which is not to be revealed to anyone. Unlike ordinary yoga, basic TM does not require any special asana or posture. Advanced classes, which teach a technique called TM-Sidhi, or yogic flying, do require the student to sit cross-legged on a floor mat, in the familiar lotus position. The advanced course is by no means necessary in order to practice TM. Many, possibly most, meditators never take it.

The Maharishi gained considerable notoriety in the 1960s when for a short time he was spiritual advisor to the Beatles, England's super-famous rock 'n' roll quartet.[25] In the 50 years since then, TM has acquired many accolades and also some criticism. Perhaps the best testimonials come from those who have actually practiced TM and given it a fair trial. The following quotes are from "Case Histories: Using the Transcendental Meditation Program with Alcoholics and Addicts," a scientific article written by Catherine R. Bleick:

!*Nothing*, including prayer, Twelve Step meetings, talking to other alcoholics, or exercise is so effective as TM in controlling my chemical abuse problem and associated feelings of "insanity." ~Tom, a "success story"
!I have a lot less anger and a much clearer mind. This has enabled me to make the right decisions, whether it be on the spur of the moment or whether it requires long-term planning. I believe that TM has been a major factor in my being sober today. I cannot express in words the rewards that I received through daily meditating. ~Sam, another "success story"
!TM is one of the most valuable tools of my recovery. At first I meditated in order to stay off drugs, but now I stay off drugs in order to meditate. It keeps me centered – sometimes I feel

a blissful state – and allows me to focus on the day, one day at a time. ~Pedro, a third "success story"

!I had some rather hard, difficult times during my first year of sobriety. Facing reality sober is not an easy task. However, through practicing this very natural and easy method of relaxing, the business of living has been much easier to handle. ~Frank, a "success with irregular meditation"

! I do not believe I could have become this open with just AA and not meditation. I am eternally grateful that I was ready for TM. ~Jill, another "success with irregular meditation"[26]

Finally, George A. Ellis, who successfully taught the TM technique in Central American prisons and to over 1,200 Mayan Indians, had this to say: "If the TM program could be that successful in the prisons and among the Mayan people, in the midst of grinding poverty and extremely difficult circumstances, then the TM program can certainly be used to reduce substance abuse in any environment, anywhere in the world."[27]

Deepak Chopra: Quantum Recovery?

Deepak Chopra met Maharishi Mahesh Yogi in 1985 and from then until January 1993 he was one of the Maharishi's favored disciples. There are various accounts of why the two separated, the most common being that Chopra left because it was interfering with the success of his other businesses.[28] According to Chopra's 1988 book, *The Return of the Rishi,* Transcendental Meditation helped him to overcome his own dependence on alcohol and tobacco.[29] While he admits to being a heavy smoker and coffee drinker, he seems never to have quantified his intake of alcohol. However, it may be noted that he doesn't claim to have ever been an alcoholic or a drug addict.

Even after separating from the Maharishi, Chopra continues to use methods that incorporate mantra meditation and Ayurveda, the "science of life" based ancient Hindu writings. Although he holds an M.D. degree, Chopra hasn't practiced western medicine for many years. His first large-scale foray into addictive medicine came in 1997 when he published *Overcoming Addictions: The Spiritual Solution*. In that book Chopra describes how meditation and Ayurveda can be used to conquer addictions; and in it Chopra also reveals that he is not altogether in agreement with the Twelve Steps. Although the book is cautious about ruffling feathers, Chopra gently offered a negative observation about Twelve Step programs. First, he softened any criticism by lauding AA extravagantly: "The Twelve Steps of Alcoholics Anonymous are not just a program for becoming a sober person. They are about becoming a truly *great* person in all areas of life." Then, he commented that:

> Much as I admire these aspects of AA, I am less comfortable with what seems to be a fear-based element in the recovery program. Certainly many alcoholics have developed self-deluding ego mechanisms that need to be broken down, but AA's emphasis on the powerlessness of the addict seems troubling. As he walks a tightrope between the evil strength of alcohol on one side and the saving grace of a higher spiritual power on the other, the addict's true inner nature remains unknown and perhaps even irrelevant. Quite simply, he is what he does – and he himself can never be sure what he's going do from one day to the next. As AA's best-known maxim puts it, "One day at a time."[30]

Overcoming Addictions concludes by offering Chopra's own "twelve points for replacing addictive behavior with true joy in living."[31]

"Because I don't want these suggestions to seem in any way like a list of commandments etched in stone," Chopra said, "I've put them in the form of questions."[32] Chopra's twelve questions follow. The quotations after each question are intended only to show the "flavor" of the discussions in the book. For the complete set of comments see *Overcoming Addictions,* pages 223-228.

1. *Did you get the right amount of sleep last night?*
   "If you're sleeping more than ten hours a night, or less than six, this is probably an area in which you can make some positive adjustments."
2. *Did you start your day with nurturing activities that strengthened you in body and in spirit?*
   "The first hours are crucial in determining your state of mind throughout the day."

3. *Did you find real pleasure in your work?*
   "Even if you can't make radical career changes at this point, look for areas outside your present job that you may be able to develop over time."
4. *If you felt angry at someone or something, were you able to express this in a constructive way?*
   "According to Ayurveda, anger should be 'digested' just like anything else that's taken into the body."
5. *Were you able to experience nature today with awareness and appreciation?*
   "Even if you live in an urban area, you can keep in touch with nature through contact with plants and flowers, by walking in a park or near a body of water whenever there's time, or even simply by being out in the sunshine for a while each day."
6. *Did you find time for enjoyable activities or exercise?*
   "Your improved physical condition will make you much less inclined toward self-destructive activities."
7. *Were you able to spend some quiet time by yourself?*
   "...gaining access to the silent space between thoughts is the real purpose of Ayurvedic meditation."
8. *Did you laugh with real pleasure today?*

"Laughter can truly be a positive addiction, and its presence can overshadow the impulse toward other addictive behaviors."

9. *If you felt tired or under stress, were you able to rest for a while?*
"The world won't collapse if you simply take it easy for a [time]."

10. *Did you take your meals in pleasant surroundings, with company you enjoyed?*
"According to Ayurveda, the food that comprises a meal is less significant than the emotions that accompany it."

11. *Did you show love today to friends and family members?*
"Human beings best perceive affection through the sense of touch, and physical contact is clearly a wonderful way of expressing love."

12. *Did you freely and joyfully receive their love in return?*
"Compared to love, no addictive substance has any power whatsoever."[33]

In 2007 Chopra partnered with co-author David Simon to publish *Freedom from Addiction: The Chopra Center Method for Overcoming Destructive Habits*. Under the Heading "What's New in Recovery," Simon and Chopra wrote:

> Over the past seventy years, millions of people seeking to overcome addictive behaviors have embarked on a Twelve Step program.... The Twelve Steps are not for everyone, however. For some, the religious overtones are incompatible with their core personal beliefs, while for others, the Twelve Steps are not religious enough. The most common reason we hear at the Chopra Center for why people do not resonate with A.A. is its emphasis on personal powerlessness... The implication that people with bad habits must consider themselves lifelong victims

of an incurable condition is, for some, untenable. For those who believe free will is a distinguishing feature of human beings, admitting that one has lost free will stops the recovery process before it begins.[34]

They also wrote: "We think it's possible to reconcile the opposing viewpoints of choice verses powerlessness. The Chopra Center philosophy and approach to addiction highlights the paradox that every life seeks to resolve – the apparent conflict between our individuality and our universality."[35] In explaining the Chopra Center's philosophy, Simon and Chopra present several helpful lists, usually lists of seven things, ideas or questions. Two of these helpful lists are:

(1) Core Needs and Beliefs

Somewhat echoing the Abraham-Hicks philosophy, Simon and Chopra wrote: "The first compulsion that you want to release is self-disdain." Then they added:

> In terms of core needs, people with addictions are no different than other people. The primary distinction is that they have chosen a socially unacceptable or biologically undesirable way to meet their needs. Do not add insult to injury by wasting time or energy denigrating yourself over your addiction. Instead let's use that energy for healing and transformation.[36]

To counter this, Simon and Chopra created a list of seven *authentic beliefs*. They recommend reading these several times and then memorizing them. The seven *authentic beliefs* are:

1. I am doing my best given my current psychological and spiritual resources.
2. I have no desire to hurt anyone, including myself, as a consequence of my addiction.

3. Although I am good at rationalizing my addiction, I know at the core of my being that my habit is not serving my body, mind, or soul.
4. I recognize at some level that my addiction is a substitute for love.
5. I would free myself of this life-damaging habit if I could find a life-honoring substitute of equal or greater efficacy.
6. Although at times I may doubt it, I know at the deepest level of my being that I am capable of releasing this negative habit and replacing it with positive ones.
7. Seeking relief through substances is an expression of my essential spiritual nature.[37]

(2) The Seven Essential Components of Transformation

"Our experience working with many people," Simon and Chopra wrote, "have convinced us that the following actions are essential components underlying all lasting change:"

1. Make a commitment to transform.
2. Make a commitment not to repeat the mistakes of the past.
3. Face the harsh reality of the present.
4. See the infinite possibilities available in the present moment.
5. Envision where you want to be.
6. Ask yourself what choices need to be made to actualize your vision.
7. Create an action plan to execute your choices.

"For your world to change, you need to translate your intentions into actions," Simon and Chopra say. "Envision what you want to see unfold in your world and execute it. Be the change you want to see in your life."[38]

Reworking the Twelve Steps

From the Chopra Center's point of view, each of us has two "I's." One is the self-image or ego and the second is our higher self or soul. "Indeed, the conditioned 'I,' or our ego's self-image may be powerless over addiction," Simon and Chopra explain, "but there is another part of us over which addiction has no power." This second "I" they call the soul or the higher self. "The power that is greater than ourselves is our own higher self," they assert. "To seek this power we don't have to look for it externally."

To clarify this, Simon and Chopra reworked and expanded each of the Twelve Steps. Their rewritten version of the Steps, along with the original Twelve Steps of AA, are presented here side-by-side:

ALCOHOLICS ANONYMOUS TWELVE STEPS	CHOPRA CENTER TWELVE STEPS
1) We admitted we were powerless over alcohol—that our lives had become unmanageable.	*1) As a spiritual being, I recognize that my ego is not the real me and has no real power. An ego based life seeking security through control, power, or approval is difficult to manage.*
2) Came to believe that a Power greater than ourselves could restore us to sanity.	*2) Underlying and giving rise to my ego is a field of awareness with infinite possibilities Surrendering to this field within myself, I become safe, centered, and balanced, and I am capable of making life-supporting choices.*
3) Made a decision to turn our will and our lives over to the care of God AS WE UNDERSTOOD HIM.	*3) [I] Make the commitment to expand my external reference point, from a skin encapsulated, ego seeking control and approval to a unique expression of universal Being.*

4) Made a searching and fearless moral inventory of ourselves.	*4) I commit to exploring, healing, and transforming the hidden dimensions of my heart and soul through the regular practice of recapitulation [a method of self-review that enables us "to learn from our past, access creativity, and recognize the transitory nature of emotional reactions."]*
5) Admitted to God, to ourselves, and to another human being the exact nature of our wrongs.	*5) I commit entirely to cultivating nourishing relationships with others and with myself, so I am able to make healthy choices without the burden of regret, resentment or grievance.*
6) Were entirely ready to have God remove all these defects of character.	*6) I commit to accessing the aspect of my being that embraces and transcends the duality of my nature, so I may consciously choose to express those qualities that resonate with my higher self.*
7) Humbly asked Him to remove our shortcomings.	*7) I commit to acknowledging the light and dark elements of my nature as an expression of a deeper reality that is beyond duality. Accepting my capacity for duality and unity empowers me to make life-supporting evolutionary choices.*
8) Made a list of all persons we had harmed, and became willing to make amends to them all.	*8) I commit to taking responsibility for the choices I have made that had unintended consequences, including creating pain for others and myself.*

9) Made direct amends to such people wherever possible, except when to do so would injure them or others.	*9) I commit to a life of healing and transformation. Through my thoughts, words, and actions, I will demonstrate my awareness of the interrelatedness of life.*
10) Continued to take personal inventory and when we were wrong promptly admitted it.	*10) I commit to a spiritual practice of responding to life with greater awareness so my choices will be increasingly self-supporting.*
11) Sought through prayer and meditation to improve our conscious contact with God AS WE UNDERSTOOD HIM, praying only for knowledge of His will for us and the power to carry that out.	*11) Through meditation and reflective self inquiry, I commit to immersing myself in expanded awareness, thinking and behaving in the world as an expression of the universe.*
12) Having had a spiritual awakening as the result of these steps, we tried to carry this message to alcoholics, and to practice these principles in all our affairs.	*12) I commit to exploring the sacred dimensions of my soul and expressing my higher qualities in my relationships with others and myself.*[39]

Now, if you read the Chopra Center's steps quickly and superficially they are likely to sound like so much New Age gibberish, but if you read them slowly and reflect on the idea that your Higher Power is not necessarily outside and above you, but can also be within (inmost *and* most high), then they are apt to make more sense, not only in light of Eastern wisdom but also in light of Christianity. For example, see St. Paul's rhetorical question in his first letter to the Corinthians: "What? know ye not that your body is the temple of the Holy Ghost *which is* in you...?"[40]

The So-Hum Meditation Technique

The remainder of *Freedom from Addiction* is dedicated to explaining Ayurvedic techniques that are used at the Chopra Center for Well-Being. Most of these procedures are too complex to be summarized here. However, an exception may be a form of meditation that Simon and Chopra call the "So-Hum Meditation Technique," which is intended as a meditation for those who do not have a secret mantra given to them by a qualified teacher. They present the "So-Hum" technique in a series of ten steps. The steps are:

1. Find a comfortable place to sit where you will not be disturbed.
2. Close your eyes and take a few deep breaths.
3. Survey your body and adjust your position so you are not feeling any tension in your muscles.
4. Begin observing the inflow and outflow of your breath.
5. Introduce the internal thought "So" on each inhalation and the thought "Hum" on each exhalation.
6. Once you have established some rhythm to the silent repetition of SoHum, release your attention on the breath.
7. When you realize you have stopped thinking the mantra and have been lost in trains of thought, gently shift your attention back to the mantra.
8. When you realize your awareness has gone outward to a sound in your environment, gently bring it back to the mantra.
9. Treat the interruption of thoughts or noises with an inner attitude of "Whatever happens during my meditation is okay."
10. Practice the meditation for about fifteen to twenty minutes twice each day, in the morning and the evening.[41]

The "So-Hum" method is *not the* same as the "Primordial Sound Technique" that is taught at the Chopra Center, but the authors suggest it for those who cannot attend the Center or learn from one of its instructors. The two authors flatly state that they "have never seen a person relapse who is meditating regularly."[42]

The Sedona Method:® The Art of Letting Go

Lester Levenson was mad as a wet cat. He practically shouted at his doctor: "You're sorry? Well, so am I! You saved my life ... for what? So that I can be an invalid for the rest of it? What the hell kind of life are you giving me back anyway?"[43]

The doctor had just told Levenson that he could go home from the hospital, but it wasn't very good news. Lester was only 42 years old, still relatively young and something of a playboy; *and he was being sent home to die.* His health was a mess. He had suffered a second heart attack. He was depressed. He had an enlarged liver, kidney stones, spleen trouble, hyperacidity, and ulcers that had perforated his stomach.[44]

"[Y]ou cannot expect to live a normal life from here on," the doctor had told him. "You've just had a very serious coronary [and] you're lucky to be alive at all... I wish there were something else I could say; I wish I could tell you that in a few months you'd be back to normal and could pick up where you left off, but in all good conscious I can't tell you that... you could live for a year or two or you could go tomorrow. I just don't know."

"Thanks for being honest with me," the demoralized patient replied. "I'll be seeing you."[45]

But the doctor was wrong. Lester Levenson was to live for another 40 years and more, not dying until January 18, 1994, when he peacefully expired at the age of 84. Hale Dwoskin, a Levenson protégé, wrote about Lester in his 2003 book, *The Sedona Method:*

> Lester was a man who loved challenges. So, instead of giving up, he decided to go back to the lab within himself and find some answers. Because of his determination and concentration, he was able to cut through his conscious mind to find what he needed.

What he found was the ultimate tool for personal growth – a way of letting go of all inner limitations. He was so excited by his discovery that he used it intensively for a period of three months. By the end of that period, his body became totally healthy again. Furthermore, he entered a state of profound peace that never left him...[46]

After recovering his health, Lester decided that for the rest of his life he wanted only one thing: to teach others his method of finding health, happiness and peace. He had discovered that his happiness was the fruit of love – *not* the love Levenson received but the love he gave to others. According to Robert Ullman and Judyth Reichenberg-Ullman, authors of *Mystics, Masters, Saints and Sages*: "Realizing that his problems were self-caused by his own erroneous thinking, Lester found freedom. When he was able to release negative thoughts and feelings, he felt tremendous relief and inner peace."[47]

In the late 1950s Lester moved from his New York penthouse to the high desert around Sedona, Arizona, where he taught his method to a small number of disciples. Upon Lester's death in 1994, those of his students who chose to do so passed along his teachings by forming organizations of their own. One such organization is the Sedona Method founded by the aforementioned Hale Dwoskin. Although there are others who are also teaching Levenson's methods of "letting go" or "releasing," the Sedona Method appears to be the only one that places an emphasis on breaking habits and overcoming addictions.

The basics of the Sedona Method can be boiled down to just five simple steps, which are explained on pages 39-40 of *The Sedona Method:*

> **Step 1 -** Focus on an issue that you have, and then allow yourself to *feel* whatever you are feeling at the moment.

Step 2 - Ask yourself *one* of the following questions:
- *Could I let this feeling go?*
- *Could I allow this feeling to be here?*
- *Could I welcome this feeling?*

Step 3 - No matter which question you chose, ask *Would I let it go?* Or *Am I willing to let go?*

Step 4 - Ask yourself: *When?* (This is an invitation to answer "now.")

Step 5 - Repeat the procedure as often as necessary until that particular feeling is released, let go of, or gone.[48]

Note that the above summary is just a very bare bones presentation of the Sedona Method, which is described more completely in Dwoskin's 400+ page book. The basics of the method can also be summarized as "five basic releasing questions." If, for example, you are having an urge to drink and/or to use drugs, ask yourself:

What is my NOW feeling about this?
Could I welcome/allow it?
Could I let it go?
Would I let it go?
When?
Then repeat as necessary until the feeling is released or let go.

"All the questions used in this process are deliberately simple," Dwoskin explains. "They are not important in and of themselves but are designed to point you to the experience of letting go, to the experience of stopping holding on [or the experience of not holding on anymore]."[49]

In dealing specifically with addictions, Dwoskin recommends making a pact with yourself that indulging the habit may be allowable *if you release first*. "The reason for releasing first,"

Dwoskin says, "is that all habit patterns are locked in by patterns of feeling. Certain feelings come up in our awareness, and the way we compensate is by taking a particular action.... So when you release, you let go of the underlying cause or motivation for that particular habit."[50]

Such is the Sedona Method theory. However, an exception is urged in cases where you are addicted to illegal drugs, are under medical or other professional care, or a member of a Twelve Step group.

But the Sedona Method does have one relatively strong disagreement with the Twelve Step method. It is the often-heard objection to saying "I am an alcoholic." Dwoskin explained:

> The one disagreement I have with various 12-Step programs, is the continual affirmation and reaffirmation by people speaking in their meetings of "I am a _____ (insert your particular addiction, e.g., alcoholic, sex addict, or overeater.)" This may be extremely helpful in the beginning to break through denial, but after someone has completed the steps of the program, and kicked his or her particular habit, it would be much better to affirm: "Hi, I am _____ insert your name) and I *used to be* a _____ (insert the particular addiction).

Despite this difference, Hale Dwoskin insists that the Sedona Method is intended to be used *as an addition to* – not as a substitute for – competent medical assistance, professional counseling, and support groups such as Alcoholics Anonymous.

Emotional Freedom Technique:
The Tapping Solution

EFT stands for Emotional Freedom Technique which is an offshoot of TFT, Thought Field Therapy, which is a form of acupressure that is based on acupuncture, the ancient Chinese method of healing. There, in one sentence, is the 5,000 year history of the evolution of EFT, an allegedly new and untested method of healing.

Because EFT is rooted in Chinese philosophy, it is important to understand that while most of western medicine is based on manipulating the body's *chemistry*, Traditional Chinese Medicine is based on adjusting bodily *energy*. According to ancient Chinese medical science, the human body has twelve "Principle Meridians" and eight "Extraordinary Channels" through which life-energy or Qi^* flows. There are about 360 acupuncture points located along these meridian lines. They are the points where acupuncturists insert their needles according to the art and science of acupuncture.

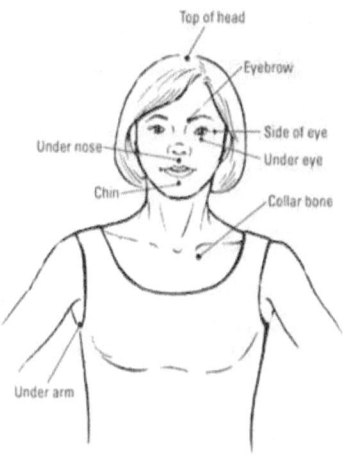

Basic EFT Tapping Points

Like acupuncture, acupressure seeks to stimulate certain acupoints and thereby increase the flow of *Qi*. Pressure may be applied manually or with various hand-held instruments. Thought Field Therapy (TFT) is a form of acupressure that was developed in 1981 by Roger Callahan. It uses a complex system of algorithms to

---

* *Pronounced chee as in cheese, rhymes with glee.

determine which set of acupressure points are to be used for which specific psychological problems. TFT does not come anywhere near using all of the 360 acupoints. Instead it uses seven tapping points on the face and upper body and four points on the hands.[51]

Virtually the same points are used by the Emotional Freedom Technique (EFT), which adds a point at the top of the head (see the Basic EFT Tapping Points diagram, above left). They also use the "karate chop" point on the little finger side of the either hand.[*] Significantly, EFT does not use algorithms.

EFT was developed in the 1990s by Gary Craig, a Stanford engineering graduate and an ordained minister.[52] Craig was studying Thought Field Therapy when he must have asked himself something like this: Why is it necessary to have all these complex algorithms when using all nine of the tapping points is so quick and easy? Indeed, the algorithms are *not* usually necessary and their elimination has the added benefit of allowing lay people to use the procedure on themselves.

The EFT approach uses a five step process. The basic five-step EFT tapping recipe follows:

Step 1. *Identify the Issue.* Make a mental note of your problem. Examples might be an embarrassing moment from your childhood such as your father ruining a birthday party by showing up drunk. Or an insatiable desire to drink at 5:00 o'clock every day.

Step 2. *Test the initial intensity.* Establish the *before* intensity of your issue on a subjective scale of zero to ten.

Step 3. *The setup.* Compose a simple phrase to say while continuously tapping the "karate chop" point on the side of your hand. This phrase has two goals:

1. acknowledge the problem

---

[*] The "karate chop" point is on the fleshy underside of your hand (either hand). It is the spot you would use if you were trying to "karate chop" a piece of wood.

2. accept yourself in spite of it. The formula for this *setup phrase* is:

"Even though I have this _____, I deeply and completely accept myself" where the blank is to be filled in with whatever problem you are having.

So your completed *setup phrase* could go something like this:

"Even though I have this *drinking problem,* I deeply and completely accept myself." Try to be as specific as possible.

At about this time you will also need to create a *reminder phrase,* which is an abbreviated version of the *setup phrase.* Examples of a *reminder phrase* might be: "my ruined birthday" or "my five o'clock drinking problem." The *reminder phrase* is to be used when tapping on the remaining acupoints.

Step 4. *The Sequence.* To perform this, you tap on each of the Basic EFT Tapping Points shown in the diagram on page ??. You tap each point from seven to nine times (no counting is necessary). While you tap you repeat the *reminder phrase.* The sequence is from the top downward:

1. -Top of head
2. -Eyebrow
3. -Side of eye
4. -Under eye
5. -Under nose
6. -Chin
7. -Collar bone
8. -Under arm

Step 5. *Test the intensity again.* Assign a second number to your problem using the same zero to ten subjective scale. If you are not down to zero then repeat the process until you reach zero or plateau at some level.

The above brief description is based largely on Gary Craig's "Free EFT Tutorial" but it is not sufficient training for using EFT on yourself or others. There are many books and Internet sites devoted to EFT, including numerous videos. The EFT method is not completely standardized and different purveyors may have slightly different formulas for its practice. Furthermore Gary Craig –who, you recall, is EFT's founder– cautions: "EFT is still in the experimental stage and, while a growing number of PhD's and MD's are adopting it, we cannot claim that it is risk free."[53]

Drum Therapy: "Drumming Out Drugs"

"Kids who were down got pumped up, and kids who were a little too pumped up, got mellowed out – all without a prescription."[54] So spoke Ed Mikenas, a youth counselor and drummer with a group called *Conga*. Mikenas's opinion of therapeutic drumming is very high as the above quotation and others reveal in "Catching the Beat of the Drum," an article by Brion McAlarney. But with the exception of that excellent article, much of the literature on drumming as a complimentary addiction treatment method was either written by a different man, Michael Winkelman, or references Winkelman's work, particularly "Complimentary Therapy for Addiction: 'Drumming Out Drugs,'" which was published in the April 2003 edition of the *American Journal of Public Health*.

In that paper, Winkelman concluded: "Although systematic evaluations of the effectiveness of drumming activities are lacking, experiences of counselors and clients indicate that drumming can play a substantial role in addressing addiction."[55] His research methods included observing drumming activities in a number of substance abuse programs and interviewing program directors and counselors. Winkelman described the activities of the programs he observed, including Mark Seaman's "Earth Rhythms of West Reading, Pa":

Seaman's program begins with his drumming as people enter the room. They pick up drums and are free to play them as they choose. He then introduces warm-up exercises to make people feel comfortable with the drums, teaching people how to hit the drums without emphasizing anything technical... A subsequent activity gives each participant the opportunity to briefly drum to express feelings... Seaman ends his program with an application of Alcoholics Anonymous' 11th step (meditation), using meditation music and a variety of percussion instruments to reinforce a visualization process to connect with a higher power.[56]

"I get people to relax," Seaman says, "give them permission to leave their body and go on a journey. I talk about forgiveness, acceptance and surrender. I work [on] release of guilt from the wreckage that they have produced through their addictions."[57]

Of course, others in addition to McAlarney and Winkelman have contributed to our knowledge on this subject. Michael Drake in "The Therapeutic Effects of Drumming," a paper published on August 5, 2009 on the SelfGrowth.com website, declared that drumming has many positive effects. Among these are that drumming:

- Reduces tension, anxiety, and stress
- Creates a sense of connectedness with self and others
- Helps us to experience being in resonance with the natural rhythms of life
- Provides a secular approach to accessing a higher power
- Releases negative feelings, blockages, and emotional trauma[58]

Drumming may be done in groups, usually with a professional leader, or individually. Concerning solo and group drumming, Robert Friedman, author of *The Healing Power of the Drum,* had this to say: "Whether you play with others or alone, the drum provides the perfect communication tool, unencumbered by the restrictions of verbal language, and creating an environment where your emotions can flow freely."[59]

Kudos for Drumming

I've previously made the point that individual praise or testimonials do nothing to establish a program's statistical success. What they do show is that such programs have gained the enthusiastic support of some people. And if they work for some people, they could work for you. Really, what use is it to know that a program works for, say, 52 percent of the population (which is far better than most programs perform)? What you're really after is not necessarily something that works for the majority, *of which you may or may not be a member,* but something that works specifically for you. Keeping that in mind, the following testimonials may (or may not) entice you to try therapeutic drumming.[60] Either outcome is OK, so read and decide.

- I thought the drum circle was very relaxing. Drum circles are awesome. ~ Chris, age 28
- It was very good… I learned how to deal with stress… how to think positive ~ Kevin, age 38
- It was very therapeutic for me… [I] got to learn how to do something as a team. I felt very free and healthier. ~ Robert, age 30
- I learned a new way to let certain things go. ~ Steven, age 36
- It was fun and a stress reliever ~ Anonymous, age 31
- [The drumming brought back my] memory of having a good time without using ~ Richard, age 20
- [I] Got to release bad energy and get my creative side out ~ Anonymous, age 21
- I felt free and relieved during the experience ~ Chastain, age 28
- You release stress, clears your mind, [and] gives you the opportunity to leave garbage behind ~ Frances, age 49
- I felt an uplifting of my spirit - I was able to let go of certain things ~ Stefini, age 36

- It made me realize the importance of positive affirmations - I wish we could do it more often ~ Sara, age 24
- Cleansing, healing, mind freeing, heart pounding Beauty ... the feeling of being One and Whole ~ Larissa, age 23

Pagan Recovery: "Here There Be Pagans," *Sober* Pagans

Paganism is sometimes called the "Old Religion" because it resurrects or recreates the religion that was practiced by Europeans prior to their conversion to Christianity. It is an earth based religion and a polytheistic religion, which means that it allows for the worship of numerous goddesses and gods.

As with some other non-Christian groups, such as the Jewish people, for example, Pagans (or Neo-Pagans, also Neopagans) who fall victim to an addiction sometimes find that Twelve Step programs are not compatible with their religion. Polytheistic Pagans in recovery have to deal with the assumption that one's Higher Power should be a singular, male deity. And some Christian rituals, such as recitation of the Lord's Prayer, are often found to be inappropriate for Pagans. Furthermore, AA's Third and Eleventh Steps may imply an understanding of the will that runs counter to the Pagan Path.

Both the Third Step and the Eleventh Step talk about the will. The Third Step – "Made a decision to turn our will and our lives over to the care of God AS WE UNDERSTOOD HIM" – implicates the personal will as part of the addiction problem. And the Eleventh Step – "Sought through prayer and meditation to improve our conscious contact with God AS WE UNDERSTOOD HIM, praying only for knowledge of His will for us and the power to carry that out" – assumes that the personal will is something that is at odds with the Devine will. This is summed up in a thesis paper by Charlotte Turvey titled "Twelve Stepping on the Margins: A Neo-Pagan Case Study in Overcoming Adversity."

Neo-Pagans have a very different worldview from the Christian one that influenced the founders of AA and Al-Anon. Neo-Pagans seek to honor the divine feminine, are polytheistic and view the divine as imminent [present in all things, especially people].[61]

There is no accurate assessment of how prevalent recovering people may be in the Pagan community, but Isaac Bonewits made this somewhat tongue-in-cheek estimate:

> I would guesstimate that if we added up all the Neopagans who are currently recovering alcoholics or drug addicts, adult children of alcoholics and/or drug addicts, adult survivors of childhood abuse (physical, emotional, spiritual and/or sexual), have eating disorders (such as anorexia or compulsive overeating), who are sex and/or love addicts, etc., that we would wind up with 95% of the entire Neopagan community – and 150% (sic) of our clergy.[62]

A more serious indicator may be the fact that best-selling author Starhawk revised her popular book on Neopaganism, *The Spiral Dance: A Rebirth of the Ancient Religion of the Great Goddess,* to make the Pagan Path a safer place for Pagans in recovery.

"Another healing challenge that the Pagan community has begun to face over the last decade," Starhawk wrote, "is that of confronting our addictions." She explained:

> The language of the Twelve Steps and the traditional forms of meetings may not always work for Pagans... [and] one of the overall changes I have made in this edition of the book [is] the substitution of other drinks for wine in the rituals and the change of what we used to call Cakes and Wine to Feasting. I do this not because I think no one should ever drink

but so that ritual becomes a safe space for those who are struggling toward recovery from Addictions. [63]

Some Pagans in recovery adjust by modifying their understanding of the Steps or by making subtle changes to their ritual practices. There are also some Pagan Twelve Step groups, both face-to-face and Internet based, and at least two books that spell out different step programs for Pagans. In no particular order, the following four programs are briefly described.

The Spiral Steps
Unlike some of the other Pagan recovery programs that will be discussed here, the Spiral Steps program is not a group for working rituals or practicing other aspects of the esoteric arts. It is simply a support group of like-minded, earth-based spiritualists who are recovering from an addiction. Spiral Steps was founded by Dj, who has been a practicing Pagan since 1984 and a sober practitioner since 1987.

The Spiral Steps program has face-to-face meetings and an email list. They seem to be a bit reclusive, only wanting members who have been screened for compatibility with their philosophy. Like other Pagan recovery programs, Spiral Steps have re-written AA's basic Twelve Steps and Twelve Traditions. The Spiral Steps include a focus word, which is apparently the principle upon which each Spiral Step is based. There is also an added Thirteenth Step and an added Thirteenth Tradition. The Thirteen Steps of the Spiral Steps program are:

1. We admitted that we had a problem and made the decision to reclaim our lives.
   FOCUS: HONESTY
2. We came to believe that there was hope for healing, health and balance.
   FOCUS: HOPE
3. We now honor our connection with the divine, as we understand it, and we accept the process of change.

FOCUS: COURAGE
4. We make a searching, fearless and honest inventory of our behavior and beliefs.
FOCUS: INSIGHT
5. We admit to ourselves and another human being what is both healthy and unhealthy in our lives and we make a daily commitment to heal ourselves in body, mind and spirit.
FOCUS: COMPASSION
6. We are willing to seek our Highest Good and to grow both spiritually and emotionally.
FOCUS: INTEGRITY
7. We let go of dysfunctional thoughts and behaviors and we consciously welcome joy, love and peace into our lives.
FOCUS: FREEDOM
8. We make a list of all beings we have harmed, including ourselves, and we become willing to make amends to them all.
FOCUS: JUSTICE
9. We work to restore balance in our lives. We make direct amends to others whenever possible and we value and care for ourselves.
FOCUS: BALANCE
10. We continue to take personal inventory and promptly acknowledge both our mistakes and our achievements whenever they occur.
FOCUS: EMOTIONAL AWARENESS
11. We continue to grow in compassion, strength and understanding. We learn to celebrate our lives and our connection to all living things.
FOCUS: SPIRITUAL AWARENESS
12. Having had a spiritual and emotional awakening, we work to help others along the path and we practice these principles in all our affairs.
FOCUS: SERVICE
13. We seek to find our Calling and to develop the will and the wisdom to follow it.
FOCUS: WISDOM [64]

The Recovery Spiral

Not to be confused with Spiral Steps, *The Recovery Spiral* is the title of a 2004 book by Cynthia Jane Collins. In it she presents a Pagan version of the Twelve Steps and some radically different ways of working those steps. Her version of the Steps addresses many of the issues that Pagans have with the traditional Twelve Step program, including its insistence upon a monotheistic, apparently male God.

Among the innovations that Collins has made is the use of Tarot card readings for advice on how to take a step. She also recommends rituals to be performed prior to taking each step. Altogether, these additional tools may enhance the Twelve Step program, making the Recovery Spiral less ambiguous than traditional ways of working the steps.

Recoven

"Recoven" is apparently a word made by combining "recovery" and "coven" (a gathering of witches). It is also the title of a book. *Recoven: The Wiccan Recovery Program* is a 2005 book by Medicine Hawk Wilburn, a Wiccan and, among other accomplishments, a university professor in Southern California. Like *The Recovery Spiral*, *Recoven* rewrites the Twelve Steps to make them more compatible with Pagan philosophy. And also like *The Recovery Spiral*, *Recoven* presents rituals to be performed with each step.

In essence the Recoven steps are changed very little from the AA Steps, except for Step Eleven, which is an added step, making thirteen Recoven steps in total. Recoven's Step Eleven reads: "I will seek the cause for my actions in the review of my past lives that I may better understand my karma and dharma in the past, present and future of this life."[65]

Medicine Hawk justifies this step by saying:

> There are two schools of thought regarding the inclusion of past life information in a recovery program. Some believe that the process of recovery

is so complicated that we should simplify it by concentrating only on the "present" life. Others are of the persuasion that all the information necessary to fully explain dysfunction is not contained in the memory of the "present" life. In keeping with the latter statement, perhaps recovery is so difficult because we do limit our interpretive discoveries to the "present" life. Perhaps the process would be expedited by investigation of past lives.[66]

Nine Step Pagans

Nine Step Pagans (NSP) is an organization of Pagan and Pagan friendly individuals who recognize in themselves a tendency toward addiction or compulsive behaviors and who have a desire to overcome this tendency. NSP started as an Internet e-group support list with the hope that it would grow into an organization with face-to-face meetings in physical space. The Nine Steps of the Nine Step Pagans are:

1. We came to feel enslaved by excessive behaviors which were harmful to us, throwing our health and relationships out of balance through addictions, compulsions, or both.
2. We realized that resources were available to help us win our freedom, if we were willing to use them.
3. We became willing to reach out for help, physically, emotionally, and spiritually.
4. We sought help from our Deities, fellow humans, healers, clergy, groups, or whatever source necessary, to aid us toward freedom and health.
5. We established a pattern of life-affirming behaviors, avoiding the sorts of isolation which would make us vulnerable to relapses, creating a foundation of supports which could help us recover from whatever lapses we might have.

6. We considered, acknowledged, and took full responsibility for harm we had done to others and ourselves in the time of our slavery.
7. We considered and discussed with a neutral adult, the harm we had done, and how we might make restitution or otherwise restore balance, facing the fact that in some situations no direct redress was possible.
8. Where possible, and using whatever supports necessary, we endeavored to restore balance in those situations and relationships previously harmed by our servitude to addiction or compulsion.
9. Remaining constructively vigilant in our self-regard, we continued to grow strong in health and freedom, eventually becoming a source of support for others seeking to bring their own lives into healthy balance.[67]

Buddhist Recovery: Noble Paths to Overcome Suffering

"[O]nly in very trivial and easily overcome ways does Buddhism not fit squarely within the same process as 12-Step programs in general."[68] So spoke Buddhist writer Taiyu in a 2013 article titled "A Buddhist's Views on AA."

Now the above statement may be true –probably is true from the point of view of Taiyu– but it is not the whole story. Some Buddhists simply don't want to translate their beloved Buddhism into the language of the Steps. And some addicts turn to Buddhism specifically *because* they are looking for an alternative to AA and/or other Twelve Step programs. As practicing Buddhist and addiction counselor Darren Littlejohn put it: "I no longer insist that people who ask me for help become full time 12-Steppers. While I participate in 12-Step, I respect the feelings of those who might not like it. In fact, they seem to be in the majority."[69]

Thus recent years have seen an increase in books and articles describing how Buddhism can be used *instead of* Twelve Step recovery programs.* Two recent books in particular offer this option. They are: *Eight Step Recovery: Using the Buddha's Teachings to Overcome Addiction* by Valerie Mason-John and Dr. Paramabandhu Groves, and *Refuge Recovery: A Buddhist Path to Recovery From Addiction* by Noah Levine.

Eight Step Recovery

Valerie Mason-John and Paramabandhu Groves created an Eight-Step Addiction recovery model that relies heavily on Buddhist philosophy and the teachings of Siddhârtha Gautama, who is called the Buddha, a name that means "the enlightened one." Siddhârtha, or Buddha, was born in Northeastern India about 2500 years ago, give or take several hundreds of years. His namesake religion is now practiced by 360 million adherents around the world, making Buddhism the world's fourth largest religion.

Mason-John's and Groves' Eight Step Recovery program is similar to the famous *Noble Eight Fold Path.* Those who have some familiarity with Buddhism will know that the *Four Nobel Truths* and the *Noble Eight Fold Path* are basic teachings of the Buddha. The *Four Noble Truths* are: 1) life is suffering; 2) suffering is caused by desire; 3) suffering can be eliminated; 4) suffering is eliminated by following the *Noble Eight Fold Path.*

The *Noble Eight Fold Path* is not a series of steps that are to be taken but a way of life that needs to be lived. The elements of the *Noble Eight Fold Path* are: Right view; Right intention; Right speech; Right action; Right livelihood; Right effort; Right mindfulness; and Right concentration (or meditation). In contrast, the Eight Step Recovery program may be taken as a series of steps. Bearing in mind that the quotes accompanying each step are merely samples of the chapter-long detailed discussions that are given in the *Eight Step Recovery* book, the Steps of the Eight Step Recovery program are:

---

* There are also many books on how Buddhism and the Twelve Steps can work together. See for example: *One Breath at a Time* by Kevin Griffin, *The 12-Step Buddhist* by Darren Littlejohn, and *The Zen of Recovery* by Mel Ash.

1. Accepting that this human life will bring suffering
   "Step one highlights the teachings of the first noble truth. That there is suffering."
2. Seeing how we create extra suffering in our lives
   "The key to freedom from the trap of suffering is to realize that we are responsible for multiplying our suffering."
3. Embracing impermanence to show us that our suffering can end
   "In Steps One and Two we explore suffering in great detail. The good news is, in Step Three, we come to see how there is an end to suffering."
4. Being willing to step onto the path of recovery and discover freedom
   "Everything changes. We can relate to change in a fearful way that keeps us on the path of suffering, or we can open up to change. We can get a glimpse of a different sort of life: a life without addiction and one that has the taste of freedom."
5. Transforming our speech, actions, and livelihood
   "Transforming our speech, actions, and livelihood is part of the ethical and moral spring cleaning we need to help maintain recovery and cultivate sobriety of mind."
6. Placing positive values at the center of our lives
   "We recognize that our addiction is a false refuge and cannot bring about true happiness or contentment. We go for refuge to a community that offers the ideal of recovery, sobriety, and abstinence."
7. Making every effort to stay on the path of recovery
   "We ride the harrowing waves of recovery with calm, and know that, every time we surf the pain of recovery, the waves will become calmer. We surf the waves with calm by preventing unhelpful states of mind from arising, eradicating them when they do arise, and cultivating and maintaining helpful states of mind."
8. Helping others by sharing the benefits we have gained

> "Helping other people can draw us away from self-preoccupation and can be one way of providing a sense of meaning to our lives."[70]

The Four Truths of Refuge Recovery

Recovered addict Noah Levine has also created a Buddhist recovery program that is modeled on the *Four Noble Truths* and the *Noble Eight Fold Path*. Levine's Four Noble Truths are: 1) Addiction creates suffering; 2) The cause of addiction is repetitive craving; 3) Recovery is possible; and 4) The Eight-Fold Path is an abstinence based path and philosophy that leads to the end of suffering.[71]

> The Eight-Fold Path of Refuge Recovery, which is summarized on pages 24-26 of the *Refuge Recovery* book is clearly patterned after the *Noble Eight Fold Path* of regular Buddhism. It is not a linear path where the steps need to be taken in order. Rather, according to Refuge Recovery, all of the factors need to be developed and applied simultaneously or concurrently.[72] It consists of:

1. **Understanding.** We come to know that everything is ruled by cause and effect. The Four Truths are an ongoing practice. In this step, we gain insight into the impermanent, unsatisfactory, and impersonal nature of life. Forgiveness is possible and necessary.
2. **Intention.** We renounce greed, hatred, and delusion. We train our mind to meet all pain with compassion and all pleasure with nonattached appreciation. We cultivate generous, kind, and compassionate wishes for all living beings. We practice honesty and humility and live with integrity.
3. **Communication/Community.** We take refuge in the community as a place to practice wise communication and to support others on their paths. We practice being honest, wise, and careful in our communications, asking for help from the

community, allowing others to guide us through the process. We practice openness, honesty, and humility about the difficulties and successes we experience.

4. **Action/Engagement.** We purify our actions, letting go of the behaviors that cause harm. The minimum commitment necessary for the path toward recovery and freedom is renunciation of violence, of dishonesty, of sexual misconduct, and of intoxication. Compassion, nonattached appreciation, generosity, kindness, honesty, integrity, and service become our guiding principles.
5. **Livelihood/Service.** We try to be of service to others whenever possible, using our time, energy, and resources to help create positive change. We work toward securing a source of income/livelihood that causes no harm.
6. **Effort/Energy.** We commit to the daily disciplined practices of meditation, yoga, exercise, wise actions, kindness, forgiveness, generosity, compassion, appreciation, and the moment-to-moment mindfulness of feelings, emotions, thoughts, and sensations. Through effort and energy we develop the skillful means of knowing how to apply the appropriate meditation or action to the given circumstances.
7. **Mindfulness/Meditations.** We develop wisdom through practicing formal mindfulness meditation. This leads to seeing clearly and healing the root causes and conditions that lead to the suffering of addiction. We practice present-time awareness in all aspects of our life. We take refuge in the present.
8. **Concentration/Meditations.** We develop the capacity to focus the mind through the practice of loving kindness, compassion, and forgiveness to focus on the positive qualities we seek to uncover. We utilize concentration at times of temptation or craving in order to abstain from acting unwisely.[73]

According to Noah Levine, the creator of the Refuge Recovery Program, The Eight Steps of Refuge Recovery can be used with, or instead of, the Twelve Steps of Alcoholics Anonymous.

Taking These Roads

While writing this chapter I took some time to try out several of the techniques and meditations that are described herein. For TM's and Deepak Chopra's approaches to addiction recovery, I tried doing the So-Hum meditation technique. Here I must confess that mine is not the mind of a natural mantra meditator. Almost always my mind would drift or, often as not, I would simply fall asleep. Although it is said that anything that happens while you are meditating is OK, I did not find this to be a rewarding practice. No doubt the results would have been much better if I had taken a Transcendental Meditation class or had the advantage of being taught by one of the Chopra Center's instructors.

I also tried the Sedona Method's "letting go" technique. This was interesting and I do believe that "letting go" or "releasing" old thoughts and memories does have a calming effect on the mind. The EFT or Emotional Freedom Technique method is easily learned and can be practiced on one's self. The tapping and the repetition of a phrase does seem to help to quiet the mind and after the exercise one gets the feeling that *something* has happened. I also tried EFT on my wife, who also said that "it worked."

Finally, I actually bought a djembe drum to practice the "drumming out drugs" technique. Even drumming alone and with no training except for a U-Tube video, the drumming seemed to have an effect. After drumming for a while and then stopping, the subtle "ringing" or "tone" in the ears is silenced and the mind is calm.

So much for my first-person accounts of New Age recovery practices.

Since **Father Divine's** passing in 1965, the **Peace Mission Movement** has been shepherded by his second wife, Edna Rose Ritchings, who is better known as Mother Divine. The *Peace Mission Movement* is headquartered at 1622 Spring Mill Road, Gladwyne, PA 190351021 and its website is at: http://peacemission.info/.

Abraham-Hicks' Second Twelve Steps are available on *"Beyond the 12 Steps: Breaking Free of Addiction,"* a DVD and/or a CD from Abraham-Hicks Publications. Furthermore, *Abraham-Hicks* is almost literally *all over* the Internet. There are many blogs, discussion lists, videos and audios. Although I do not personally know of any face-to-face groups, it would not surprise me to learn that there are such groups for devoted "Abrahamers," as the disciples of Abraham sometimes call themselves. The official Abraham-Hicks Internet address is at: http://www.abraham-hicks.com.

Addiction Alchemy is headquartered at 1939 Park Meadows Dr., Ft. Meyers, Florida 33907. Their website is at http://www.addictionalchemy.com/index.html. It includes a list of "gatherings" you may want to attend and a list of "clans" that are currently forming. For more information, you can email them from their *Addiction Alchemy* Website.

In the past, the fees charged by ***Transcendental Meditation*** have been criticized for being too high. At one time they were up to $2,500 in the US, but they were reduced to around $960 in 2013. The fees also vary greatly from country to country. The official ***TM*** website is at: http://www.tm.org/.

Deepak Chopra's website is at: https://www.deepakchopra.com/ and the website for the *Chopra Center for Well Being* is at: http://www.chopra.com/. Besides the Chopra Center, most of Deepak Chopra's work is available through his many books and audio/visual media. The two books that speak directly to addiction recovery are Chopra's *Overcoming Addictions: The Spiritual Solution* (1998) and *Freedom From Addiction: The Chopra Center Method for Overcoming Destructive Habits* (2007) by David Simon and Deepak Chopra.

To find the ***Sedona Method's*** website go to: http://www:sedona.com or just search for "Sedona Method." As mentioned earlier, in addition to Hale Dwoskin's *Sedona Method,* there are others who are carrying on Lester Levinson's basic teachings. One of the more successful of these is Larry Crane. His *Release Technique* website is at: http://www.releasetechnique.com/.

Whatever you choose, or before you choose, take your time. If you like what's on the Internet, buy the book. If you like the book, buy the CDs. And if you like the CDs, then sign up for a retreat if you want.

There are many websites devoted to the ***Emotional Freedom Technique (EFT),*** so many that I choose not to mention any for fear of being biased or of leaving out some of the more appropriate ones. Search the Internet and follow up on those sites that seem to interest you.

There is no one particular website or central office for ***Drumming Out Drugs.*** Individuals are basically on their own when it comes to finding therapeutic drumming groups. Local treatment centers or professional counselors may know of such programs, or you could try asking New Age bookstores who sometimes sponsor drumming circles. But be very careful, some drumming groups are havens for active drug addicts. My advice is that it's better to drum alone than to drum with a group of active stoners.

Unless you are already a member of a Pagan community, ***Pagan Recovery Groups*** can be reclusive and hard to find. One clever suggestion that I ran across is to contact local hospitals to ask if they have a Pagan Chaplain onboard. If they do have such a Chaplain, she or he is likely to know about local *Pagan Recovery Groups.* There are also Pagan e-groups on Yahoo and possibly other places on the Internet. Furthermore, a couple of the groups discussed here have Internet sites. The site for ***Spiral Steps*** is: http://www.spiralsteps.org/; and for ***Nine Step Pagans*** it is: http://www.ninesteppagans.faithweb.com/. Books about the other two programs, *The Recovery Spiral* and ***Recoven,*** have been discussed already.

Concerning the two programs representing ***Buddhist Recovery,*** *Eight Step Recovery* has an excellent website at: https://thebuddhistcentre.com /eightsteps; and also at: http://windhorsepublications.com/eight-step-recovery-audio. Among other things, the websites have a number of audio meditations. According to page ix of *Eight Step Recovery,* the publisher grants to individuals who have purchased the *Eight Step Recovery* book non-assignable permission to stream and download the audio files.⁷⁴ According to Valerie Mason-John, there are already some face-to-face *Eight Step Recovery* meetings in the UK and Canada and the second edition of *Eight Step Recovery* will contain a suggested meeting format.⁷⁵

Refuge Recovery: A Buddhist Path to Recovering from Addiction was published in 2014 and even before then there were meetings in Nashville, Tennessee (http://againstthestream nashville.com/category/refuge-recovery-talks/), Los Angeles (https://www.facebook.com/RefugeRecovery) and Oklahoma City (http://rrokc.wordpress.com/). An appendix to the *Refuge Recovery* book contains a suggested format for *Refuge Recovery* meetings and there is a *Refuge Recovery* treatment center opening in Los Angeles and possibly other cities.

Finally, although Martial Arts are not usually thought of as "New Age" activities, almost all of the genuine martial arts have a spiritual foundation. This, of course, excludes Mixed Martial Arts or MMA, which is sometimes more or less accurately described as "brawling." It's just a suggestion, but if you should find yourself in recovery with extra time and energy, you may want to try *Tae Kwon Do, Karate, Kung-Fu, Tai Chi, Aikido,* or *Muay Thai,* all popular types of genuine martial arts.⁷⁶

Certainly there are many *New Age* roads to recovery. As you consider all these, may all the choices you make be wise and healthy ones. Namaste!

Chapter Endnotes

1 Schneider, Daniel B. (Sept 27, 1998) "Life With Father Divine," *New York Times.* Retrieved 3/10/2014 from: http://www.nytimes.com/1998/09/27/nyregion/fyi-025666.html

2. Father Divine" (29 Nov 2013) *Wikipedia.* Retrieved 2/21/2014 from: http://en.wikipedia.org/wiki/Father_Divine. And "Father Divine Facts" (2010). Retrieved 3/4/2014 from: http://biography.yourdictionary.com/father-divine.

3. McLoughlin, William G. (n.d) "the resurrection of father divine," a book review retrieved 3/5/2014 from: https://journals.ku.edu/index.php/amerstud/article/viewFile/2551/2510.
4. "President of Nazareth Mission Church of Australia Acclaims Supreme Teaching of GOD FATHER DIVINE in Recognition of America's Bicentennial Celebration" (Feb 28, 1976). *The New Day*. Retrieved 3/6/2014 from: http://fdipmm.libertynet.org/word8/760228lt.html
5. Weisbrot, Robert S. (1997) "Father Divine and the Peace Mission." In Pitzer, Donald E., ed.(1997) *America's Communal Utopias,* Chapel Hill: The University of North Carolina Press, pages 347-348.
6. Erickson, Keith V. (Dec 1977) "Black Messiah: The Father Divine Peace MissionMovement," *Quarterly Journal of Speech,* Vol. 63, page 437.
7. Watts, Jill (1992) *God, Harlem U.S.A.: The Father Divine Story,* Berkeley, CA: University of California Press, pages 102-3.
8. Erickson (Dec 1977) page 432.
9. "Esther Hicks" (13 Jan 2014) *Wikipedia.* Retrieved 2/22/2014 from: http://en.wikipedia.org/wiki/Esther_Hicks.
10. O'Neil, Michelle (Feb 24, 2010) "My Journey to the Abraham-Hicks Hot Seat." Retrieved 3/8/2014 from: http://fullsoulahead.com/2010/02/24/my-journey-to-the-abraham-hicks-hot-seat/
11. "About Abraham-Hicks" (1997-2014) *Abraham-Hicks Publications.* Retrieved 2/22/2014 from: http://www.abraham-hicks.com/lawofattractionsource/about_abraham.php.
12. Abraham-Hicks (2011) *Beyond the Twelve Steps: Breaking Free of Addiction,* audio CD recorded at Abraham-Hicks Art of Allowing workshop, held in Asheville, NC, on May 6, 2007, Abraham-Hicks Publications. (Transcriptions available on the Internet were also consulted).

13. Ibid.
14. Ibid.
15. Alchemy (2014) *Mirriam Webster Dictionary.* Retrieved 3/13/2014 from: http://www.merriam-webster.com/dictionary/alchemy
16. "Addiction Alchemy, A different Approach to Recovery" (Aug 17. 2007) *Eclectic Recovery.* Retrieved 8/9/2014 from: http://eclecticrecovery.blogspot.com/2007/08/addiction-alchemydifferent-approach-to.html
17. "Frequently Asked Questions" (2006). Retrieved 3/30/2014 from: http://www.addictionalchemy.com/addiction_alchemy_overview.html 18. *Supra,* "Native North Americans"
19. "Frequently Asked Questions" (2006). Retrieved 3/12/2014 from: http://www.addictionalchemy.com/addiction_alchemy_overview.html.
20. Retrieved 3/13/2014 from: http://www.addictionalchemy.com/pattern_on_the trestleboard.html. Addiction Alchemy credits: Case, Paul Foster (1947) *The Tarot,* Richmond, VA: Macoy Publishing.
21. "Addiction Alchemy Recovery Meditations" (n.d.) Retrieved 3/13/2014 from: http://www.addictionalchemy.com/addiction_recovery_meditations.html.
22. Williams, Patrick Gresham (2002, 2006) *The Spiritual Recovery Manual,* Palo Alto, CA: Incandescent Press, pages 88-92.
23. "Inner Peace and Wellness, What is the TM® technique?" (2014). Retrieved 3/20/2014 from: http://www.tm.org.
24. "Transcendental Meditation" (Jan 20, 2014) © 2005 Maharishi Vedic EducationDevelopment Corporation; © 2009 SpiritStep Publishing. Retrieved 3/19/2014 from: http://11thstepmeditation.org/meditation_styles/transcendental_meditation.php.

25. "Maharishi Mahesh Yogi" (7 Mar 2014) *Wikipedia*. Retrieved 3/25/2014 from: http://en.wikipedia.org/wiki/Maharishi_Mahesh_Yogi.
26. Bleick, Catherine R. (1994) "Case Histories: Using the Transcendental Meditation Program with Alcoholics and Addicts, in O'Connell, David F. and Charles N. Alexander, eds. (1994) *Self Recovery: Treating Addictions Using Transcendental Meditation and Maharishi Ayur-Veda,* New York: Harrington Park Press, pages 246, 248, 251, 253, 256.
27. Ellis, George A. and Pat Corum (1994) "Removing the Motivator: A Holistic Solution Substance Abuse," in O'Connell, David F. and Charles N. Alexander, eds. (1994) *Self Recovery: Treating Addictions Using Transcendental Meditation and Maharishi Ayur-Veda,* New York: Harrington Park Press, page 283.
28. "Deepak Chopra" (19 May 2013) *The Skeptic's Dictionary*. Retrieved 3/16/2014 from: http://www.skepdic.com/chopra.html.
29. Chopra, Deepak (1988) *Return of the Rishi: A Doctor's Search for the Ultimate Healer,* Boston: Houghton Mifflin Company, page 125.
30. Chopra, Deepak (1997) *Overcoming Addictions: The Spiritual Solution,* New York: Harmony Books, page 53.
31. Chopra (1997) page 122.
32. Chopra (1997) page 123.
33. Chopra (1997) pages 123-128.
34. Simon, David and Deepak Chopra (2007) *Freedom from Addiction: the Chopra Center Method for Overcoming Destructive Habits,* Deerfield Beach, FL: Health Communications, Inc., pages viii-ix.
35. Simon and Chopra (2007) page ix.
36. Simon and Chopra (2007) page xv.
37. Simon and Chopra (2007) page xvii-xx.
38. Simon and Chopra (2007) pages 19-20.
39. Simon and Chopra (2007) pages 17-59.
40. I Corinthians 6:19, KJV

41. Simon and Chopra (2007) pages 68-69.
42. Simon and Chopra (2007) page 72.
43. "Lester Levenson's Story" (n.d.) Retrieved 4/3/2014 from: http://www.releasetechnique.com/wordpress/wp-content/uploads/lester-levenson-story.pdf
44. Dwoskin, Hale (2003) *The Sedona Method: Your Key to Lasting Happiness, Success Peace and Emotional Well-being,* Sedona, AZ: Sedona Press, page 7.
45. "Lester Levenson's Story" (n.d.)
46. Dwoskin (2003) pages 7-8.
47. Ullman, Robert and Judyth Reichenberg-Ullman (2001) *Mystics, Masters, Saints and Sages: Stories of Enlightenment,* Berkeley, CA: Conari Press, page 163.
48. Dwoskin (2003) pages 39-40.
49. Dwoskin (2003) pages 39-40.
50. Dwoskin (2003) pages 301-302.
51. Callahan Techniques, Ltd. (2011) "Algorithm Level Training Manual," page 40. Retrieved 4/19/2014 from: http://www.tappingtherapy.com/elearning/pdf/TFT-Algorithm-Manual.pdf.
52. Craig, Gary and Tina Craig (1995-2014) "About the Authors Gary & Tina Craig," in *Free EFT Tutorial.* Retrieved 4/19/2014 from: http://www.emofree.com/eft-tutorial/before-begin /authors.html.
53. Craig, Gary and Tina Craig (1995-2014) "What Can I expect from EFT Tapping?"
54. McAlarney, Brion (Jun 2006) "Catching the Beat of the Drum." Retrieved 5/19/2014 from: http://www.addictionpro.com/article/catching-beat-drum.
55. Winkelman, Michael (Apr 2003) "Complimentary Therapy for Addiction: 'Drumming Out Drugs,'" *American Journal of Public Health,* 93(4): 647-651.
56. Winkelman (Apr 2003)
57. Winkelman (Apr 2003)

58. Drake, Michael (Aug 5, 2009) "The Therapeutic Effects of Drumming." Retrieved 4/21/2014 from: http://www.selfgrowth.com/print/554100
59. Friedman, Robert Lawrence (2000) *The Healing Power of the Drum: A Psychotherapist Explores the Healing Power of Rhythm,"* Gilsum, NH: White Cliffs Media, page 30.
60. Jadus, Joel (2010-2014) "Drum Therapy," *Enter the Sun.* Retrieved 4/20/2014 from: http://www.enterthesun.com/DRUM_THERAPY_TESTIMONIALS.htm
61. Turvey, Charlotte (May 2013) "Twelve Stepping on the Margins: A Neo-pagan Case Study in Overcoming Adversity," Master of Arts in Anthropology Thesis, California State University Northridge, pages 1-2.
62. Bonewits, Isaac (1996, 2005) "Pagans in Recovery" (version 2.7). Retrieved 5/27/2014 from: http://www.neopagan.net/PIR.html.
63. Starhawk (1979, 1989, 1999) *The Spiral Dance: A Rebirth of the Ancient Religion of the Great Goddess,* New York: Harper Collins, page 21.
64. "A Comparison Between The Spiral Steps & The 12 Steps of AA (n.d.). Retrieved 6/4/2014 from: http://www.spiralsteps.org/comparison.html
65. Wilburn, Medicine Hawk (2005) *Recoven: The Wiccan Recovery Program,* Longview, TX: Three Moons Media, page 101.
66. Wilburn (2005) page 101.
67. "Welcome to Nine Step Pagans" (n.d.). Retrieved 6/2/2014 from: http://www.ninesteppagans.faithweb.com/main.htm
68. Taiyu (Aug 4, 2013) "A Buddhist's Views on AA." Retrieved 6/8/2014 from: http://aaagnostica.org/2013/08/04/a-buddhists-views-on-aa/.
69. Littlejohn, Darren (2012) *Perfect Practice: How Everyone Can Use Buddhist and Recovery Tools for Greater Happiness,* [Kindle Version]. Retrieved from Amazon.com.

70. Mason-John, Valerie and Dr. Paramabandhu Groves (2013) *Eight Step Recovery: Using the Buddha's Teachings to Overcome Addiction,* Cambridge, UK: Windhorse Publications, pages: 17-18, 25, 61, 79, 95, 117, 161, 177, 184.
71. "Refuge Recovery" (n.d.) Retrieved 5/18/2014 from: http://againstthestreamnashville.com/refuge-recovery/.
72. "Refuge Recovery" (n.d.)
73. Levine, Noah (2014) *Refuge Recovery: A Buddhist Path to Recovering from Addiction,* New York: Harper One, pages 24-26.
74. Mason-John and Groves (2013). Page ix.
75. Vimalasara, a.k.a. Dr. Valerie Mason-John (June 2, 2014) "Eight step recovery meetings." Retrieved 6/22/2014 from: http://www.wildmind.org/blogs/recovery-monday/eight-steprecovery-meetings.
76. "Martial Arts in Recovery/Alcohol Rehab" (2008-2014). Retrieved 6/23/2014 from: http://alcoholrehab.com/addiction-recovery/martial-arts-in-recovery/

www.ingramcontent.com/pod-product-compliance
Lightning Source LLC
Chambersburg PA
CBHW020941230426
43666CB00005B/115